AMERICAN LABOR

FROM CONSPIRACY TO COLLECTIVE BARGAINING

ADVISORY EDITORS

Leon Stein   *Philip Taft*

ORGANIZED LABOR AND PRODUCTION

Morris Llewellyn Cooke and Philip Murray

ARNO & THE NEW YORK TIMES
NEW YORK   1971

Reprint Edition 1971 by Arno Press Inc.

Reprinted from a copy in
The ILGWU Research Department Library
LC# 73-156409
ISBN 0-405-02918-7

American Labor: From Conspiracy to Collective Bargaining—Series II
ISBN for complete set: 0-405-02910-1
See last pages of this volume for titles.

Manufactured in the United States of America

ORGANIZED LABOR AND PRODUCTION

ORGANIZED LABOR
AND
PRODUCTION

Next Steps in Industrial Democracy

By

MORRIS LLEWELLYN COOKE

CONSULTING ENGINEER

and

PHILIP MURRAY

PRESIDENT OF THE CONGRESS OF INDUSTRIAL ORGANIZATIONS (CIO)
AND PRESIDENT OF THE UNITED STEEL WORKERS OF AMERICA

REVISED EDITION

*"In the coming times an economist and
the expert in politics may have the beauty
and wisdom old men have known in poems
and strange tales"*

HARPER & BROTHERS PUBLISHERS
NEW YORK   LONDON

ORGANIZED LABOR AND PRODUCTION

*Copyright, 1940, 1946, by Harper & Brothers
Printed in the United States of America*

All rights in this book are reserved.

No part of the book may be reproduced in any manner whatsoever without written permission except in the case of brief quotations embodied in critical articles and reviews. For information address Harper & Brothers

REVISED EDITION

G-W

TABLE OF CONTENTS

Editor's Preface	vii
Authors' Preface	ix

I. Blazes on the Path to a Great Industry
   1. The Substance of Our Approach … 3

II. The Roots of Our Industrial Future
   2. The Evolution of American Enterprises … 9
   3. The Industrial Revolution … 24

III. The Estate of Labor
   4. The Labor Union Set-Up in the U. S. A. … 39
   5. Some of Labor's Controversial Practices and Attitudes … 51

IV. The Equipment of Management
   6. Organization, Management and Planning … 69
   7. Essentials in Administrative and Managerial Authority … 84
   8. Some of Management's Controversial Practices and Attitudes … 94

V. Matters for Joint Union-Management Study and Determination
   9. Wage Systems … 109
   10. The Hours of Work … 123
   11. Operating Control … 136
   12. Safety and Health in Industry … 144

VI. Two Make-or-Break Factors
   13. The Impact of Technology on Employment … 159
   14. Electricity and Human Labor … 173

VII. Toward Solutions
   15. The Current Practices of Collective Bargaining … 185
   16. The Wagner Act … 196

TABLE OF CONTENTS

17. Tapping Labor's Brains — 211
18. Adult Education for Management and Men — 222
19. A Free Society and a Better Life — 234

A Dialogue Between the Authors — 250

Notes and References — 266

Index — 271

EDITOR'S PREFACE

THIS book has a new timeliness. Four years of war have matured its message and given it inescapable pertinence. Written originally as this country was moving into a vast productive effort unequalled in human history, the new edition now comes as America faces uncertainly the problem of adjusting that productive power to peacetime needs. Never has the country faced a more critical problem. The message of this book has, perhaps, more importance than ever.

Productive efficiency, high purchasing power, and the wide diffusion of industrial and agricultural products are to the advantage both of labor and management: This is the central message of this book. This unity of interest of labor and management will be as necessary to planning a successful economy for peace as it was to the victorious economy of war.

The authors have entered new areas of responsibility since the first edition of the book was published. Morris Llewellyn Cooke, in Washington during the four years of war, is an indispensable consultant of many of those who govern the country, from Presidents down. In the fields of internal economy, scientific management, technological planning and development, and human needs in relation to industrial progress no person's judgment is more respected, no one's advice more sought. He is an engineer with a long history of significant public and private service. He was Philadelphia's Director of Public Works, chairman of the Storage Section of the War Industries Board of World War I, a Trustee of the Power Authority of the State of New York, Director of the Giant Power Survey of Pennsylvania, chairman of the Mississippi Valley and of the Great Plains Committees, the first Administrator of the Rural Electrification Administration, Adjudicator in the Mexican Oil Dispute, head of the American Technical Mission to Brazil. In Washington today he is, so to speak, an expert, one-man pressure group for the public interests of the people of the United States.

Philip Murray during the four years of war has come to pre-eminence as a labor leader in America. He was elected President of the C. I. O. in 1940. His strong but temperate policy in the problems following the war gives confidence to those who wish this country well. During World War I he served as a member of the National Coal Production Committee and on a subcommittee of the National Defense Council. He was also a member of the National Industrial Recovery Board and the N. R. A. Advisory Council. For more than twenty-five years he has been a member of the Pittsburgh Board of Education.

Written with the cooperation of authorities in various special fields, this book is in a sense an effort by specialists to overcome "specialism." Until the general interest of the people of America and the general philosophy and value of living are given priority over the disintegrative special interests and special areas of research that are characteristic of our modern culture there will be little chance for social and human integrity. One way to attain that integrity is through such cooperative projects as this by the specialists themselves.

Baker Brownell
Supervising Editor.

AUTHORS' PREFACE

THIS book was written just prior to World War II, at a time when it was generally recognized that we were on the threshold of a new era, even the outlines of which were far from clear. This outlook, at no point too reassuring, is still unfolding, more recently with the release of atomic energy as the driving force. Peace and plenty for all for the first time in history appear to be realizable, with the debacle of civilization itself the probable price of failure to cope competently with the global situation. One of the most important phases of this titanic struggle implies the welding together in times of peace of all production factors into one unified, dynamic, and unconquerable enterprise for the satisfaction of human wants, comparable to that which during the war made industrial America the envy and ultimately the saviour of mankind.

Quoting from our Preface to the first edition:

"This book is the effort of two Americans representing supposedly conflicting interests, labor and management, to seek out some of the bases for constructive industrial statesmanship. They are gratified to find so much common ground when the problems are considered calmly and objectively. The public has frequently been mislead as to the possibilities of reconciliation because of past controversies arising in the hurly-burly of a developing industrial society."

With the declaring of war—just before our publication date—everything depended on the rapid conversion of our economy to make possible an unprecedented volume of munitions and supplies for the use of ourselves and our allies. Management and labor were thrown together unceremoniously, and almost over night, into novel and intimate associations with each other and with government. Out of this pooling of minds and effort has come newer and more vital concepts (1) of technology and of production possibilities,

(2) as to the relations between the several parties engaged in industry, and (3) as to the interpretation of democracy itself.

In the matter of technology we witnessed the breaking up into relatively simple constituent parts tens of thousands of craft operations, permitting the recruitment of a vast and new labor force, the individual members of which could be trained in weeks, or months at the most. This was effected through a new type of foremanship resulting from a synthesis of skills easily taught and uniform over a great variety of industries and geographical locations. It is estimated that 50 per cent of the machines and tools used in wartime production were designed and built to meet volume necessities. This process has apparently only begun. To put it bluntly, machines and processes are designed eventually to be discarded.

The great discovery as to production is that there are no limits when the brakes are taken off and all parties pull to a common purpose. The urge for an output of munitions on the grand scale gave to both workers and employers a powerful incentive to pull together. The fact that never before have we seen so little opposition on labor's part to increased production was due in no small measure to the increased confidence which the workers have acquired through their organizations in securing an equitable distribution of the fruits of increased productivity. The employers, on their own initiative, and through the adoption of procedures recommended by government, facilitated this development. This book exerted some genuine influence in this situation, advocating and illustrating as it does the techniques by which conflicts in the employer-employee relationship can be avoided or adjusted when they arise. We have indeed discovered something about our potential capacity to produce in order to destroy our enemies. This war-acquired "know-how" must now be directed toward producing for purposes of life—not death—for peace and the good life.

Through tri-partite committees and boards encouraged and sponsored by Government agencies, such as War Manpower Commission, War Production Board, Office of Price Administration, and the Shipbuilding Stabilization Committee, management, labor, and Government have worked together. This has been true on joint production committees, industry and labor advisory committees, manpower policy committees, price control, war bond issues, Red Cross activities, tire and gas rationing, and other policy formulations. The war period thus provided golden opportunity for teamwork between labor, management, and Government in a way that had never even been thought of before.

The encouragement extended by the War Production Board to labor and management to establish Labor-Management Committees or Joint Production Committees (as they are called in Canada), proved highly successful. If these Committees made the contribution to increased war production that they are given credit for, surely there is something in this experience that is valuable for peace-time production.

As of March 15, 1944, there were 451 of these Committees in the iron and steel industry alone, representative of 719,530 employees. With the exception of the ordnance industry (542 Committees representing 1,098,290 employees) the largest number of these Committees were in the iron and steel industry. But actually over 5,000 such committees functioned throughout American industry. Probably between 500 to 1000 of these functioned effectively in production matters. All of them were effective in breaking down bulkheads between management and men.

This increasing recognition of labor in our national counsels is best exemplified by the legislation setting up the Office of War Mobilization and Reconversion—known as the George bill—wherein membership is provided for both labor and agriculture with the appointees confirmed by the Senate. A new pattern for the organization of our democracy seems to be evolving. Such committees provide an opportunity for enlarged participation by functional groups. They provide as well opportunities for the training of both labor and management people in the operation of a democratic industry.

Out of the dislocation and destruction of war we are becoming more conscious of many types of weakness in our industrial structure. New concepts of human values are finding expression. Such agencies as the National Planning Association—with its committees on agriculture, business and labor—and the Committee for Economic Development, are pressing their non-partisan inquiries into all phases of our economic setup. There is a new interest among the colleges and universities in labor-management relationships. Witness the Harvard Graduate School of Business Administration Trade Union Fellowships. Cornell University, under the authorization of the New York State legislature, has set up a well-financed School of Labor and Industrial Relations. The University of Chicago has organized a competently staffed Industrial Relations Center. Yale University's Labor and Management Center, the University of Illinois' Industrial Relations Program, and the University of Wisconsin's labor faculty are agencies which fully attest the growing interest.

The status quo in industry is definitely out. Nothing is taken for granted, or considered beyond remedy through understanding and concerted action. And we no longer assume that a single factor, such as capital or labor, has the authority, the power or the competence by itself to right the wrong or straighten out the tangle. More and more our national life, and especially our industry has become recognized in a broad sense as a joint undertaking. This is actually more vital than a joint undertaking where there is the implication of co-operation between separate entities. What is inherent in this situation is the co-operation of organically related parts of a single entity—the organic relations of which are being forced on our recognition.

With this heightened consciousness of shared responsibility goes increasing concern as to full employment and regularized employment. This latter expresses itself in interest as to the possibility of more general adoption of the guaranteed wage. We no longer assume the ability of our free enterprise system to provide the amount of employment necessary for such a sustained purchasing power as will avoid periodic depressions with all their baneful effects. The dilemmas call first for understanding and then for cooperative effort.

That industrial America is growing up is indicated by the difference in character between the gathering held in the Fall of 1945 in Washington under call from President Truman and the commission authorized by Congress and set up early in President Wilson's administration to seek the causes of industrial unrest. Thirty-five years ago the facts of our industrial life were so little understood even by the leaders on both sides that it proved desirable for this commission to hold hearings at industrial centers throughout the country. Through this means both the leadership and the general public were let in so-to-speak for the first time on the broad points of contention and given a reasonably unbiased appraisal of the merits of the controversy between the employers on one side and the labor unions on the other.

At the recent gathering, however, there appeared to be no reason for travel because the general situation stands out with the necessary clarity. The conference, through its several joint labor and management committees, assumed the basic facts and contented itself with an attempt to find out how far labor and capital might be willing to go in defining their respective positions, and how far each would go in making concessions in the interest of peace and security, both as to wages and returns on investments. While no joint statements resulted, positions were clarified, and next steps in many directions were indicated. One can gather too that as a result of these weeks of joint effort to discover the way out of industrial disorder, one unanimous if unpublished conclusion was reached, i.e., that any nation-wide or even widespread conflict between management on the one hand and labor on the other is unthinkable.

The vastly expanded labor union movement now claims to number 14 million members and the increasing power and influence it may be expected to exert under wise leadership gives added meaning to this development. If allowance is made for families, this union group represents a large, if not the largest, segment of our population. No wonder then that organized labor increasingly seeks to identify its interest with the public interest.

As one detailed example it may be cited that in the period since the book was written—five years—the United Steel Workers of America has become a constitutional union (1942) and has 700,000 dues-paying members. Two hundred thousand members have been in the armed services and were relieved from paying dues while in the services, making a total of nine hundred thousand members.

Collective bargaining contracts are in effect with some 1300 companies, many of which have been renewed and improved three and four times.

This International Union has a staff of 400 people in the field, plus 200 employees in 70 field offices in 38 states and 4 Canadian provinces. It has a technical staff of 40 specialists dealing with production and such industrial engineering problems as job classification and evaluation, rate relationships, incentive systems, etc.

It has $5 million in its treasury. It employs a nationally known firm of certified public accountants to make semi-annual audits which are sent to all members of Congress, the Governors of 48 States, and to all others who request copies. Through joint agreement with the U. S. Steel Corporation, a Board of Conciliation and Arbitration of three members was set up with a member of the faculty of the University of Chicago as Impartial Chairman (Chairman's salary $25,000 annually). All costs are shared equally and jointly by the United States Steel Corporation and the Union.

It is the considered judgment of the authors that both labor and management can each well afford to give more thought to and deal more generously with the problems and difficulties of the other. The workers now recognize that their own prosperity inevitably grows out of the prosperity of the concern by which they are employed as well as that of the industry with which the concern is affiliated. And ultimately their well-being must be affected by the state of the nation—prosperous or depressed as the case may be. Recognizing that management has its own authority and responsibilities which it alone must carry, labor has to be made increasingly conscious of and sympathetic with management's difficulties. Similarly, of course, while labor also must be master in its own house, the effectiveness of the national productive effort will be enhanced by a better understanding on the part of management of labor's objectives and the difficulties within labor's own ranks which always accompany their accomplishment. In other words, the Biblical injunction "Be ye members one of another" must be increasingly observed.

AUTHORS' PREFACE

At this moment many grave issues are pressing for settlement in reasonable harmony with some common plan. Near the top of this list certainly is the relationship between ownership and the working force in industry. In this situation the authors could hardly feel that they had been quite frank with their readers were they not to express the opinion that in any fruitful study of industrial relations one must recognize a qualitative difference of momentous significance as between the claims of the contending parties.

To the casual observer, or to one not acquainted with human history, it all seems to boil down to an uncomplicated fight: wages versus profits. At times it may be just this. On occasion collective bargaining may degenerate into a struggle for mere money advantage. There is to be seen in this attitude of course no relation to an historic struggle of countless millions seeking to raise themselves by their own bootstraps first from the degrading conditions which attended the early days of the Industrial Revolution, and then through the long era of subsistence wages.

At the present time when the entire world envisions the possibility of plenty in place of scarcity, the struggle is on a somewhat higher level—liberty for all and everything done to safeguard increasingly the dignity of the individual. It would in our opinion be wholly impracticable as well as unethical not to recognize adequately the legitimate rights of property to rewards in all dealings between the worker and his employer. But we see in the struggle of the workers through the centuries for a better life, a more important participation in human affairs and a wider recognition of the dignity of labor, a cause to which all men of goodwill may well dedicate themselves.

Through our wartime experiences it has been fully demonstrated that without democracy at the workplace democracy at the higher administrative levels is all but impossible. In fact, democracy at the top is only possible as it originates at the bottom and spreads its benign influence throughout the organization. Similarly, efficiency at the top is quite out of the question except as it stems from the work of the rank and file. But efficiency at workplace or machine has deep roots and is affected by widely ramifying influences. Our main purpose in writing this book was to explore some of these fundamentals of good management.

Without repeating their names the authors desire to express once again their appreciation to the considerable number of authorities who assisted in the preparation of our original manuscript. The passing months have not in any way lessened the importance of these contributions.

January 10, 1946

Morris L. Cooke
Philip Murray

I. BLAZES ON THE PATH
TO A GREAT INDUSTRY

CHAPTER I

THE SUBSTANCE OF OUR APPROACH

BETWEEN the powerful group which own private enterprises and the numerically much larger group which operates them for a wage or its equivalent, wide differences are to be expected. These differences will be in general outlook, in the interpretation of facts pertinent to any industrial situation and even in regard to the facts themselves. Out of these differences grow the problems on which the struggle between capital and labor is based. But these few words give no idea of the complexities involved nor of their constantly developing character. Acrimonious disputes and even bitter conflicts arise. This means simply that the employer-employee relationship is something relatively recent as human history goes. It means that democratically conceived rules for its conduct have yet to be fully worked out.

The authors of this book are two technicians each trained in a different discipline. They hope that the cause of industrial peace and progress may be advanced by facing the situation frankly and working on it somewhat as a baffling problem in science. We have no thought of dealing in last words. We hope, rather, to make this group of problems more intelligible by narrowing the area of legitimate controversy and by developing the large area of common ground which either actually exists or which lies just below the horizon.

One of us is a labor leader; the other is an engineer. The normal differences in our education, industrial training, and clientele should keep us from oversimplification of the problem. Our lifelong association with industry has given us a profound appreciation of the beneficent influence which sound relations between the employed and their employers may exert both on the daily lives of the workers and in increasing the volume of production of the American people. Right at hand lies the opportunity for a large increase in production, and through it of a higher standard of living. Organized cooperation as envisioned in this book may prove a master key to open this door of opportunity.

The authors are firm believers not only in the cause of organized labor but in the usefulness of the organized labor movement to the public and in the further development of the democratic process. Our references throughout the book to the "workers" and to "labor" mean organized workers and organized labor.

John Chamberlain says in the *New Republic*, "Little practical good can come of trying to create a blueprint-perfect society overnight: engineers of social change must work with institutions as they now exist and the future can only grow out of the exceedingly imperfect present." Our program envisages unions and managements bound together by collective bargaining. Normally we would hope it to be a good union and a good management cooperating through good collective bargaining techniques. Irrespective of the conditions at the start, each of the three elements should constantly grow in its ability to perform its allotted function. If not, the scheme probably will not work. At any rate in spite of occasional failures "union-management co-operation is becoming an accomplished fact."[1]

The plan of the book provides for just enough of the history of industry to give roots to the current situation. Then follows: first, an intimate picture of labor's set-up; and second, a description of the function of management in industry. Essential to these two sections are chapters in which the controversial practices of both management and labor are listed and frankly discussed. In a scene spreading as wide and far as do industrial relations it has not been possible to mention every one of Tom's and Dick's and Harry's pet aversions—whether the practice be one perpetrated by the employing group or by the labor unions. But the effort *has* been made to mention every essential practice bothersome to the two contending parties and debated by the public, to give its purpose and discuss its tendencies, toward and untoward.

THE SUBSTANCE OF OUR APPROACH

One must bear in mind that techniques change. Under the methods of mass production, and as the organization of the workers is put more and more on a national and even international basis, the modes by which each side exerts its power inevitably alter. Some practices resorted to in the early days of the industrial struggle have completely disappeared. For instance, the employers no longer use the whip to enforce obedience nor do the workers seek to destroy machinery. We do find, however, that some practices persist here and there long after they have become essentially obsolete. For instance, right at this minute there are employers still insisting that there shall be "No conversation between employees during working hours"—a rule not only inhuman and anti-social but virtually impossible to enforce. Similar outworn and wholly useless customs are encountered among labor unions, especially among the older and smaller groups. Unfortunately, such practices, whether followed by the employers or the unions, have an effect entirely out of scale to their inherent importance in that they antagonize right-minded folk and detract attention from vital current problems and really significant current strategy.

There are chapters in this book devoted to common problems such as wages, hours, safety, health, production control and to the challenge afforded by the impact of technological improvements on satisfactory industrial relations. These follow the outlines of the respective fields and functions of labor and management in the whole industrial picture. Finally come discussions of the remedial measures, such as collective bargaining, adult education and a new status for the workers through which a new industry and a new society may be built.

The ideology of conflict in our opinion is most harmful to all concerned. Any satisfactory solution of the problem of labor relations, whether for the nation as a whole, a single industry or an individual plant, is well-nigh hopeless if approached with the psychology of battle. The results of fighting against things are picayune compared with what can be produced through cooperation. In the long run it will be discovered that the techniques found effective in creating a satisfactory life for the family are applicable to industry.

6 ORGANIZED LABOR AND PRODUCTION

Agelong experience calls for give and take, the ignoring of minor shortcomings, restraint from taking petty advantages, the adoption of the long-time point of view, of one for all and all for one, and the individual advantage merged in the group advantage. That there are today cases in the industrial world where these principles and practices have been put into fairly complete operation makes it possible to picture the results of a more widespread application. Of course there exists a very real basis for differences of opinion and interest in the division both of the proceeds and authority in an industry operated for profit. We will suggest procedures through which such may be accommodated with the minimum of heat.

While we have advocated cooperative attitudes throughout, our book will have been misunderstood if collective bargaining is looked upon either as a pink tea or a petting party. Labor's struggle for status and the good life in a world dominated by tool power and private financial concentrations will go on and should go on. Our hope has been to set up techniques of law and order, to recognize science, to intrigue the best in the contending parties and to plan that industry should produce more and more to the end that there shall be more and more to divide. But we have had never a thought that the deeper conflicts of a people seeking ever more freedom for mind, body and soul should be compromised.

This book is published at a period of world-wide disillusionment. In one field after another the devastating conclusion has been reached that former ways of doing things have been the wrong ones, with results sometimes worse than futile. Certainly no one viewing the American industrial scene dispassionately can avoid the conclusion that there is a better way. This book it is believed points in that direction.

And so in the following chapter we turn for a few pages to the past in which are to be found the roots of the present, and first to that part of the past during which a people exclusively agricultural at the start, occupying a small part of the present continental United States, has been transformed into the mightiest industrial nation on earth.

II. THE ROOTS OF OUR INDUSTRIAL FUTURE

CHAPTER 2

THE EVOLUTION OF AMERICAN ENTERPRISES

"I WAS never so discouraged in my life. In a flash I saw my savings go, and then my home. I saw myself beginning all over again. Of course there's been no chance to begin over again. We're on the bread line. But at that time I didn't see so far ahead."

John Smith was talking to a new friend as they were leaving the relief office. John Smith is not his real name. But the man, his wife and their two children are real people.

They live in the Middle West in one of the smaller cities where automobiles are made. After he finished high school, John got a job in a factory making certain automobile parts. He became a skilled, steady worker and earned good wages. He was not the kind who spent all he earned. When the firm set up a savings plan he joined the group. In a few years he was able to marry. Later he bought on contract a little cottage with space for a garden on the outskirts of the city, and with his young wife started to make a real home of it. They and their children lived simply, but they enjoyed a decent standard of living and their children went to school in clothes of which they were not ashamed. John even bought on contract a tiny plot of land on a lake in the country near by, and built a little camp in which the family could spend summer week ends. The automobile business boomed during the twenties and everything appeared promising. Everybody talked prosperity; a good worker with a prudent wife could soon get the cottage and lake camp paid for. Some big men who ought to know talked about two chickens in every pot and two cars in every garage.

Then came the crash of 1929. At first it did not affect John—he was one of the most skilled workers and was kept on. But eventually the blow fell—John was laid off. "It ought not to be for long," the employment office said; "we'll soon get going again, and you skilled, steady fellows will be the first called back."

A few months later John read in the local paper that the firm was taking back some of the men. He had not received a notice, and went to see about it. "Your turn will come soon," he was told. Again the newspaper said a few more men had been taken on. Again John visited the plant's employment office. "We have decided to take back the men whose families are in need; you fellows who have savings accounts and homes can get along better than the other fellows." The personnel man said nothing about John's savings account being small, the house only partly paid for, the months of unemployment the family had already suffered. That was John's black moment. He knew the balance of his savings could last only a short time; he did not dare make further payments on the home and cabin, and when his payments stopped, he would lose the places and all he had put into them.

Such was the story John told his friend as they walked away from the relief office. "We live in a screwy world," he added; "there may be something wrong with the whole system—I don't know about that. But put this in your pipe and smoke it—something is wrong with our company. We've given them the best we have—the best years of our lives—and now they throw us to the dogs like that!"

John was right. There is something wrong with the system, and there is something wrong with the attitude of employers as a class toward workers. Although this book is concerned primarily with relations between employers and workers, in this chapter we want to consider the American industrial situation in somewhat broader fashion.

On the face of it there should be nothing seriously wrong with the United States. It has a greater supply than any other developed nation of all the elements required for a busy people; for full employment and a high living standard. Its area is greater than that of all the countries of western Europe combined. There are no tariff walls between states, no serious barriers to free communication and there is a highly developed transportation system; the country generally has most favorable conditions for the production and exchange of goods. It has the greatest abundance of varied raw materials required by industry—fertile soil for grains, cotton, fruits and other crops; coal, petroleum and water power; iron ore, copper, lead, zinc and bauxite; timber; salts, sulphur and other elementary chemicals. At hand is nearly every mineral, plant and animal basic raw material. Its hundred and thirty million inhabitants are the most vigorous and efficient in the world, capable of producing any desirable commodity and disposed to use all that man knows how to make. Within the past century these people have produced and saved more capital per person than any other people, in the form of cleared land and farm buildings, highways, railroads, bridges, factories, machines, tools, stores, office buildings and other forms that capital takes. They have additional working capital, ready for any kind of use. Their managers and engineers have developed the most effective and productive methods of making things. In all history there has never before been in one nation such a balance among materials, equipment, labor power and skill, and a people's desire to enjoy things; never before such a foundation for a busy nation making and consuming every variety of product. Judged by fundamental facts there should be nothing wrong with the United States.

Yet judged by other clear facts there is something wrong. There is something wrong with the whole machine when a sixteen-cylinder nation is limping along on six or eight cylinders; when a nation that has produced an eighty billion dollar annual income has during the past few years been producing only forty to sixty billion; when ten to twelve million John Smiths cannot find employment and over twenty-five million—about one-fifth of all the people—have no income other than public relief with which to maintain a bare subsistence. When we set these facts alongside the facts of the preceding paragraph, can any situation appear more stupid?

However, it is not fair to indict a whole nation. One must

be generous. The social machine is ponderous and complicated. Mass ideas and mass habits change slowly. Circumstances change more rapidly than ideas and habits. Changes in conditions creep up with small steps and are not noticed; then eventually it is realized that conditions have changed so radically that the old ideas and ways of doing things do not suffice. A nation may be in serious difficulties before it awakens to the extent of the change. That is the generous way of explaining the present situation.

When John Smith's great-grandfather William went into business—set up a little plant to make wagons and carriages—every relationship was direct and simple, and the interest of everybody concerned entered into his management. He had saved from his earnings as a worker and had a nest egg of capital. He enlarged this by a small loan at the local bank. As his business grew he added to his capital out of the small plant's earnings by living simply and withdrawing little for his own use. He knew his limited market and what it would take, and regulated output accordingly. Of course it was an expanding market and did not require close calculation—only a common-sense conservatism. The business grew because the market grew. He knew every one of his twenty to forty workers personally; knew them, their wives and children. If one of them came to him, first names were used: "Will, the wife isn't feeling so well today and I guess I'd better go back and help her out." "All right, Sam, I'm sorry to hear it; hope she's better tomorrow. If you don't show up, I'll know she isn't better, and the wife will come over and see if there's anything she can do."

It should not be inferred that we believe employers of that day were at bottom a better lot of people than employers of today. There were the usual proportions of all kinds. But the circumstances surrounding the small business in the small village or city in a developing region were different; and these differences permitted employers naturally to express that spirit of neighborliness that almost everybody has. William Smith could pay good wages because business was good in an expanding economy. He knew his workers because the plant was small and was in a small village. The banker knew not only Will, but also every worker. Everybody was interested in the business and knew how it was going. If a depression came everybody helped everybody else according to his means; and everybody, including the banker, had gardens, poultry and a cow to fall back on. The natural spirit of humanitarianism could find more ways to express itself in personal relations.

Nor would we have it inferred that the workers of today are at bottom a better lot of individuals than the workers of William Smith's day. Human nature does not change that rapidly. But circumstances may change rapidly. In the earlier day, as in the case of employers, circumstances tended to bring out the best in workers and to suppress the less desirable individual traits. But today, in the case of workers as in the case of employers, the complexities of society have given greater opportunity for undesirable as well as desirable traits to have influence. Workers, like employers, have learned the advantages of organization and how it can bring mass power to bear on a situation of conflict. While the trend in labor leadership is distinctly in the direction of cooperative, creative action, now and then leadership of the opposite types comes into power, and constitutes an obstacle to constructive efforts both of other more statesmanlike leaders of labor and of statesmanlike leaders among employers.

This book makes every effort to avoid impugning motives back of individual actions on the part either of employers or of workers. It is interested in the present and the future, and would let the dead past bury its dead. Its purpose is to aid employers and workers alike to a better understanding of the problems of livelihood, and, through understanding, to a joint effort toward the realization of the economy of full employment and abundance which science has made possible.

One important feature of business in William Smith's day should be noted particularly: business got a large part of its capital without anybody having to earn and save it. The bulk of the natural resources of the country belonged to all the people, with title in the national and state governments. These governments gave it away virtually for nothing. Therefore a man who staked out eighty acres of good

14 ORGANIZED LABOR AND PRODUCTION

farm land, or a section of forest land, or a mine, required only modest capital. He inherited his basic asset from nature. He only needed cash enough to get the equipment to develop this inheritance. Sometimes he had to earn and save this working capital but generally his appreciating physical property was acceptable security for a loan at the local bank. It was not difficult to get a start in business.

Of course no government gave William Smith his little wagon factory—that is, directly. Indirectly it did. This factory was in a small village growing rapidly because of the settlement of the surrounding farm land and because of some profitable lumbering operations near by. Government gave the farmers and the lumbermen their properties and because of this they had more cash to spend. The village became a thriving little market center. These conditions of expansion led William Smith to believe that a reliable and able man ought to develop a good wagon and buggy business. The banker agreed with him and was ready to lend Will the additional capital he needed. The total situation was one in which practically every business started with a gift of basic assets from nature and could expect increase from the growth of the country.

The situation today is different. All the desirable farm lands, forests and mines are owned and held at a good price. He who would start in business today must purchase them, and must have considerable capital to do so. Some enterprises require very large blocks of capital. For this, among other reasons, business has passed more and more into the hands of large corporations, which pool and control the savings of a great many people.

Today the businesses that dominate employment are the great corporations. Each plant may represent an investment of several million dollars. Nobody is the responsible owner because thousands of stockholders scattered all over the country are irresponsible owners. There is no personal relation between these owners and the workers. William Smith's great-grandson is but one among five or ten or twenty-five thousand workers. The capital is not furnished by the local banker, but by a group of great banks and investment houses in New York or Chicago where savings are assembled and

EVOLUTION OF AMERICAN ENTERPRISES

distributed. The principal concern that the thousands of stockowners have is that they get the dividends and that their shares do not decline—preferably that they increase—in value. So the financial interests that circumstances sometimes permit to get essential control, especially in influential key industries, put the pressure on the management of the plant—demand lower costs, more dividends, greater value of the securities on the ticker tape. The top management of the business passes the pressure along to the superintendents and they to the department heads. The pressure finally reaches the employment office. There the cost-reducing urge says not to employ one man more than is needed; to lay anyone off who is not essential. Sometimes a large number are laid off at one sweep, as in the years immediately following 1929. Under the general circumstances in modern industrial centers there is no other work to which discharged employees may turn; no gardens to help keep the pantry stocked; only local or national government relief. The personal interest and the personal touch are all but gone.

A fundamental aspect of the trouble is that the spirit of self-interest has been permitted to work unrestrained during the century of magnificent development which has passed, while conditions have so changed that this spirit is no longer the wholesome force it once was. In the day of John's great-grandfather self-interest embraced more than self: to an appreciable degree the local banker's self-interest included Will, the employer, and his workers; Will's self-interest included the banker and Will's workers; the workers' self-interest included Will and the banker. Everybody understood and helped the entire situation. It was a sort of family give and take, with fellow feeling and generosity a vital part of the situation.

However, with the growth of great corporate employers this spirit has become smothered. Not that the typical businessman is hardhearted; he is generous among those with whom he is acquainted. He believes in justice—in the abstract. He believes workers should have steady employment and good wages—in the abstract. But concretely, if a dividend on one of his holdings of stock is passed, or if the financial page of his daily paper shows a drop in the quoted price of a stock in which he is interested, he is apt to sell or to write a condemning letter to someone. These sales or condemnations from stockholders start a series of pressures that finally bear on the management. More profits; lower costs; reduced wages; stretchout. Dividends and stock values must be maintained. Shut down the plant if it will reduce bookkeeping losses. The individual worker is helpless. It is all impersonal. Business is business.

Of course there are many medium-sized and small plants in which the owners are not so completely governed by such impersonal motives. They would manage better if they could; would have more concern for workers' interests if they could. In fact, many of them have good work-a-day relations, although unfortunately, many of them have not. But these smaller concerns on the whole are not independent of what the big concerns do, especially in the matter of regularity of employment.

It is the big concerns that extract and convert the basic materials, develop the processes of mass production, and employ workers in huge numbers. It is their relations that are so impersonal. When for any reason one of these huge concerns lays off its workers an important flow of wages is stopped, local business declines, the local merchant orders less, and distant producers feel the effects. If many of these larger concerns lay off their workers at the same time the effect on business all over the country is serious. There is a heavy decline in merchants' orders and a correspondingly large decline in the business of many producers; these producers have to lay off their workers, which causes a further decline in business, additional layoff of workers and widespread unemployment. Nobody is to blame; yet everybody is to blame.

Of course there are many complicating factors which need not be considered here in detail, for this book is not a treatise on economics. Yet several of these complicating factors should be brought into the picture, for when industrial relations again become less impersonal and workers share with employers some of the responsibilities of policy and management, these complicating factors will have to be considered by both parties.

First; the past century has been one of magnificent development of production facilities that lessen the drudgery of work and increase man's capacity to produce, and that make possible a society of abundance. However, this economy of abundance will require an equitable distribution of social income among all the people on the payrolls of a nation in order that widespread purchasing power may absorb the vast output of modern industry required to keep everybody employed and to establish a high standard of living.

Yet our wage system generally is still that set up when a principal contribution of workers was muscular energy, and it still rests on that base. There have been increases in rates largely through the influence of labor organizations, but the base has not been essentially modified. It is not a base suitable for a society in which a man's contribution to the social income is determined by his skill in applying powerful natural energies. It cannot bring about that distribution of the social income required to establish an adequate and widely distributed purchasing power. Modern mechanized, mass-production industries call for a distribution of the social income in accordance with the principle of functional contribution in place of the principle of energy contribution. Here is a complicated problem for solution.

Second; during the past century maximum freedom was given businessmen to develop the corporation. This was called for by the newly discovered production processes, which require huge, expensive equipment, which in turn requires huge blocks of capital investment, the combined savings of millions of people. Individual employers and partnerships cannot assemble such masses of capital. Therefore the corporation developed as a most useful social institution.

But the corporation has been permitted to develop without socially desirable direction, with the result that a powerful instrument has been placed in the hands of self-interest which has been becoming less personal in its relations, and less self-controlled by considerations of the common weal. It has come to think more and more in terms of making money and less and less in terms of making commodities for use. Sometimes it can make more money by monopoly control and high prices. Sometimes it can make more, without being outright monopoly, by formal or informal agreements among competitors for maintenance of higher prices. Sometimes it can make more money by refusing to reduce prices in the face of declining demands; by closing the plant (and causing unemployment) with the idea of recouping later through the maintained higher prices. Available evidence indicates that in most lines manufacturers could make more money by reducing prices and keeping workers employed and in a position to continue purchasing. However, this is not what many manufacturers believe, and they have the power to act in accordance with their belief. Altogether, the beliefs, policies and administrative methods of these great employers are an obstacle to the development of the purchasing power that modern productivity requires. Here also is a problem calling for solution.

Third; perhaps the greatest problem of all is that of the mental attitude of business. As we have explained, nature gave the pioneers, with little cost, the basic capital of agriculture and industry—something like the young man who inherits a million. We know from observation what this young man's mental attitude is. So great a part of business in the United States has had a like mental attitude as to have set the tone for the whole. Getting capital through appropriating natural resources; excessive valuations, high prices, high dividends, waiting for capital to increase "naturally"; these have been and remain the controlling content of the business mind. It has largely forgotten what "earned income" means.

Recently circumstances have so changed that the nation's income must be of the earned variety rather than capital appropriated from nature's reserve. But business generally does not realize this. It still thinks in terms of getting capital in other ways, and of waiting for it to increase in value. The activities of business are largely directed by such thinking. It has until recently got much of its capital and then increased its value through high prices. Not by the owners living simply and drawing little from the business, as in the case of William Smith many years earlier, but by charging prices that yield good dividends and in addition extracting new capital from consumers, which becomes the property of the owners. Although this mode of capital formation has not been so prevalent since 1929, business still thinks in terms of its restoration. Several prominent industrialists recently testified before a congressional committee that much less than half the capital of the great corporations they represent has been contributed by the owners; that more than half has been unknowingly contributed by purchasers of the company's products. Their testimony was essentially an argument for legislation favoring the earlier conditions. Such excessive extraction of capital from consumers will not succeed in the long run, because it is an obstacle to the creation of that widespread purchasing power necessary to keep everybody employed. Here again is a serious problem calling for solution.

These problems and others related to them must be attacked in many ways; simultaneously and along a broad front. One of the most important ways of attacking them is to make every effort to restore, so far as possible, the sound relations of the day when William Smith the employer, his banker and his workers knew each other personally and knew all the ins and outs of the business. When some counterpart of such relations becomes again established in American industry, all interests of all parties, and therefore the common weal, will be taken into consideration in determining business policies on all levels, and in working out production, distribution and other procedures.

But, you say, the same kind of personal relations cannot be restored; the intimate contacts of the small plant of William Smith's day cannot be duplicated in the modern corporation. It is today impossible for many employers to know all their workers and form contacts with them to sense their interests and problems. And the corporation has come to stay, for properly used it is one of the instruments which make possible the modern industrial organization and methods giving high productivity and a large social income. Let us accept these facts; the problem is to achieve in the modern situation the values lost in the transition from the old to the new.

We can get a clue to the solution in our political experience. The town, village or school-district meetings are the

20 ORGANIZED LABOR AND PRODUCTION

only survivals in the United States of the original pure democracy in which everyone knew everyone else, and worked together in familiar give and take. For state governments and the national government a form of representative democracy has been developed. The people as a whole vote on broad issues and for executive and legislative representatives. These representatives have the personal contacts. On the one hand they "keep their ears to the ground" and ascertain the desires of the particular constituents they represent; on the other hand they meet with the representatives from other areas, learn the interests of these other constituents and come to understand their desires. Together a solution of common problems is sought through a harmonizing of all interests and desires. The important thing is that all interests and desires can be brought to bear more or less effectively on the solution of each common problem.

Some similar arrangement is required to handle the problem of relations between employers and workers. A beginning has been made. One party to such relations is suitably organized: owners are represented by directors, and directors by management. A management, representing owners, is a compact group of a size suitable for the solution of common problems in conference with workers.

However, only a beginning has been made in similar organization of workers for the purpose. In many plants the workers are not organized. In many others such organizations as exist cover only a fraction of the workers, and many of them are of such a nature that the interests and desires of all classes of workers cannot be brought to bear on a specific problem. There should be in each plant an inclusive organization of all the workers, with compact representation similar to that which management affords to owners. Likewise there should be for each industry and for the total business of the nation similar compact groups representative of the two interests. Then each party could bring to bear on each problem at different levels the numerous interests and desires of employers and of workers. If such an arrangement could be worked out, many of the problems that seem at present not to be problems of industrial relations—large economic problems such as those we have mentioned—would be on the way to solution, for industrial relations would then be organized on a basis favoring industrial statesmanship.

In another respect the political parallel is important. In the development of representative democracy the representatives chosen by the people through universal suffrage represent all the people. Different parties offer their own candidates and work for their election. But once a contest is decided, the elected representatives represent all the voters and all the voters are bound by their decisions. A representative democracy could not survive any other arrangement. Similarly, when representative democracy is established in industry the sets of representatives chosen to speak for workers on the one hand and owners on the other, must represent all concerned at a particular level. Then only can all interests and desires be reflected in negotiations, sound relations established within plants, statesmanlike decisions made at all levels, and a stably expanding economy developed.

Various significant first steps have been made in the cooperation of managements and organized workers in industrial government. These point to what is possible through more extensive and better organized efforts along the same lines. Prior to the World War there was a general situation of suspicion, each of the other's motives, by management and by organized labor. But during the war representatives of employers and of labor worked together on war committees and from this experience each acquired a sound respect for the other. There emerged a disposition on the part of some to work together more intimately and constructively. A society of managers and industrial engineers sought to promote the type of management emphasized throughout this volume. Employers and unions in the clothing industry set a notable example of cooperation in the development of working conditions and standards. Several of the larger railroad systems joined with their organized shop employees in a comparable development of production methods and standards. Recently the Steel Workers Organizing Committee issued a pamphlet inviting all managements to join with labor in working out better production methods; and this pamphlet is a notable little textbook on how to go about the matter. Several isolated efforts such as that of the Naumkeag

Mills in Massachusetts, did not carry through, but they left lessons which will be of definite value in guiding the inevitable trend toward cooperative management.

Democracy in industry is essential. We have learned that it is essential in political affairs—a people cannot survive half-slave and half-free. Industry is another big and important aspect of life, and we are coming to realize that an economy cannot survive in which the participants are without the freedom appropriate to American citizenship.

Democracy in industry would open the way for solution of most of our distressing problems. Today the parties at interest are finance, ownership, management and labor. As a result of historic circumstances finance has come to occupy the commanding position. As long as finance occupies that position and ownership is dependent on finance for its investment and working capital, ownership will line up with finance. But the real community of interest is among ownership, management and labor. Their interests are essentially identical. Labor wants employment and a good standard of living, and that means high production, for a living standard depends directly on the goods and services created. Management wants high productivity because production and distribution is its job—its reason for existence. Unemployment and part-time production is what management most abhors. Management's interests are far more closely identified with labor's interests than with those of finance, or even with those of ownership if the latter be of the absent kind and not actually engaged in management. At bottom, however, even ownership's interest takes on the quality of that of labor and management. It wants stable, regular profits, and these come from the same arrangements that promote the interests of labor and management.

Ownership, management and labor should join forces in the pursuit of optimum productivity. Optimum productivity means the highest possible balanced output of goods and services that management and labor skills can produce, equitably shared and consistent with a rational conservation of human and physical resources. Democracy in industry will open the gates to the highway that leads to optimum productivity.

EVOLUTION OF AMERICAN ENTERPRISES

So much for the "where-we-are-at" of American industry and the route by which our present status was reached. But, it must be remembered that for the first one hundred years of our national existence we were very largely an agricultural people. Only after the Civil War came the real beginnings of the large-scale industrial development which is now recognized as our dominant characteristic. Hence to understand fully the situation out of which a new industrial era is to grow we must know something of the evolution which went on in the industry of other nations at a time when we Americans were clearing our lands and planting our crops. If it were not for the lessons of the industrial revolution as developed abroad, even more emphatically than at home, our future path would not be so clear.

CHAPTER 3

THE INDUSTRIAL REVOLUTION

IN 1790 a supposedly standard-sized cylinder was furnished to James Watt which proved to be almost half an inch too small. Today, one hundred and fifty years later, standard reference gauges, using the principle of the length of light waves, are accurate to one-millionth of an inch. This is the industrial revolution. At the close of the eighteenth century, steel was still produced by the slow and expensive process of baking the impurities out of the molten iron in sand boxes. Today, in a modern steel plant, a 4000-ton press, in Stuart Chase's words, "picks up a log of steel as though it were a lead pencil, holds it by the throat, and sinks a hammer twelve inches into its glowing mass, squeezing out a gush of molten metal like water from a wet rag." This, too, is the industrial revolution. In 1790, to send a ton of coal from Manchester to Liverpool cost forty shillings. Today, thanks to improved transportation and communication, a few rupees spent for thread in Calcutta sets a spindle going in Fall River. And this, too, is the industrial revolution. Well might Dr. Shotwell ask, "What is the Renaissance or Reformation, the empire of Charlemagne or of Caesar, compared with this empire of mind and industry, which has penetrated the whole world, planting its cities as it goes, binding the whole together by railroad and telegraph, until the thing we call civilization has drawn the isolated communities of the old regime into a great world organism, with its afferent and efferent nerves of news and capital reaching to its finger tips in the markets of the frontier?"

These twentieth-century miracles are not the result of a modern Aladdin's lamp, but the products of momentous events extending back through hundreds of years. These

THE INDUSTRIAL REVOLUTION

events lie back of our technological triumphs and our tremendous wealth, back also of our depressions, our bread lines, our strikes. In the aggregate they constitute the industrial revolution—a historical epoch which in a sense was neither industrial (since it embraced much more than merely industrial expansion) nor revolutionary (since there was no overthrow of existing institutions but rather a steady procession of events). Yet we shall use the name that has stuck—if only because it *has* stuck—without trying to reduce a profound and intricate historical phase to too glib a description or too neat an intellectual bundle.

There is no exact starting point. The origins of the industrial revolution seem to go back as far as the exploits of Columbus and the other great explorers which opened up vast new fields for colonization. Europe stirred and slowly awoke from a heavy sleep to partake of fabulous riches from the New World. Better ships were built and new processes were introduced in order to distribute limited quantities of goods throughout what was still a localized economy. In the seventeenth century commercial and financial improvements laid the basis for modern capitalism. This was the commercial revolution, a necessary prelude to the revolution in industry.

Despite this progress, Europeans in the early 1700's still were dealing with a limited supply of goods and a static population. There was a smooth and serene harmony between the three factors of population, natural resources, and technique. Until there was sharp expansion of one of these factors, the sparks kindling the industrial revolution could not be struck. Finally, in the eighteenth century, the intensive colonization of sections of the New World began to affect European industrialization. Natural resources were tremendously increased, and this compelled similar expansion of population and the industrial arts.

Before this time, the chief problem facing the merchant or craftsman was that of improving already existing processes. He devoted himself to selling or making better shoes, pottery, or carriages rather than more of them. But the increased availability of raw materials from the colonies set off a cycle of events which demanded not better goods, but more of them. This change was of crucial importance, because it led to enlargement of the factories. Consequently, with every addition to plant capacity, the activities of each worker were reduced to a simple or more nearly automatic operation—a process which, like the modern assembly line, greatly increased the efficiency of each worker.

It was precisely here that the machine came in. As long as each worker pursued a variety of individual tasks, the potentialities of the machine were greatly reduced. But the more nearly automatic the operation, the easier and more profitable to substitute a machine. So during the 1700's the demand for improved machines steadily increased, and was rewarded toward the end of the century with a burst of inventive genius. From this period on it is difficult to trace any single strand of cause and effect, for industrial progress depended on incessant interaction between new processes, greater demand and increased supply. Underlying the whole development, however, was one dominant theme: increase of cheap raw materials augmented the size of the factory; this led to further specialization of the industrial process; more actions were specialized, isolated, and replaced by machines; this led to greater efficiency and lower prices; and this in turn led to an enlargement of the market, and repetition of the cycle. While this cycle took many different forms, it represents the basic rhythm of the early part of the industrial revolution.

Put in this form, the early industrial revolution, as Hobson has pointed out, dispels the "heroic" theory of invention— "that of an idea flashing suddenly from the brain of a single genius and effecting a rapid revolution in trade."[1] Although Wyatt's roller spinner, Hargreaves' spinning jenny, Watt's steam engine, Arkwright's mill, Crompton's mule, Cartright's power loom, Whitney's saw gin, Roberts' self-acting mule, and a few others stand out as landmarks in inventive progress, actually these steps represented improvements over former types rather than wholly new inventions. Almost every one of the great textile inventions is of disputed authorship. Thus by the middle 1800's, spinning machinery was already a compound of about eight hundred inventions, and carding machinery comprised about sixty patents. The pres-

THE INDUSTRIAL REVOLUTION 27

sure of circumstances compelled men of meager ability to adopt common-sense methods of increasing efficiency. Necessity was the mother of invention, producing gradual but systematic perfection and elaboration of simple techniques. Faced with the economic imperatives of the day, practical men by rule of thumb hit upon contrivances to get over one difficulty after another.

Aware of this tedious, unromantic kind of progress, some historians have felt that the reason for Great Britain's technological superiority over other countries lay in its possession of essentially practical men who worked out concrete industrial problems in the factory while scientific philosophers in other countries limited themselves to theory. Thus, with the exception of Arkwright, the men mentioned above were tinkerers and jacks of all trade. Watt, for example, adapted to practical use the expansive power of heat, the theory of which seems to have originated with a physicist of Marburg. It now seems clear, however, that England's practical inventiveness was one of the lesser reasons for her supremacy in the industrial field. More important was Great Britain's insular character, which gave her natural facilities for procuring raw materials. There was also the advantage of a temperate climate and excellent internal communication. Mercantilism, with its paralyzing state control, was first thrown off in England. Perhaps most important of all, while the inventions of Crompton and Cartright were transforming the industrial scene in England, her continental rivals were wasting their energies in wars and revolutions.

England's real supremacy was not so apparent during the period 1770-1790—the time of early invention—as during the decades immediately following. For the period 1790-1840 witnessed a truly breath-taking expansion of England's production and trade. The cause of this was the use of steam power to propel the new machines. The increase in productivity from 1770 to 1790—the age of the great mechanical inventions—was tremendous compared to the preceding decades. But it shades into insignificance when contrasted with output during the period 1790 to 1840. For no matter how refined the machinery, large-scale production was an impossibility until the power of millions of horses had been harnessed and put to work. This was the job of steam, and it did its job well. British importation of cotton amounted to 35,000,000 pounds in 1790 and to 490,000,000 in 1841; importation of wool totaled 2,500,000 pounds in 1790 and 50,000,000 pounds in 1850; iron output increased from 61,300 tons in 1788 to 1,347,790 tons in 1839.[2]

Britain had the industrial game to herself until well into the nineteenth century. Once the initial mechanical problems had been solved, the technicians of the "workshop of the world" eagerly faced the demands of an ever-expanding world economy. Situations that once had involved problems of physics and mathematics now demanded knowledge of the new sciences of biology and chemistry. It was in these latter fields that the continental nations found their industrial self-expression. France can claim the discovery and development of silk-throwing machines, the Jacquard loom, the tubular boiler, the water turbine, chemical bleaching, and other mechanisms and processes. But the Napoleonic Wars, the individualistic inheritance, and the lack of fuel, raw materials, and capital, kept France well behind England in industrial progress. Although pioneering in the application of agricultural chemistry, Germany also remained stationary until the 1850's. Holland lacked sufficient resources, and Italy was too crippled by political disunity, to enable these countries to duplicate Britain's industrial achievements.

Just as the Americans revolted against Britain politically in the 1700's, so they revolted industrially in the 1800's. At first economic development had been slow, since the settlers were obliged to make most of their own tools and clothing. With improvement in transportation, the farmer steadily abandoned various by-occupations—shoe making and brewing, for example—which in turn were assumed by factories. The Revolutionary War had stimulated domestic production, and tariffs after 1815 helped the textile and iron industries over the hurdle of foreign competition. While agriculture and commerce remained the chief interests until the Civil War, by 1850 American machine tools were entering the European market and English observers were marveling at the "fearless and masterly manner" in which "correct principles" were applied by American engineers.[3]

The flowering of industrialization in the United States came after the Civil War, which in itself was a major factor stimulating industry. During the following decades the expansion of the railroads linking the West with the more settled part of the country, facilitated the exploitation of our tremendous natural resources, and led to an increased demand on the part of an expanding population. Our industrial development was meteoric. The value of manufactures increased steadily from three billion dollars in 1869 to seventy billion in 1929. Agricultural products rose in value from two billion in 1870 to twelve billion in 1930. The amount of primary horsepower used productively grew from nineteen million in 1869 to four hundred million in 1929. In 1860 we exported a third of a billion dollars of goods and imported about the same amount; in 1930 both figures had been multiplied tenfold. Our population jumped from thirty-one million in 1860 to one hundred and twenty-two million in 1930. These figures, of course, indicate only the spearheads of the movement, the economic skeleton of a revolution which covered the whole range of politics, science, learning, culture, and the arts as well.

America's intensive and far-flung industrialization not only challenged Britain's supremacy; it also illustrated what was to be one of the central phenomena of the industrial revolution. Thorstein Veblen, the brilliant sociologist noted for his original and critical diagnoses of capitalism, called this "the penalty of taking the lead"—the disadvantage accruing to the nation which blazed the industrial trail by expending its capital and genius on new inventions, only to find its equipment obsolete when placed in competition with other nations which, starting afresh, could reap the benefits of the latest advances.[4] An excellent example of this was the narrow-gauge railway system in Great Britain, a great handicap which was irremediable because the expense of widening the gauge was considered too great.

The United States was a major beneficiary of the "penalty of taking the lead," only to be penalized in turn. In Japan the state fostered industrialization on an elaborate scale, and here again the latest techniques were borrowed from older industrial nations only to be used to beat them at the competitive game. The most recent case has been the Soviet Union where, as Heaton has pointed out, "the logic of large scale production, the factory system and the machine technique are being adopted more completely . . . through their extension to agriculture, than anywhere else."[5] In all these instances an underlying motive can be seen: while advanced industrial nations exported machine goods, most countries preferred to import industrialism, for the industrial revolution shifted the major emphasis to the importance of large productive capacity and self-sufficiency as basic to the awakened nationalism of the times.

Despite its talent for turning head over heels so many phases of society, the industrial revolution brought with it no reversal of the condition of the workers. While long hours, insanitary conditions, low wages and other evils had existed long before the introduction of factories, misery was now concentrated and made more visible. Intent on profit making and faced with unorganized employees, the employers bothered little with the condition of their workers. The inevitable result was a record of social degradation and general misery without parallel in history.

The hastily erected factories had practically no provision for the comfort or health of the workers. Low ceilings, narrow openings, poor ventilation were the rule. Rest rooms and sanitary toilets were unheard of. Fatal accidents were frequent owing to lack of protection from machinery, but there was no compensation system and damages could be collected only if it was proved that the employer was directly at fault! On returning from the factory the worker had no park or playground to go to, but bleak and foul industrial slums close to the dirt and smoke of the hearths. Within the factory a heavy discipline hemmed in the actions of the workers. In one plant fines of a shilling apiece were levied on the spinner who opened his window, whistled, was five minutes late, or was found "in another's wheel gate"—to mention only a few of the crimes.[6]

The conditions of women and children were particularly atrocious. Control by foremen over the giving of jobs led to a common saying in England, "Every man's factory is his harem." Wages of women and children averaged from four

THE INDUSTRIAL REVOLUTION

shillings to nine shillings ($1 to $2.25) a week—about a third of the men's wages. Often the head of the family sat at home jobless while the rest of the family eked out some sort of living. Sixteen- and eighteen-hour days were not uncommon for children under fourteen. Ten-year-old girls went insane in the darkness of mines, chimney sweeps were smothered in flues or burnt to death, half-naked women hauled coal cars on their hands and knees—all without exciting pity from the employers. A father testified before factory commissioners in 1833:[7]

> My two sons (one ten, the other thirteen) work at the Milne's factory at Linton. They go at half past five in the morning; don't stop at breakfast or tea time. They stop at dinner half an hour. Come home at a quarter before ten. They used to work till ten, sometimes eleven, sometimes twelve . . . I have been obliged to beat 'em with a strap in their shirts, and to pinch 'em, in order to get them well awake . . .

One observer summed it all up: "The children lived the life of a machine while working, and at other times that of a beast."

This is a harrowing picture, relieved by only a few bright spots. Robert Owen showed that better conditions of work and higher pay were not only morally desirable but profitable as well. In the smaller plants employers tended to be more considerate of their workers' welfare. But unquestionably the greatest single aid to the employees was the trade-union.

Detestation of action by workers—whether organized or not—apparently did not originate with the factory system. There has come down to us a statement made by John Gower around 1385:

> The world goeth fast from bad to worse when shepherd and cowherd for their part demand more for their labor than the master-bailiff (himself) was wont to take in days gone by. Laborers of old were not wont to eat of wheaten bread: Their meat was of beans or of coarser corn and their drink, of water alone. Cheese and milk were a feast to them—then was the world ordered aright for folk of this sort. Three things, all of the same sort, are merciless when they get the upper hand: a water flood, a wasting fire, and the common multitude of small folk— Ha, age of ours, whither turnest thou? for the poor and small folk, who

should cleave to their labor, demand to be better fed than their masters!

This feeling did not become more pronounced during the following centuries because in England, at least, industrial labor was never a menace before the industrial revolution. Not the common people but the skilled workers and traders formed associations. These combinations of the fifteenth and sixteenth centuries included masters and merchants with journeymen for the purpose of regulating quality, quantity, and price of product. No revolutionary ideas were bred in these organizations, but schemes for protecting the privileged position of the skilled. Later the guilds gave way to workingmen's associations, but still the emphasis was on welfare functions and social activities among the members.

Here, as in so many other fields, the industrial revolution wrought a major change. As the "common multitude of small folk" were herded into factories, as their habits and attitudes were disciplined by a common environment, the ground was prepared for trade-unionism in the modern sense. But the vested interests of the day were well aware of the threat offered by the organization of hungry and desperate men and women. Fearful that the older workingmen's associations would supply the leadership for the new industrial wage earners, the government took swift action against "Republicans and Levellers." In 1799, national associations with branches were made illegal. This was followed by the Combination Acts of 1800, which suppressed by law all forms of trade-unionism.[8]

If the unions had been strong and well entrenched, these laws would have met with organized resistance amounting almost to civil war. As it was, the young and feeble organizations were broken into fragments. The natural result was a series of sporadic strikes and riots. The most notable protest took the form of machine smashing. Led by "King Ludd" of Sherwood Forest, a mythical leader with a Robin Hood reputation, the Luddites organized attacks on what they supposed to be the basic cause of unemployment and starvation wages. For a time Parliament sought to abolish unrest by force, but as economic conditions grew worse, especially after 1815, pressure for reform grew stronger. The Combination Acts were repealed, which paved the way for rapid advance in factory legislation.

Economic conditions in the United States at this time were but little better, although there was a greater scarcity of labor. The first workingmen's associations followed the traditions of the old English guilds and concerned themselves less with the improvement of working conditions than with social activities and financial help for their members. With the rise of more intensive competition following the Revolutionary War, incipient capital-labor antagonism became evident. It was not until after the Civil War, however, that trade-unions managed to survive the periodic economic storms that swept the Atlantic seaboard.

Meanwhile the American worker was trying to adjust himself to changing conditions. We have seen in the preceding chapter that the growth of huge concerns widened the gap between employer and employee. Simultaneously, there was a steady decrease in the number of workers who were independent, under nobody's orders, masters of their own fate. The "independent" class in the United States (composed of proprietors and officials, the professional group, and farmers and their children) decreased from 43.3 per cent of the working population in 1880 to 32.4 per cent of the working population in 1930. The "dependent" class, on the other hand (made up of farm laborers, industrial wage earners, domestic workers, and lower-salaried groups) increased from 48.5 per cent of the working population in 1880 to 62.2 per cent in 1930.

It should be noted, however, that since 1920 there have been, in general, relatively fewer persons working in manufacturing and mines, while a relatively greater number are to be found in transportation and communication, in the clerical occupations, and in the trade or service occupations.[9]

This development may or may not mean more class consciousness in the United States. Many of the newer occupations lead to personal contact with the "independent" class, a sense of superiority to ordinary wage earners, and consequently to "capitalism-mindedness," even though wages in this group may not be higher. On the other hand, it seems clear that if occupational groupings become more rigid and barriers are set up preventing passage from one classification to another, the clash among economic interests will sharpen and class feeling will develop. Magazines may still feature stories of office boys rising to a partnership and marrying the boss's daughter, but for millions this will have no meaning unless opportunity for education and advancement is left open to them.

The increase in the percentage of the "dependents" reflects what is a central characteristic of recent economic history—the supremacy of the corporation, which received its chief impetus from the industrial revolution. Appearing in the United States before the Civil War, the corporation has personified the rise of industry on a vast scale. Its present power is sufficient to make it the rival of government as the dominant means of social organization. And as Berle and Means have suggested, just as the factory deprived labor of its control over conditions of work and amount of remuneration, so the corporation has deprived the bulk of the stockholders of their control of policy.[10] This development has speeded up the placing of more and more power in progressively fewer hands, so that by 1927 nearly half of the wealth and income of corporations (excluding banks and other financial corporations) was owned or controlled by two hundred companies.

Thus we have the makings of an economic dictatorship in a political democracy—an uneasy alliance. Undoubtedly the centralization of economic power has led to more coordination, stability and efficiency. But at the same time there has been a growing feeling that our economic overlords have not sensed the obligations placed upon them. The very strength of the corporation often makes it impervious to the demands of its stockholders, to the complaints of the employees, to the needs of the consumers. Its actions, furthermore, reach into the darkest areas of our society and arouse to action men hitherto untouched by its industrial and financial policies. In John Steinbeck's *The Grapes of Wrath* the corporation's employee who has come to take over the farmer's mortgaged land can say only: "The bank isn't like a man . . . The bank is something more than men, I tell you. It's the monster. Men made it, but they can't control it." In a sense this is a continuation of the old anti-machinism of the Luddites, except that now antagonism is directed against something more powerful and farther removed from the control of the people.

There is always a tendency to use the past tense in speaking of the industrial revolution. Yet it may properly be asked whether this great phase of man's development is really at an end. Surely our technological advance is not over. As described in a later chapter new materials—glass, rubber, fiber, plastics, alloys—are revolutionizing industry, just as steel did years ago. New techniques, inventions, processes, formulas, are offering positive proof that industry still continues to rebel against its own trappings, continues to break through its shell into new ways.

But we must not become too complacent in our expectation of continued technological advance. Such progress is best ensured in a society that provides opportunity for change and does not stifle inventive or artistic talent. The machine itself sets up a discipline which tends to militate against further progress. The far-off struggles of the Luddites still pose questions of heavy consequence. Unless we rule the machine and make it the instrument for the attainment of a democratic and humanitarian culture all effort will more and more center on making men only efficient cogs of their machines and on allowing our economy to run on oblivious of their needs and wants of the people.

To achieve the potentialities of our technology we must harness it to the will of the people. So perhaps the industrial revolution that continues will demand painstaking efforts at social engineering of the same caliber as the technical engineering of Watt and Compton and Cartright. This inventiveness and leadership must come from the ranks of the employers as well as from the organized workers. The next few chapters will attempt some picture of the approach of each of these groups to this high task. First let us take a look at the unions.

III. THE ESTATE OF LABOR

CHAPTER 4

THE LABOR UNION SET-UP IN THE U. S. A.

When labor organizes, it is sharing with other social and economic groups the need for collective action. Only under primitive conditions in a frontier economy does the individual in substantial measure control his own destiny. Even then, collective action within the family and among neighbors is essential to comfort and security. As specialization and the consequent interdependence increase in an advancing economy, collective action becomes more and more necessary to the security of individuals and groups. Farmers, tradesmen, employers, consumers, investors, taxpayers, bankers, lawyers, doctors, wage earners all discover among themselves common objectives which can be achieved only through common action.

Workers began to organize as such almost as soon as the wage status appeared in our society. Organization started among local groups of relatively well-informed, skilled and culturally homogeneous craftsmen. During the first half of the last century, these local craft groups began slowly to come together, with other groups of the same craft in other localities or with other crafts in the same locality. Organizations of the first type became national craft unions and of the second, trades councils. The typographical workers of Philadelphia, Baltimore and New York, for example, having formed locals of their craft in the vicinity of each of these cities, gradually began to establish connections with each other which eventually resulted in a central office, officers, treasury and annual convention to which an increasing degree of importance was delegated. Among other crafts—carpenters, mule spinners, and foundry workers, for example—similar developments took place. Paralleling this evolution, and beginning somewhat earlier, was the appearance of trades councils in the larger communities. These councils were composed of delegates from various local crafts. Their common interests were primarily political, while those of the craft nationals were largely economic.

Somewhat later came the beginning of common action, local and national, among different crafts, in the same industry—mule spinners, loom fixers, weavers and carders in the cotton textile industry, for example. On a local basis, councils of textile craft representatives were established to consider matters of mutual interest. Nationally, the craft unions first exchanged views and correspondence, then formed loose federations and, finally, amalgamated into associations. From these amalgamated craft unions grew up industrial or semi-industrial unions with occupational lines obliterated or greatly diminished in importance. The Amalgamated Association of Iron, Steel and Tin Workers of North America, for example, was formed in the 1870's as a result of the consolidation of a number of craft organizations in the iron and steel industry. The Iron Puddlers' Union; the United Sons of Vulcan; the Associated Brotherhood of Iron and Steel Heaters, Rollers, and Roughers of the United States; the Iron and Steel Roll Hands' Union, composed of catchers, hookers, helpers, and others; and the United Nailers all joined hands and invited "all men working in and around rolling mills, (etc.) . . ." to join the new association. Thus, locally, industrial unions take in all those who work in and around a given mine, mill, factory, shop, or a group of such producing units. Nationally, an industrial union asserts jurisdiction over an entire industry or even a group of related industries such as cotton, woolen, silk and rayon. The rise of industrial unions represents a higher degree of common action among workers. In an industrial union the interests of the individual are merged, first with those of other workers in his own occupation, second, with those of other occupations in the same local unit of the industry, finally with the interests of the workers throughout the industry.

Beyond the collective action of the industrial unions are the federations of national unions such as the American Federation of Labor and the Congress of Industrial Organizations. Both of these are composed of workers organized both geographically in local, state or regional councils and economically in national or directly affiliated trade unions. In passing it should be noted that the American Federation of Labor contains both craft and industrial unions.

A fairly accurate measure of the degree of commonality of action among workers in a particular union may be found in its financial arrangements. The primary source of union income is membership dues. These are paid into the local union treasury by employed union members. A share of the dues is paid by the local to the regional or national treasury as a per capita tax. If the national union is affiliated with the CIO or the A. F. of L., it pays to the treasury of one of these organizations a per capita tax upon its total membership. The larger the proportion of membership dues which is paid upward from the local to the national organization, the greater the importance and responsibility of the national and the greater the degree to which the individual worker has merged his interests with those of others. In some unions, the national office does not play an important part, the local unions retaining most of the funds and providing most of the services for its members. In other unions the bulk of the funds goes to the national or district offices which direct the major functions of the organization and assume its obligations. Obviously the probability and the strength of common action throughout the industry or trade is far greater in the second case than in the first. Historically, the trend has been from the looser toward the firmer bond throughout the American labor movement.

The most recent instance is to be found in the fact that the monthly per capita tax from constituent national unions to the CIO is five cents as compared with one cent to the A. F. of L. This means that, constitutionally, and insofar as it is aided by financial resources, the younger federation is capable of greater solidarity than the A. F. of L.

The development of group action among American workers has been intensely realistic. The forms of organization in different industries or trades tend to conform to the nature of the industry or trade. Consequently there is wide variety among different unions or even within the same union. In the United Textile Workers, for example, pure craft, amalgamated craft, industrial locals, a craft national, industrial departments and an almost autonomous industrial national union persisted side by side for years within the same general structure. In the United Mine Workers, all district organizations except one are geographical units. One "district," however, is made up of coke and by-product chemical workers, wherever they may be employed and without regard to geography.

To the extent that business had become integrated, specialized, interdependent, huge and centralized, American labor has followed in its footsteps. The United Mine Workers of America, for example, found their organization imperiled by the anti-union practices of the steel masters who were closely allied with the coal operators. It was as much to protect their organization as to help a fellow worker build his own that the miners sponsored a campaign to establish collective bargaining in the steel industry.

In the beginning all labor organization was spontaneous and under fellow-employee leadership. Groups of workers grumbling about their long hours, short pay, and harsh working conditions set the stage for unionism within their craft or industry. If the union survived, its officers continued to work in the shops, attending to union affairs after hours. (If the union failed, the officers were usually discharged.) With the growth and amalgamation of various streams of the movement the need for full-time, experienced leadership became more and more urgent. The professional executives developed in the trade-unions were quite different from those of business or government. The last two have always been able to hire brains and knowledge from any walk of life. They can draw new blood from the universities, and enlist men who have proved their ability in other fields. Not so the labor union. Its officials are elected by popular vote or convention, and, as a rule, candidates must spring from the membership within the craft or industry. In other words, the trade-union leader has worked his way up from the mine or factory. For the most part he has had no training for labor leadership except experience in the smaller units of his organization. The chances are that his education stopped with

THE LABOR UNION SET-UP IN THE U. S. A. 43

grade school. Recently, however, as unions have extended their activities, there has been a tendency to enlist the services of sympathetic college graduates for specialized tasks. Some of the newly established union papers have secured their editors from outside the membership. Occasionally union research directors are not workers themselves though they may have a wage-earner background; and the union legal department is almost exclusively without trade experience.

The modern labor union has, in many respects, become a big business. And while its annual income may not approach that of Standard Oil, it is nevertheless a sizeable institution. The story of the Steel Workers Organizing Committee, because it is new and unfettered by tradition, illustrates many recent trends in labor organization.

The SWOC was created on June 3, 1936, by an agreement between the Amalgamated Association of Iron, Steel, and Tin Workers and the Congress of Industrial Organizations. The CIO was to furnish funds for an organizing campaign to enroll new members into the Amalgamated. The membership recruited by SWOC, however, was at first to act independently of the Amalgamated and to have its own national officers and conventions. Within one year membership in the steel union rose from 8,000 to 450,000, and 230 companies signed their first union contracts with the SWOC. The first convention of the SWOC was held at Pittsburgh in December, 1937, and at that time it was able to report a membership of 500,000 and signed contracts with 445 firms. The convention, composed of delegates from each of the then 700 lodges, elected or rather reaffirmed the national officers and set the policies for the future. In the summer of 1939 the SWOC had a membership of 550,000 and 595 iron and steel producing and fabricating companies under written contract. The SWOC was well established and could turn its attention to the problems of industrial union activity.

Today the national headquarters of the SWOC has a staff of 246 persons, thirty of them attached to the national headquarters at Pittsburgh, the remainder stationed at some sixty field offices. In appearance the national office is not unlike that of any steel company. The auditing and lodge departments are well equipped with business machinery, including a teletypewriter connected with the printer in Indianapolis. The shelves of the research department are lined with source material on the iron and steel industry, and the editorial offices of the SWOC paper, *Steel Labor,* have a "morgue"* complete for its field.

The primary function of the labor organization—collective bargaining—is a day-to-day relationship based upon a contract periodically renewed. The union's national officers, together with a committee of local lodge representatives, negotiate the contract with employers or employer associations. This agreement outlines the terms and conditions under which the employees are to work during the ensuing period. The rights and duties of management as well as of men are usually set forth, and almost invariably there is a clause forbidding strikes or lockouts during the term of the contract. But the indispensable section of the agreement is that establishing the grievance adjustment machinery. Without this, even a primary form of collective bargaining cannot exist. The contract corresponds in many respects to the constitution, and the written settlements of important grievances serve the same purpose as the body of common law and court interpretations. That is, an issue once settled serves as a precedent for similar questions unless the decision is modified by the next contract.

The grievance adjustment machinery is primarily the responsibility of local union lodge officers and grievance committeemen. They meet daily with local management of supervisory staffs and thresh out difficulties or complaints which may have arisen in the plant. Grievances, like taxes, may be reduced but they cannot be eliminated. The best intentioned corporation policy will trip somewhere along the line down to the "straw boss" or "pusher" (rank and file designations for assistants to the foreman whose special duty it is to expedite work). In such a case the grievance machinery acts as a safety valve relieving resentment before it reaches the explosion point. Technological changes are a fertile source of grievances. An old machine is replaced by a

* "Morgue"—newspaper vernacular for a collection of pictures and clippings relating to people and organizations likely to be in the news again.

new and faster one. The company wishes a change in the rate structure, pointing out that less effort now produces more units, and that the concern is entitled to a return on its investment. The worker may claim that the new rates reduce his earning capacity while increasing his responsibility. Here is where joint time studies and thorough discussion are extremely useful.

Grievances that cannot be settled locally are appealed, in stages, to the national officers of the union and the top executives of the company. Agreement is generally reached here, for failing agreement the case will be settled by arbitration which, relatively speaking, is both expensive and uncertain.

At this writing, the SWOC has 1,100 local lodges with some 25,000 local officers and grievance committeemen. These are men who were formerly obscure wage earners. Most of them lived in communities dominated by their employers. Their rights in the mill were practically non-existent and their rights in their communities severely circumscribed. Under such conditions they took little interest in improving either their towns or their work places. But recognition of their labor organization has kindled ambition. Being able to make their influence felt, they are now both mill and community conscious.

The union health and safety committee works with management for the elimination of hazards and careless operation. These committees have changed the viewpoint and the practice of many an obstinate worker who refused to wear safety appliances.

The union relief committee looks after the interests of fellow employees who have been laid off and are without means of support. The workman's compensation committee helps injured employees in making their claims for disability. The union social committee seeks to instill a feeling of good fellowship among the employees. Company facilities are frequently used, and many union picnics are held on company grounds. In the past, social and recreational opportunities offered by the employer were often shunned as "paternalistic"; today employer cooperation is welcomed and appreciated.

The local unions have engendered a new civic pride—a

sense of responsibility for community welfare. Unions are taking an interest in politics and good government. Many of their leaders have been elected to public office. Few are the steel towns now without wage-earner representation on the council or school board. The local unions take an interest in the schools and in cultural and recreational activities, frequently in cooperation with local educators and clergymen. The local unions urge well-rounded programs of social legislation and do much to spread understanding of their objectives. In short, unionism in steel is leading to a wide-awake citizenship and as a result is greatly strengthening the forces for democracy in America.

The SWOC was fortunate in being able to draw upon the experience of the long-established unions in the CIO. It has also had a greater sphere for action because the company town was more frequent in steel than in most American industries, except coal mining. However the accomplishments of the SWOC are not unusual. Other unions, particularly the newer ones, are doing more or less the same things.

The organizational activities of a labor union consist essentially of conveying to particular groups of wage earners the philosophy of group action; that is, advertising the benefits of unionism. The approach necessarily is personal. A representative of the union, the organizer, directs the efforts in a given locality. It is his duty to explain what trade-unionism means and to answer questions. He must encourage the natural group leaders around whom the local union lodge will develop in the plant. Although this is the basic organizing technique in all labor groups, it usually is supplemented by other appeals. Leaflets, pamphlets and newspapers, mass meetings with well-known speakers, radio and sound truck appeals, the establishment of workers' education and recreation projects, house-to-house canvasses, shop and mill gate meetings may all be used by the organizers. But the birth and the adolescence of the new organization depend for their success upon the efforts of a relatively small number of active local leaders who do the work, run the show, take the praise or the blame and build the young effort into a permanent enterprise.

After the union has been recognized, the contract defining

the relationship between the employer and the union commonly becomes an aid to maintaining organizational unity. Employers opposed to unionism have traditionally maintained what has been called an "open shop" position. This has frequently meant that the shop has been in fact closed to union members, or that the employer through his hiring and firing policies has kept the union so weak that its bargaining efforts have been futile. Under these conditions, no pressure can be exerted by union members upon non-union workers. On the contrary, the economic power of the employer is used to prevent organization.

If, however, by the terms of its contract a union is recognized by the employer as sole bargaining agent for his employees, the prestige of this position is frequently effective in breaking down fear in the workers who want a union. Under the National Labor Relations Act a union having a majority of the workers in a bargaining unit is granted sole bargaining powers. While recognition as sole bargaining agent adds prestige and power to a union and may therefore attract new members, it is unnecessary for workers to join and pay dues to a union in order to secure its services as bargaining agent. All that they have to do is to vote for it in an election under the auspices of the National Labor Relations Board each time the majority status of the union is challenged. With the union thus established, workers may persistently neglect to pay dues or to attend meetings, leaving the union to hold the bag of responsibility, anxiety, toil and expense. Union members are no different in this respect from taxpayers who are sometimes forgetful of the obligation they have assumed. Citizens of a government realize that something more effective than patriotism is necessary to sustain the exchequer. They therefore provide for the compulsory collection of taxes or dues to the nation. Everybody benefits from the protection and services of the government, but not everybody is always willing to pay his share of the expense, particularly when it involves some inconvenience in doing so. The same is true of union members.

There is therefore a strong motive for union members and leaders to seek a closed shop contract. Under such a contract workers are required to join the union at the time of employment or within a stated period afterward. If employment is slack, this may mean that only workers on the union's membership and seniority lists will be employed. The traditional reasons for union insistence upon a closed shop contract are, first, to prevent an anti-union employer from whittling away the union's strength by gradually replacing union members with non-union workers and, second, to compel all workers receiving the benefit of union activities to pay their share of the freight. The first of these reasons has become less weighty because of the protection afforded unionism by the National Labor Relations Act. The second reason, however, has become even more compelling for the reasons indicated above. For some time to come, therefore, the closed shop is likely to be insisted upon as an important tool for preserving collective action among organized workers.

There is a third reason, compelling to union and employer alike, for the closed or union shop. Under a "members only" or even "sole bargaining rights" contract the status of the union is insecure. It owes its continued existence to the day-to-day benefits it can confer upon its membership. There is a tendency therefore for the union to take up grievances indiscriminately and make vigorous efforts to win them all, for if it does not do so, it will lose support and membership. The shortsighted employee who has no justifiable complaint but is pressing for "action" will say, "All right, if you won't take up my case, I'll stop paying dues and get my friends to do the same." Under a closed shop contract this is impossible. The union then is in a position to take up cases on their merits alone, ignoring threats of this kind. A variant of the closed shop agreement is the preferential union shop contract under which the employer binds himself to give preference to union members in hiring and layoffs, but under which no worker is compelled to join the union in order to secure a job.

The check-off of dues is frequently associated with the closed or union shop. The fact should not be overlooked that employers first made use of the check-off to deduct from employees' wages amounts owed to the firm for tools and supplies purchased at company stores. Even where no union contract exists, it is a usual practice for employers to check off from employees' wages premiums for group insurance, medical and hospital services, and even in some instances, pew rent in churches.

Under the check-off the company deducts dues from the pay checks of the employees and forwards the money directly to the financial officer of the union, largely as a matter of accommodation. The check-off is an auxiliary device rather than a compulsive weapon. It regularizes collections and does away with much inconvenience. It also diminishes the possibility of misuse of union funds, for it eliminates transactions in currency and substitutes payments by check. Although the check-off may be compulsory under union contract, the authorized or voluntary check-off is coming into increasing use. Under this arrangement the individual worker signs a statement authorizing the employer to deduct stated amounts from his pay.

In concluding this chapter it should be emphasized that the reasons for labor unions lie in the necessity for group action among workers as among other social or economic groups in a society so vast, complex and interdependent that the individual is practically powerless. Wherever and whenever the process of production ceases to be small, self-sufficient and simple, the worker can influence the conditions under which he gains his livelihood only by common action with his fellows. To some groups in some situations, this fact is obvious and there organizational work is spontaneous and easy. Other groups require long educational effort and "outside" assistance. But whatever the case, as soon as the local union or lodge is established, officers elected, and a contract signed with the employer, the real business of unionism begins. If management has stoutly resisted the collective bargaining efforts of its employees, if it has discriminated against union members, and forced all but the boldest to crouch in the background, then it is likely to be rewarded by a set of officers and a committee noted best for their fighting qualities and only secondarily for their administrative ability. On the other hand if management has not opposed organizational activities and thus permitted the calmer and less spectacular leaders to come to the fore, it will be rewarded by a set of officers and committee which have no sores to heal and no background of antagonism to management. Under such condition the transition, for management from arbitrary control, and for men from docile submission, to joint responsibility and cooperation will be much easier and with a minimum of misunderstanding and suspicion. Little of permanent value can be accomplished if labor must be constantly on guard against attack.

For the third time in a third of a century circumstances are again ripening for a common endeavor to resolve the major problems of industrial relations and production. The first two—the National Civic Federation and the World War period experiments—ended disastrously for labor. Labor has learned much in its two false starts and will not make the same mistakes again. One of the purposes for the writing of this book is to demonstrate that this new effort has not only a much greater chance of success than the previous two but is designed to influence the common weal more effectively.

Now given its organization let us turn and review labor in action—especially those practices and attitudes most discussed by the proverbial "man on the street."

CHAPTER 5

SOME OF LABOR'S CONTROVERSIAL PRACTICES AND ATTITUDES

THE controversial practices and attitudes of labor have very largely grown out of its struggle to survive. Reduced to desperation in the past, labor used whatever weapons were available. When labor was forbidden the right to strike or make effective petition for redress of grievances under the old anti-combination acts of the first quarter of the nineteenth century, groups of workers in England took matters into their own hands and devised their own methods to protect their interests. The Luddites in England destroying machine frames, because they saw these new contraptions taking away their livelihood, is one illustration. Under similar legal and economic restraints the Molly McGuires engaged in another kind of furtive guerrilla warfare in the anthracite fields of Pennsylvania some fifty years later.

With the extension of democracy, and the institution of sound practical trade-unions, these early tactics were discarded, and new and more realistic principles of organization defense were introduced; principles the fundamental purpose of which was to advance or protect the cause of labor. Even so, forthright steps were taken to keep to a minimum injury to employer or public. In a strike, for example, the union committee furnished maintenance men to keep the plant in order during the stoppage and to prevent unnecessary loss. And if a public service is affected, care is taken to see that hospitals, doctors, and others are not hindered in their duties.

As a rule restrictive instruments in the hands of labor originate in corresponding and pre-existing practices of the employer. For the strike there is the lockout; for the slow-down there is the speed-up; for sabotage there are the *agent provocateur* and labor spy; for the boycott there is the black list. It is a case of "Bloody instructions, which, being taught, return to plague the inventor."

The Republic Steel strike of 1937 was finally precipitated by the lockout of the workers at the strongly organized plants at Canton and Massillon, Ohio. Indeed these workers independently declared themselves on strike one day before the general walkout was voted.[1] The objective in this strike was union recognition embodied in a signed contract. The signed contract was insisted upon as the only way to put an end to the employer's abuse of his economic power. In it discrimination is specifically outlawed. Also the terms and conditions of employment are definitely set forth, and machinery for adjustment and, if necessary, arbitration of grievances is provided. Such a contract is labor's constitutional guarantee against arbitrary treatment as within a given plant or industry. For this reason labor is willing to fight to secure it, and for the same reason the more irresponsible men in management have fought to withhold it.

And significant is the way larger, more responsible and democratic unions prepare for a projected strike. The railroad brotherhoods require the signing of a ballot indicating whether the member is "for" or "against" the proposed strike and at the same time authorizing over his own signature an executive officer of the brotherhood to act in his behalf in all negotiations with employer representatives. The semi-industrial unions in the clothing industry place the issues involved before the membership in a series of meetings out of which authority is voted to union officers to call a strike when all other efforts to effect a settlement have failed. In the steel industry a national convention of more than 900 delegates elected by the membership of local lodges unanimously voted to vest in the national officers of the Steel Workers Organizing Committee full authority to negotiate the best available contracts with their employers to replace those expiring in 1938.

In contrast with these democratic procedures are the practices particularly of some craft unions in the building and the so-called service industries. Union business agents have either acquired or are vested with dictatorial powers. Often these powers are exercised both arbitrarily and unwisely. The practices of management in some instances provide likewise an illuminating contrast. The hiring of professional strike breakers; the stocking of arms, munitions, tear and sickening gases, of bedding and food supplies in anticipation of a strike is rarely, if ever, done with the advice and consent of the stockholders. How much such practices by management have contributed to the development of aggressive and dictatorial leadership on the part of organized labor deserves careful reflection and consideration by all interested in the preservation and extension of democratic institutions and processes.

Illustrating this point, the Republic Steel Corporation in the 1937 strike, without consulting its stockholders, hired spies to report upon the union meetings and membership; it "rough shadowed" the union leaders and organizers; it published statements to employees attempting to vilify and discredit union leaders and their purposes and policies; its police assaulted active union men; it coerced employees into signing petitions opposing outside or independent unions; it coerced civil authorities into swearing in company employees as special police officers; it incited violence and hysteria in order to terrorize union adherents; it foisted company unions upon its unwilling employees; it discharged prominent union members, and finally the company locked out its strongly organized employees at Canton and Massillon.[2] As the National Labor Relations Board has said, "The respondent (Republic Steel), not the union, had chosen the way of industrial strife."[3]

What military equipment the company had at the time of the strike is not on the record. But as of May 25, 1938—a year after the strike—it had an arsenal including 552 revolvers with 17,650 rounds of ammunition, 64 rifles with 59,350 rounds of ammunition, 245 shot guns with 5,784 shells, 2,707 sickening and tear gas hand grenades, 143 long-range gas guns with 4,033 projectiles and shells.[4]

Under modern capitalism, the strike grows out of the wage system and is not comparable to the uprisings of serfs, peasants or guildsmen. It is fundamentally related to all those conditions which have caused the rise of trade-union organization. Although strikes occurred in an early period of the industrial revolution, they became socially significant only after the rise of large-scale industry. As trade-unionism spreads to previously unorganized industries, it is often accompanied by strike waves, as witness the bituminous coal strike of 1897, the anthracite strike in 1902, and the steel strike in 1919. This does not mean, however, that the strike movement grows in proportion to the development of the trade-union movement. As the President's commission on industrial relations in Great Britain and Sweden reported,[5] as a result of its investigation in 1938, the tendency to strike diminishes as the labor unions increase in numbers and strength, both because increasing bargaining power reduces the necessity for strikes, and because responsible leadership and increasing centralization and control tend to check impulsive action. Perhaps most important in tending to reduce the number of strikes is the acceptance and general practice of collective bargaining.

The conduct of strikes varies with the circumstances out of which they arise. Some of the factors in determining the course of a strike are the nature, economic position and geographical location of the industry involved, the strength and effectiveness of the union, the economic and social conditions prevailing in the community where the strike occurs, legal restrictions, and types of industrial policing. Action which would be successful in an industry corporately owned and controlled and spread over a wide area would be inappropriate in a strike involving a single establishment under local and personal ownership. The previous status of the union likewise is significant. In a plant which is unorganized or in which only a small proportion of the employees are union members, and where no recognition has been granted the union, the strike is apt to be a spontaneous walkout without notice. Such a strike is usually the result of some sudden provocation, although it reveals a prevailing unrest. Spontaneous strikes, usually called stoppages, do occasionally take place even in well-organized industries and in open violation of trade agreements. But where relations between the employer and the union are generally satisfactory, such interruptions, if and when they occur, are likely to be of short duration. In such instances the men are ordered back to work by their own union leaders, who then take up the grievance under the orderly procedure outlined by the contract.

However, where contractual relations have been initiated because of considerations of expediency and without the intention on either one side or both of entering upon real collective bargaining various subtle devices are used to keep going the policy of warfare. In such a case the management, for instance, leaves everything up to the foreman, with the understanding that the latter will resist all threatened encroachments as heretofore. Correspondingly the unions have evolved practices through which they strengthen their position at critical times by a more or less covert show of force. "Quickies" and "slow-downs" afford illustrations. A quickie, an unauthorized stoppage of work contrary to existing contractual agreement and without a sufficiently formal authorization, was invented originally by the I.W.W. and is in current use in the West in industries where the relationship between men and management, for one reason or another—sometimes political—is not really agreeable to the union leadership. It is essentially a violation of the "no strike, no lockout" clause of the contract. The "slow-down" is of the same essential character but the workers attempt to maintain their places on the payroll by going through the motions. Neither quickies nor slow-downs can be considered features of union-management cooperation.

Once a strike is under way, its leaders are confronted with two major problems: they must maintain the enthusiasm and loyalty of the strikers and keep other workers from taking their places. To prevent this strikebreaking, strikers or their representatives picket the entrance to the place of employment. Picketing has these chief purposes: to inform those unaware of the fact that a strike is in progress and to persuade other employees to join the strike and thus keep them from going to work. Picketing methods range from mass demonstrations before the place of employment, or in the community, to individual persuasion of many different kinds. For strikebreakers who need the jobs to earn a living, appeal to the obligations of solidarity and brotherhood is normally sufficient. But where the employer uses professional strikebreakers, whose purpose is not actually to work in the plant but rather to create the impression of strike failure, and thus to demoralize the strikers, mass picketing is the usual method resorted to in this country.

The greatest disorders and most acute outbreaks of violence in connection with industrial disputes arise from what the workers hold to be invasions of their fundamental rights —the right to strike, to picket, to assemble freely, and to bargain collectively through their chosen representatives. "Picketing, of course, is not so important to union activity in Great Britain as it is in the U. S., not only because it is but rarely needed as an organization weapon but also because in England in the case of strikes involving at the outset enough workers to make a continued operation of the plants impractical, employers almost invariably shut down their plants and do not attempt to operate until the controversy has been settled by negotiation."[6]

Picketing is undoubtedly on occasion conducted by a minority of the whole body of employees. The Wagner Act tends to render this practice obsolete. But since early days, active minorities have rendered great and legitimate service to the labor movement—and to other human effort as well.

Trivial disputes whether instigated by employees or employer should be settled promptly on their merits, and as near the seat of the trouble as possible.

American labor considers its right to strike its fundamental protection. Not only has the strike been found essential to securing better working conditions, but it has also proved to be the most important bulwark against the destruction of standards already attained. Wage earners look upon their right to their jobs as an essential prerequisite to their welfare and the taking of their jobs by strikebreakers as a deprivation of their property. The National Labor Relations Act and the various labor acts have recognized the fact that a worker does not terminate his employment by striking.

There has been a significant transition in public attitude from the time, only three or four decades ago, when labor was considered a commodity, to the present recognition of a property right and interest in a job. On this point William M. Leiserson, member of the National Labor Relations Board, has said:

The three laws—Norris-LaGuardia Act, Railway Labor Act, and National Labor Relations Act—are not disconnected enactments. They are related, built one upon another, and together they constitute one solid structure of Congressional policy for the protection of legal and property rights of employees. The basis for the policy was laid in 1930 when the Supreme Court of the United States in the Texas and New Orleans case upheld the Railway Labor Act of 1926 and restrained the railroad company from interfering with the organization chosen by the employees to represent them for collective bargaining purposes. Chief Justice Hughes, speaking for the Court, said in that case:

"If it could be said it was necessary in the present instance to show a property interest in the employees in order to justify the Court in granting an injunction, we are of the opinion that there was such an interest, with respect to the selection of representatives to confer with the employer in relation to contracts of service."

Citing this decision, Judge Way in the United States District Court in Virgina ruled in 1935 in *System Federation No. 40 v. Virginian Railway Co.* that "The right of self-organization and representation in the matter of rates of pay, hours of labor, and working conditions is a property right, the loss of which would result in irreparable damage to complainants."

This decision was later upheld by the United States Supreme Court. (300 U.S. 515):

"At a time when we are greatly concerned at the threat to property rights of employers that is inherent in the sit-down strike, should we not be equally concerned about the threat to employees' property rights that is inherent in the unfair labor practices prohibited by the Labor Relations Act. Fairness and justice in labor relations cannot be achieved or maintained without regarding the property rights of employees every bit as sacred as the property rights of employers."[7]

From the point of view of the general public, strikes involve loss of workers' wages, loss of profit to employers, and further losses to the community through direct or indirect interference with its normal activities. The pecuniary cost is difficult to estimate, for not only may the employer against whom the strike is brought make up lost time, but his competitors may gain as much as he loses, and this also applies to the workers involved. In weighing the social cost it is necessary to consider the bitterness aroused between employer and workers, and between strikers and strikebreakers; the loss of morale which sometimes accompanies a prolonged strike; and the breaking of home and community ties through the migration of workers economically unable to continue the strike. Substantial as these costs may be, labor finds them on the whole less than the cost of continuing to submit to substandard working conditions or to the breaking down of higher standards already established. It must be borne in mind that the strike is not only a demand for protection in the enjoyment of rights or privileges already recognized, it is likewise an effort to secure new rights. So long as economic insecurity and inadequate avenues to opportunity are the lot of the workingman, the strike is probably inevitable.

Customarily workers leave their place of employment when a strike is called. In the last few years in certain places in this country and in foreign countries, notably France, the technique of the sit-down strike has been developed. Here the workers remain at their place of employment but refuse to work. However regrettable, this is not an illogical outcome, it must be admitted, of the bitter industrial disputes of the past. Having found that the walkout was frequently ineffective, and often resulted in violence, and having found that picketing, boycotts, and sympathetic strikes were severely restricted by law, the sit-down was resorted to, not only to increase the effectiveness of a strike, but to avoid the violence which was so likely to occur on the picket line. Such a strike further emphasizes the fact that the workers hold their right to their jobs inviolate. Whether right or wrong legally it is quite clear that sit-downers do not consider that by remaining on the premises of the employer, they are improperly depriving him of the possession of his property. They feel that they themselves have a substantial interest in the enterprise. They have spent years in obtaining their skill. They have established homes convenient to their work. They have, in effect, so conditioned their lives that their employers could make a profit. When they occupy the properties of the employer therefore, they feel that they are merely emphasizing the fact that the employer-employee relationship is fundamental, equal in importance to that of the capital investment of the owner. It cannot be claimed that such practices represent reasoned conduct or are based on a consideration of the ethics involved. Individual workmen engaged in bitter industrial disputes rarely rely on ethical considerations. That ethics are rarely considered by either side in strikes is a strong argument for other techniques.

Such manifestations of labor unrest as sit-down strikes are normally incident only to the early stages of the struggle toward unionization. It is well to remind the reader that at such times, things done and left undone are apt to be the acts of individuals and groups of individuals rather than of seasoned labor organizations. Unions have the benefit of legal advice, and individual workers seldom do. No trained unionist will countenance the infringement of recognized legal boundaries; but neither can he be expected to yield an inch in the face of injustice and other obstacles placed in his path without warrant of law. As in other matters, a strict observance of the law on one side breeds respect for it on the other.

Discussing the Fansteel sit-down strike, the U. S. Supreme Court said:

This conduct [seizure of the plant] on the part of the employees manifestly gave good cause for their discharge unless the National Labor Relations Act abrogates the right of the employer to refuse to retain in its employ those who illegally took and held possession of its property.... But reprehensible as was that conduct of the respondent [the Fansteel Company] there was no ground for saying that it made respondent an outlaw or deprived it of its legal right to the possession and protection of its property. The employees had the right to strike but they had no license to commit acts of violence or to seize the company's plant.... But in its legal aspect the ousting of the owner from lawful possession is not essentially different from assault upon the officers of an employing company or the despoiling of its property or other unlawful acts in order to force compliance with demands.[8]

The Court accordingly further held that the authority of the Board to require affirmative action "to effectuate the policies of the Act" is broad but is not unlimited and that the reinstatement of "sit-down" strikers discharged by the company for their unlawful acts in seizing the plant would be contrary to the purpose of the Act, which is to promote peaceful settlement of disputes by providing legal remedies for the invasion of the employees' rights and would tend to make abortive the plan of the law for peaceful procedure. Thus employees who are discharged because they engage in a "sit-down" strike are no longer employees as defined in Section 2 (3) of the Wagner Act.

Discussing this decision, a writer in the *Harvard Law Review* deplores—

A generalization which neglects any effort to measure the lawlessness of employees against the provocative conduct of the employer, but which excludes from the benefit of the Act all lawless employees irrespective of the degree of provocation. If experience showed that lawlessness by employees bore no relation to lawlessness by employers, such a generalization, of course, would be appropriate.[9]

The public regards the sit-down as unlawful; and the Supreme Court of the United States has since so declared it. It violates the accepted notions of property rights. At times it has seemed to be upsetting the industrial balance. There is a strong reaction against the sit-down, and labor leaders have issued warnings against its continued use. Under this pressure the sit-down strike has lost its popularity as quickly as it gained it. This type of strike, though spectacular, is limited in importance as a labor weapon. It has been used only in a restricted number of industries and localities, and only rarely has it had the approval and support of the union's national officers.

Given widespread employer opposition to labor unions, organized workers have endeavored by the use of various devices to make their organizations secure. Before the advent of mass-production methods the craft unions were built up around the skill of craftsmen. To protect themselves and maintain a preferred bargaining position craft unions required of the applicants for membership some proof of skill. To enhance their position, the unions endeavored to secure and maintain a monopoly of skill. Out of this effort came demands for restricting the number of apprentices in each trade.

The atmospheric disquietude occasioned by jurisdictional disputes certainly constitutes an outstanding objection to unionism. Of course these more or less constant altercations are deprecated by union leaders quite as actively as by those outside the labor movement.

The jurisdictional dispute and strike are the modern manifestations of craft union resistance to technological developments that threaten the security of the organization and its members. Particularly in depression periods, there are often more union members in certain industries than there are jobs. The carpenter sees prefabricated metal doors and trim being installed by iron workers or sheet metal workers. He becomes acutely conscious that his skill and his job are menaced. His fellow union carpenters employed by the same contractor refuse to work because their work is being taken by those of another craft or trade. It may be but one carpenter who is directly affected. But his fellow craftsmen see in his case a threat to their own opportunities. A singular craft solidarity is sometimes demonstrated.

The drift toward industrial unionism may put these incessant disputes—many of them quite picayune in character—in the way of more orderly settlement. At the recent CIO San Francisco Convention the report of the Committee on Appeals outlining a new and more quick acting procedure for the settlement of such questions said: "in addition to the natural desire of organizations to safeguard and protect the industrial status and integrity of their respective unions there is also another interest that cannot be disregarded. This represents the interest of an employer who is a party to a collective bargaining contract with one or more of our affiliates. Orderly and constructive collective bargaining relationships with employers must not be disturbed as a result of any inter-union controversies."

The sympathetic and general strikes are not much used now in the United States. One reason perhaps is the existence of the National Labor Relations Act which affords no protection to those engaged in such strikes. Then, too, increasingly democratic control of unions makes it difficult to call men on strike unless they are personally and directly aggrieved.

There is one form of sympathetic strike, however, which has been used fairly frequently—the refusal by water-front workers to handle non-union or "hot" cargo. Although these workers risk their jobs, and penalize themselves while penalizing their employers, they feel their efforts are fully justified. For if some day the tables are turned, and their own jobs are filled by strikebreakers, then, given their occupational situation, help from another union in the form of a boycott would be extremely useful.

In unions which have both installation and production departments the sympathetic strike or boycott is a deadly weapon. There are such organizations and on occasion they do refuse to install materials simply because they are not manufactured by their affiliated production group. This is an excellent device for building membership in a particular union but seems unduly coercive on employers and workers in fully organized factories whose only shortcoming is that they do not happen to be affiliated with a particular installation group. This spells favoritism—not labor unionism.

Some labor contracts contain clauses releasing union members from working on goods produced under unfair labor conditions. This is perhaps the best solution for the problem, since it would, in a measure, prevent underselling by sweat-shop employers while at the same time restricting the promiscuous use of this easily abused weapon.

In the United States general strikes have been limited to cities or to certain industries. During the NRA period there were two—in San Francisco, California, and in Terre Haute, Indiana. A nation-wide general strike such as England suffered in 1926 or France in 1938 has never occurred here. One probable reason for this is the limited political activity of the American workman. General strikes, in part at least, are aimed at the government, and sufficiently large numbers of employees in this country have never been stung to such protest. There have been waves of strikes, but no coordinated action covering a large territory, even a strongly organized territory. As a result of experience to date all responsible labor leaders are opposed to general strikes except possibly for a day's demonstration of strength and solidarity. It has become clear that the success of any protracted general strike is tantamount to revolution. After all somebody has not only to control but to operate.

Restriction of output may be of many different varieties and practiced both by individuals and collectively. How much there is depends largely on shop morale although the opportunities are somewhat lessened by the various methods for stipulating and measuring output quite common now in well-managed plants. Unless these appointed tasks are set competently, and with full understanding on the part of the worker, they may actually lead to restricted output. More frequently than not this is the case with piece rates.

What was formerly referred to as ca' canny or soldiering by individuals has ceased to be an important tactic of organized labor. There is of course a very common belief on the part of wage earners that the amount of work is limited and that limiting output will increase employment. Many workers continue to regulate their own efficiency and productivity on the basis of this theory. In recent years, however, trade-union leaders have realized that wages come out of the total production of the plant and that the way to get higher wages is to produce more goods. This has tended to discourage this type of restriction of output. An instance to the contrary is afforded by several international unions which insist that work once done satisfactorily must for one reason or another be done over again. This obviously is a waste. Each such situation is a study in itself and in time solutions safeguarding legitimate interests will be found. Organized labor's attitude toward the introduction of labor-saving devices is another story and is discussed elsewhere. When social security has progressed farther, labor will naturally be more enthusiastic about technological improvements.

Other widely criticized labor practices, such as the failure of unions to incorporate or to make public accounting of their funds, are controversial mainly in the sense that they provide a focus for attack on the idea of unionism. Others, such as seniority principles, on the other hand, are of basic importance in equitable industrial relations and are receiving to a greater extent the earnest and generally cooperative attention of both labor and management.

There has not always been an employer demand for the incorporation of labor unions. Indeed, in the early days of the unions the demand came from labor's camp. After suffering from the conspiracy laws labor leaders sought the protection of a government charter. This demand finally led to the enactment of a federal statute providing for the voluntary incorporation of labor unions, but the law was never used. Unions discovered that they were just as truly a legal entity without a charter as they could be with one. Their internal affairs have always been subject to review by the courts. They can sue, and be sued. They are subject to regulation just as a business is. They now see no need to incorporate and hesitate to do so. Perhaps they fear an unjustified increase in litigation; more probably an awakening on the part of hostile employers to the realization that one way to destroy a union is to sue it out of existence, as was almost the result of the Danbury Hatters and Coronado Coal cases. It will not be overlooked in this connection that a major incentive to the incorporation of business enterprise is frequently to put a limit on the responsibility of individuals.

The criticism of union accounting has even less merit. Labor unions render financial statements to their membership. These statements are published in the official journals of the unions and are included in the officers' reports at their conventions. They are available in the Library of Congress and in any other library which has requested them. Recently these financial reports have found their way into newspapers.[10] Some unions, particularly among the smaller ones, like some businesses, also among the smaller ones, do not give out financial data, and even use an archaic type of accounting. But with the growing size of unions, facilitated by industrial unionism in the mass-production industries, the practices of the smaller unions become less and less significant in the whole labor union picture. Unions do not generally call attention to their reports, particularly in trying years, any more than do ordinary businesses. The union fears an attack from an employer when it is least able to sustain

LABOR'S CONTROVERSIAL PRACTICES

a battle. Perhaps this fear is unjustified, but it will take many years of widespread acceptance of unionism to remove it.

The much discussed application of seniority rules which today are embodied in many collective bargaining contracts had its origin in the railroad industry. The rules were devised by the railroad unions to combat the practice of favoritism by railroad management. The railroads in their earlier stages of development vigorously opposed unionization. The black list was a favorite method of combatting unions by removing the "union agitator" and making it impossible for him to secure work in the industry. To make the black list effective called for an unusual degree of cooperation among railroad managements.

After the traditional struggle the railroad brotherhoods established themselves. In a period of expansion seniority rules, once accepted as a means of overcoming favoritism in the assignment of "runs," promotions, filling vacancies, etc., worked well. But with the introduction of more powerful locomotives, and longer trains, and contraction of operations as a result of motor competition the rules were given another application. Operating in reverse, they became the guide to reduction in personnel. If an employee's right to hold a job is geared to his length of continuous service, it follows that in a period of reduced operations the employees most recently taken on will be the first to be laid off. Continuation of a low rate of operations means then that in the main railroad management has to defend a force of employees whose age average is high. Management then contends that seniority and other rules developed by the collective bargaining process handicap it in the free exercise of its right to run the railroads in the most efficient, economical and profitable manner.

In this period of depression and general insecurity when hitherto unorganized industries are being unionized, the newer unions seize upon the techniques of older organizations to enhance their positions. Management resents and fears the imposition and application of such rules as an encroachment upon its prerogatives.[11] The present application of the seniority rule can be expected to yield under widespread collective bargaining to practices such as any good employer would want to use in safeguarding his older employees without jeopardizing the success of the business which is of vital interest to all employees.

Controversial practices and attitudes are gradually tapering off. Fundamentally, in so far as they are not the reflection of plain human nature they have as their inspiration employer opposition to labor unions, or the need for job security. When these problems were not recognized by the government, it was necessary for labor to improvise its own methods of protection. But now in increasing measure labor's rights and aspirations are being embodied in law, and the devices which were necessary only a short time ago are being superseded by more direct and intelligent methods.

For example, the strike to prove that the union represents a majority of a given company's employees is no longer always necessary. In the past the union feared to submit its membership records because of possible—or, rather, probable —discrimination at the hands of the employer. There was no impartial tribunal to which appeal could be taken. As is described in detail in another chapter, an election under the auspices of the National Labor Relations Board is today's peaceful, democratic method of settling the issue of representation. Similarly, other provisions of the Labor Relations Act eliminate other controversial practices, on the part of both management and labor. Other laws, such as the Norris-LaGuardia Anti-Injunction Act, the Byrnes Anti-Strikebreaking Act, various state labor relations and "labor guard" registration acts have cut down the occasion for sympathetic strikes or boycotts.

While in this country we have not progressed very far in the matter of worker security, we have made a beginning. The Social Security Act with its cooperative state unemployment compensation and welfare legislation is a long step in the right direction. When we set ourselves to deal with the problem of coordinating job distribution with technological development, we shall be definitely along the way of industrial peace and intelligent employer-employee cooperation.

So much for labor—the organized workers; now, in the following three chapters, let us look at the employers.

… IV. THE EQUIPMENT OF MANAGEMENT

CHAPTER 6

ORGANIZATION, MANAGEMENT AND PLANNING

When anyone really desires to accomplish a purpose, organization, management and planning are necessary. One does not decide to accomplish something and then do nothing about it with the expectation that the purpose will in some miraculous way accomplish itself. Housekeeping would be a pleasure if the wife could assume that the meals would prepare themselves, the beds make themselves and the children get themselves properly ready for school. She is too wise to assume any such nonsense. As she becomes experienced, she arranges all the things to be done during the day in the best manner possible in their time relations, which involves planning and organization of work. If there are older children who help her, she arranges who shall do what things and at what times, which is organization of personnel in combination with organization of work. In the making of these arrangements she is managing. When she or any assistant performs a detailed task—gets a meal, washes dishes, dusts, does the marketing—things must be arranged and manipulated, and this also is management. The arrangement of the details of work and of individual responsibilities in all their relationships is overall planning, managing and organizing combined. When each separate thing is done by someone, there is further planning, organizing and managing of the detailed activity at the workplace by the individual concerned.

Most writers have failed to note the fact that there is organization, management and planning all along the line, from the overall activities of the top executive to the detailed activities of the individual at bench or machine. Most writers have considered only the executives as managers and have referred to the contributions of the workers as, usually, just "labor." But managing at the top involves labor, and labor at the individual task involves some planning and managing.

Thus everybody in an organization plans, manages and labors. The differences are in the scope and character of these things as done by different individuals. One, for instance, may have to plan and manage the business as a whole; another the finances of the business. Another may plan and manage the credit and collection activities, and another all or some part of the production processes. A great many—all the workers—are concerned with planning and managing the actual execution of the thousand and one detailed operations which come to their machines and workplaces. Yes, the machine worker has to plan and arrange, for there are elements of skill even in tending an automatic machine; and the executive is a worker, for his mind is constantly laboring intensively to choose the significant things to do, in the reading of reports and in conferences, to find the right decisions and make the right arrangements.

Which is the most important—organization, planning, management or detailed execution? Who knows? Which is the most important part of a pair of shears—one blade, the other blade, the handle, or the rivet? What would the shears be worth if the rivet were lacking? When everyone comes to understand these relationships and the importance of each to all the others in an organization, management will be more effective, execution more precise and productive, and everybody's work relations will be more agreeable. The difference between a well-managed business and a poorly managed business is in considerable part the difference in the extent of such understanding.

When John Smith's great-grandfather William, as told in Chapter 2, began to make wagons and carriages he did not set up a factory—that came somewhat later. He was a skilled worker in wood and made the vehicles himself practically to order. He had the metal work done by a near-by blacksmith. In this situation William himself did all the organiz-

ORGANIZATION, MANAGEMENT, PLANNING 71

ing, managing, planning and executing in his jobbing business.

Eventually he got the blacksmith to join him in a partnership. William continued to handle the selling; his partner took over the metal work. They employed two assistants for woodwork, over which William kept a supervising eye. Here we have a natural division of responsibilities according to ability and experience. A task of overall organization, managing and planning emerged, and both the partners shared the responsibility for this, with William contributing most because of his larger experience. Detailed organization, management and planning remained for each man in connection with his individual tasks. The total situation generally was simple and each member of the organization understood the entire set-up of responsibilities and relationships as well as his own detailed tasks.

The region developed rapidly. The little business thrived and attracted the attention of some men of means in a neighboring city. They made the partners an offer which was accepted. The new owners were out for an expanding business, and as an historical note we may report that they got it—a successful gamble. They put in as general manager a man from the city who gave most of his attention to finance and to other general business problems. William served for a time as production manager, and he was assisted by a foreman skilled in woodwork who supervised fifteen or twenty men. The blacksmith continued for a while as a foreman of the smith's department and supervised half a dozen other men. A sales manager and two salesmen were brought from the city.

However, this new set-up began to feel the competition of a firm in the same business in a neighboring village. More distant firms were helped by new railroads to creep into their market. To get business they had to make good vehicles, yet keep the costs down. Also, there were a number of people in the city who had put money into the reorganized concern. While they did not bother the management much directly, they began a mild pressure for profits and dividends. Furthermore, operating on a larger scale the business had to arrange short-time loans at a city bank (no longer principally at the local bank) for working capital when they were accumulating inventories. These developments created problems of management on a new plane and a new scale. Organization, management and planning took on a new importance all along the line.

It is out of such beginnings that most of the big businesses of today have developed. As businesses became larger, complications developed from a mixture of uncoordinated organizing, managing, planning and detailed execution from top to bottom. This was because of one man's inability to make his work fit into that of all the others because he could not keep himself accurately informed about all going on around him—limitations in what scientists call the "span of attention." People differ in their attention spans. Of a hundred persons who pass through a room for the first time, one may be able to recall most of the objects in it but the others observe and can recall only a few. Probably not one person in a million can do what Napoleon is said to have been able to do—dictate simultaneously to half a dozen different secretaries on as many different matters. This made him a good chess player—able to keep a number of games going at the same time. In his own mind Napoleon could keep each line of thought separate from the others and pick it up where he had left off. The span of attention of most of us—businessman, manager or worker—is very limited.

As plants became larger and more complex, the number of things which each person had to observe and remember became so great that confusion resulted—doing of wrong things, doing of the right things incorrectly, making too much of one item and too little of another, and other conflicting acts that canceled each other out and neutralized the effectiveness of the whole. This frequently caused excessive costs, and losses instead of profits. For instance, as late as 1920-21 there was a short, sharp depression sometimes called the depression of frozen inventories. This depression stimulated self-examination of many businesses, which revealed gross mismanagement. Sales departments had gone wild in making commitments to purchasers. Production departments had gone wild in piling up products that the sales departments were unable to sell; and within production departments foremen had gone wild in piling up unbalanced inventories—too many of certain parts, too few of others—all because any one unit did not know with sufficient accuracy what the business as a whole required, and what the other units were doing. A business had developed to a complexity beyond anyone's span of *unorganized attention.*

Following these revelations there was a general turning by business to methods that had been developed earlier by a few concerns to reduce losses resulting from collisions in the managements of their plants. This was a type of organization and management designed to coordinate all the separate acts of planning, organizing and managing throughout a plant, so that all would be working toward the same end— the making of products required to fill the orders at the right times, in the right quantities and of the correct specifications, without waste of materials, human effort and machine time. A few leaders had discovered that a business may have an impersonal brain of its own through proper organization for management—an institutional brain, so to speak, separate from the brains of any individual member of the organization. This changed attitude toward industrial enterprize led to the adoption of radically different techniques.

The new processes involved the laying out in advance of every detail of business operations: the kinds of items to be sold; the quantity of each to be sold; how each should be made, even to the sequence of making its parts; how each part should be made; the exact kind and quantity of each material required; the number of workers and kinds of skills required; the needed machines and tools; the required working capital; and a time schedule for the performance of all essential acts most precisely, effectively and economically. Given such a layout of requirements it becomes easy to formulate and issue the instructions governing the succession of acts that will get the product made and sold without conflicts that cause waste and loss.

Now the details of conducting a business cannot be laid out in advance if the managers are not sure of the controlling facts. Layouts on the basis of hunch and guess are apt to increase confusion. Therefore in the method of management which is here described the planners and managers use every available type of investigation and research to discover the controlling facts. The market is studied, sampled and analyzed to determine the location and trend of consumer demand. Given the resulting sales schedule, the production department can work out with reasonable precision how much of each item to make each week and month to meet the sales schedule. Given the production schedule there can then be worked out schedules of the necessary kinds of machines and tools; the number of workers and kinds of skills required; the necessary raw materials; and so on. Of course the calculations depend on an almost infinite variety of detailed studies of operations—how each machine should be set up and handled for each operation within its capacity, and its dependable output of each item per hour or day.

Given this kind of detailed information, it is possible for management to control the flow of work with a precision that practically eliminates waste and keeps unit costs low. The time factors in the flow of work to the several departments, and to and from every machine in each department, can be calculated. Instructions as to who is to do what, and when and how, can be arranged in advance for each day's work. This it is that promotes dovetailing of work. From the viewpoint of ownership and management, procedures of this kind are of major importance, and such working papers as manufacturing orders, schedules, route sheets and charts, work-order slips, move-material slips, etc., have a function comparable to that of a physical tool.

Also from the viewpoint of each worker these paper tools are of major importance. They give him an enlarged freedom. A great French engineer once said that a worker does not like to be ordered but does like to work where order reigns. He does not like to be ordered in the sense that he does not like to have a foreman arbitrarily, on the basis of whim or guess, interrupt him a dozen times a day, with a now-do-this and then a now-do-that, in words that are not always clear and a manner that is not always pleasant. Sometimes such personal orders are irrational, and irrational things are most irritating. On the other hand, if work is laid out with precision in advance and given the form of written instructions which are so clearly stated that there can be no misunder-

ORGANIZATION, MANAGEMENT, PLANNING 75

standing, and are of such a nature that they supplement one another, then each worker receiving such an instruction is "on his own" within its terms and knows that he is doing something rational. He is in a situation where "order reigns." Of course these papers are "orders," but orders of the situation determined by calculation, and not orders of an individual reflecting his whims and guesses.

In most businesses it is expedient to develop specialization of work to take advantage of variations in individual aptitudes. (See Charts A and B.) Therefore in a typical manufacturing plant one small group, General Administration, will be responsible for general policies and programs. Another group, the Sales Department, will be concerned with selling, and within that group one small sub-group will be concerned with market studies and sales schedules, while another larger sub-group will do the actual selling. The Production Department makes the goods to be sold in accordance with the sales schedule, and within this department a small group is engaged in production studies and planning, while the largest group of all is engaged in making the items at machines and workplaces. A Personnel Department is responsible for employment, training, keeping of personnel records, the primary adjustment of complaints, and related matters. Other responsibilities, such as finance, are assigned to special groups.

For a coal company, a construction company, a steamship line, an insurance company, there would be a somewhat different organization. But the principle remains the same: an organization of responsibilities from the most inclusive to the most detailed in accordance with the nature of the purpose and the ways in which it can be accomplished with precision and without waste.

Looked at in the large, all these special responsibilities divide into two great classes: line and staff. The staff consists of those who conduct researches, investigations and experiments; and formulate programs, schedules, specifications and written instructions. These activities are concerned primarily with *how* and call for a special analytic ability. The line consists of those who direct and execute the doing of things. From the top to the bottom—better expressed as from the most general to the most detailed act—someone must decide *what, where* and *when* and give the go-ahead sign. This is all the more essential when there are many people in the organization and each cannot know what all the others are doing. Someone whose responsibility it is to know what everybody is doing must give the go-ahead sign for all groups; and also someone must give a similar go-ahead sign for each separate group. This responsibility calls for a special type of person: one who is energetic and alert, gets along well with people, can express his desires clearly, and can make sound decisions quickly; for unfortunately, no matter how thorough the investigations and how complete the schedules, the unexpected is always bobbing up within the whole range of possible influences from consumer reactions at one extreme to machine reactions at the other.

There is much controversy concerning the relations of line and staff into which it is unnecessary to go here. On the whole this controversy is in the realm of theory rather than reality. Any one of several kinds of relationship will work satisfactorily if all concerned want it to work; and especially if the top executive takes care of his responsibility wisely and patiently. If the staff group has the reputation of making thorough studies and of constructing dependable schedules, instruction cards and other standards, it will find the line cooperative. If the line shows a disposition to want precision and economy, and to adhere to schedules and other standards, it will find the staff cooperative and not inclined to interfere with its authority. If these conditions are not present then no kind of relationship works with entire satisfaction.

There are two principal ways in which line and staff relations may be organized. In one, the staff is an integrated group entirely separate from the line but having contacts with it at various points. In the other, the staff consists of several groups each having a definite relation with some point in the line but not much relation with each other. In an individual plant the latter is likely to be the type; in a business made up of several geographically scattered plants controlled from general offices, the first of these two types is preferable.

The accompanying charts may help to clarify these two

types of relationship between line and staff. Both are charts of a business producing, for instance, typewriters, but Chart A is of a business having one plant, while Chart B is of a business having several plants in different localities. In the latter, the staff function is pooled for all the plants. A staff unit is indicated by a rectangle made of dashes; a line unit by a rectangle made of solid lines.

It should be noted that both the line and the staff head up in the president or the general manager, who in a moderate-sized plant may be one person. This is extremely important. In fact, no line and staff organization is ever successful in which the chief executive neglects one or the other. He must be a dynamic coordinator; in the relations between line and staff he is pivotal.

We have said that both the line and the staff must be sympathetic and cooperative. That is true not only of line and staff viewed broadly, but of every individual in the organization. The very essence of good management is a well understood organization of relations that fit the situation, clearly defined responsibilities, and a spirit of cooperation throughout.

The significance of this will be understood by anyone who stops to think about the necessary foundations of an economy in which everyone is busy and enjoying a good standard of living. Everyone is busy only when goods are being made at costs that permit them to be sold at prices that permit them to be purchased; only when wages are high enough to give labor—the mass of a market population—the necessary purchasing power to take up the goods; only when the volume of production is high and the costs per unit of output are low; only when employing institutions are kept in existence and active because they realize profits. In our capitalistic economy employers must earn profits to remain in existence as employers, and workers must receive good incomes to continue as consumers whose purchases create profits. These conditions can be met only by high productivity at low unit costs, with distribution of the products at moderate profits.

Therefore it is essential that everyone in business understands these rules and plays the game fairly.

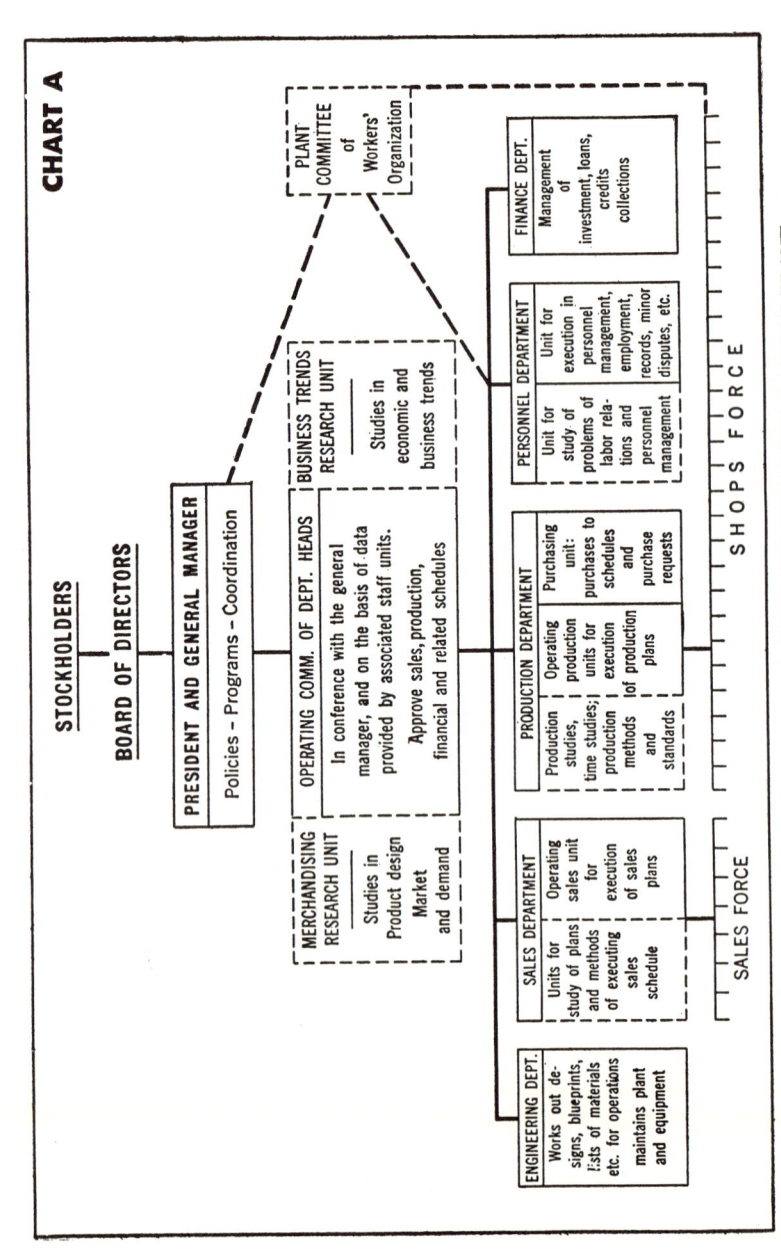

FIG. 1. ORGANIZATION SET-UP FOR A COMPANY OPERATING A SINGLE PLANT.

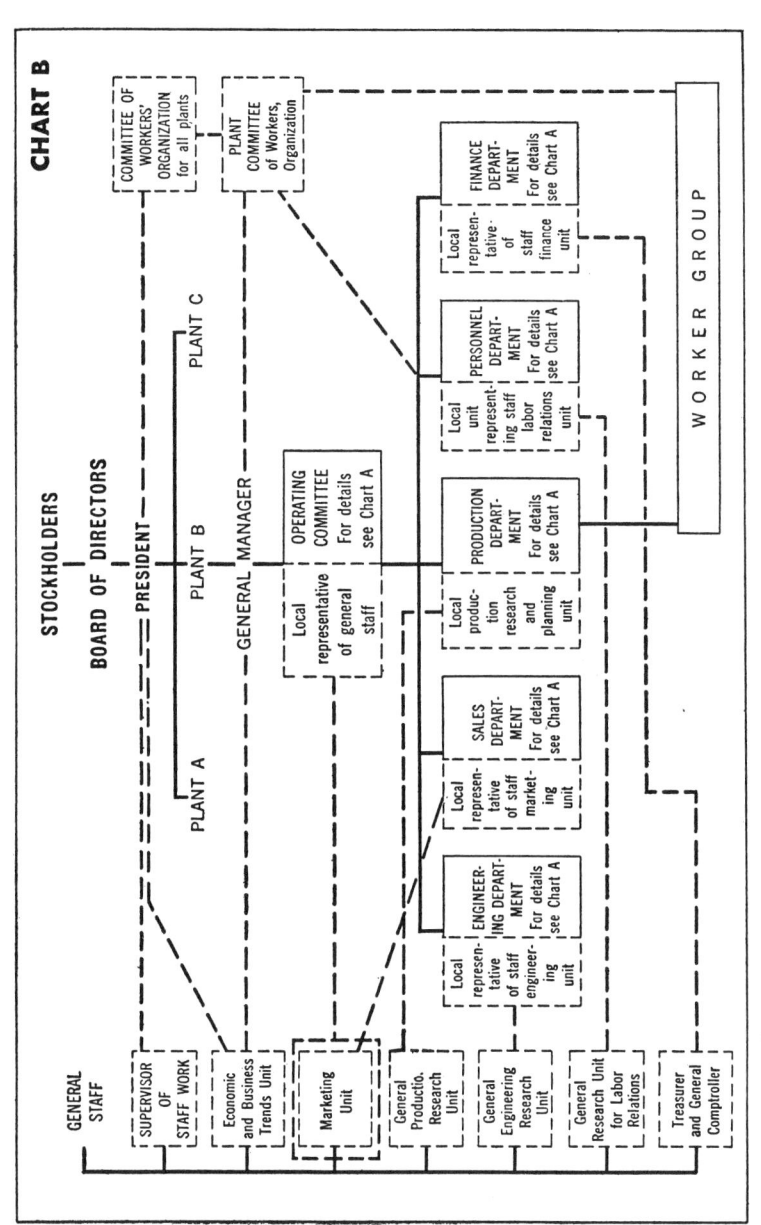

FIG. 2. ORGANIZATION SET-UP FOR A COMPANY OPERATING MORE THAN ONE PLANT.

This means that ownership must have a large perspective of the relations between opportunity and responsibility, and must accept the principles of prudent investment, fair capitalization, and moderate profits. The gains of improving technology must be passed along to the people, in part through increasing wages and in part through decreasing prices of products. Especially must there be understanding and a cooperative spirit in relations with organized labor. Only by such conduct on the part of ownership can the economic machine be kept continuously busy, productivity high, and the general standard of living high. Only in that way can the capitalistic economy evade self-destruction through the atrophy that results from failure to function properly.

It means that management—line and staff—must be large-minded, sympathetic and painstaking in its work. Its programs and schedules should be as nearly perfect as human skill can devise; the procedures it formulates should be agreeable as well as effective; its standard times and other standards worked out through time studies should be reasonable and practicable. In all it does it should have the most important factor of all—the labor group—constantly in mind. It should invite labor's cooperation in the management processes and should devise methods whereby this is made possible. There is no point all along the line, from the most general problem to the most detailed, where this is not desirable and practicable. In the final analysis, it is the workers who turn out the product.

The goal of all industrial organization must be to make it possible for every worker to give the best that he has in him. That is the meaning of individuality; the foundation of self-respect and of pride. He should see the whole picture and understand the total situation: first, that in our system of economy the employer must make profits to keep his business going and to give employment; and second, that his employer may be subject to a competition which sets an upper limit to the margin between costs and selling price. The worker must recognize that out of this margin must come any differential which can be applied to increase of wages; and that generally the only way to create this differential is to lower costs through more precise and economical ways of doing things.

The matter of wholehearted application is simple enough, but doing things in ever better ways involves several factors. First among the important elements is the worker's own individual organization and planning of work at his machine or bench. There is room here for a considerable amount of originality and ingenuity. He may now and then devise something which becomes absorbed into the general system of procedures to improve output at many points. Second—of supreme importance—is observance of the general system of procedures. These should be followed painstakingly. It is understanding of the procedures and following them faithfully that does more to reduce costs than anything else because the losses that add up to the biggest sum are the losses that result from lack of proper relationships among workplaces. The greatest source of waste is confusion and collisions among managers and among workplaces. Procedures are designed to eliminate these, just as the timetable of a railroad is designed to eliminate collisions, wrecks and loss.

The worker who follows the procedures at his workplace and in relation to other workplaces has *form*, just as a tennis player or track athlete has form. Form permits output without waste of energy. The tennis player with form can play half a dozen sets without turning a hair; the beginner may be "all in" after two or three sets. A worker who follows well-designed procedures can do a good day's work with high productivity, without undue fatigue and with genuine satisfaction.

Thus far we have been considering only the problem of organization, managing and planning in the individual business. That, of course, is of fundamental importance, for under any set of circumstances the income of a society is made up of the total of products and services created by all individual plants. And in an earlier expanding economy, such as that of the day of William Smith and for several decades after his day, attention to the managements of individual businesses was sufficient.

But circumstances have changed, and in addition to concern for the management of individual businesses we now must have concern for the management of the relations within all business—for the management of business looked at as a whole. Many managers are now talking about "cannibalistic competition," which means many things. It means, among other things, that in some businesses there are too many enterprises and a production capacity out of balance with the demand; that in other businesses concentrated ownership has established prices that upset price relations in the economy and check the flow of goods and services.

Just as once individual businesses permitted their departments to run wild and bring about wasteful disorganization, so likewise as a people we have permitted separate businesses (which may be considered departments of our total economy) to run wild and cause wasteful disorganization of the livelihood activities of the country—stagnation, unemployment, distress. And just as Scientific Management has been able to bring a reign of order to individual concerns, so the same principles and general body of procedures must be adapted to a higher plane of relationships, and establish a reign of order and balanced relationships among businesses throughout the total economy.

There is nothing in our present intra-industry or inter-industry relationships to suggest the form which the ultimate over-all business set-up will take. In 1931 the U. S. Department of Commerce listed "over 19,000 business organizations made up of 2,634 inter-state, national, and international, 3,050 state and territorial, and 13,625 local, organizations."[1] In matters of organization, planning and management, mere numbers have little significance. It is most regrettable that in this country the employers in very few industries are organized to deal with their employees on an industry-wide basis. It would make for greater efficiency and economy if there could be a national inter-industry association of employers to work out standards with a corresponding association of unionized workers. If we follow what appear to be desirable Scandinavian models, one national organization for each industry and one national organization for all industry should confine their attention to personnel matters and the regularization of relations with the unions. Perhaps when more industries are organized to carry on such work, a national federation can be brought about. Of course the study of personnel relations is only one subject that should be provided for in any adequate scheme for national inter-industry planning.

Any reorganization of the relations among businesses to establish order and stability in the midst of progress, must be under the authority, control and direction of the people as a whole expressed through their government. Full employment and a high standard of living can come only from high productivity. General restriction of production means inevitably a declining standard of living, and the development of fixed proletariat and peasant classes in our society.

There is nothing mysterious in the relation between high productivity and a high standard of living. The standard of living is made up of the goods and services we produce—the more goods and services, the higher the standard of living. Just as the more William Smith made and sold, the higher was his income and his standard of living, so the more a society makes and exchanges, the greater will be its income and the higher its standard of living. But to make high productivity result in a high standard of living instead of in a stalling of the economic machine, there must be precise and economical management in individual plants; and there must be such a reign of order in the economy as a whole as effects an equitable distribution of the total productivity.

Only organized labor and management working hand in hand can achieve a high productivity under conditions that ensure a high standard of living. Assuming managerial control of all enterprise as contemplated by the capitalistic system, what of its nature and how far must one and all yield to it that common ends may be well executed? What are the essentials of leadership in industry? We shall take up this question in the next chapter.

CHAPTER 7

ESSENTIALS IN ADMINISTRATIVE AND MANAGERIAL AUTHORITY

"ARE you going to tell me how to run my business?" is the query with which many an employer has welcomed the committees of employees initiating the era of collective bargaining in the plant. This is not only an inauspicious note on which to start a significant new relationship, but it arouses doubt as to the employer's ability to forge his managerial techniques so as to get the maximum production by securing the full and combined heart, head and hand power of the employees. The question is based on a serious misconception of the nature of authority and a flagrant misunderstanding as to the real attitude of labor.

To relieve the boss or the management of proper responsibility for making a success of the enterprise is about the last thing any group of employees—organized or unorganized—would consider workable or even desirable. The unions are on record in numerous instances as recognizing that in the last analysis management has to manage, if any concern is to be a success financially or in any other way. This is well illustrated by a clause in the contract between the Steel Workers Organizing Committee and the United States Steel Corporation:

> The management of the works and the direction of the working forces, including the right to hire, suspend, or discharge for proper cause, or transfer, and the right to relieve employees from duty because of lack of work, or for other legitimate reasons is vested exclusively in the company, provided that this will not be used for purposes of discrimination against any member of the Union.

In other words, someone has to "run the business," to use a common American expression. As between unions and management, there is never any doubt as to where this responsibility should and actually does lie. Though labor organizations do not desire, and cannot be permitted if they should desire, to run the employer's business, it is equally a mistake to assume that an employer has no need for aid from his employees in matters of management.

To accept the idea that the president of any industrial concern because of his position is competent alone to decide every question affecting the enterprise as a whole, or the employer-employee relationship in particular, is going counter to all human experience. Such an attitude is opposed to the now generally recognized theory of management by functions as contrasted with management through title, position, ownership, or salary.

Even two men owning and operating a business are well advised each to assume the final responsibility for one or more of the constituent activities such as finance, sales, manufacturing, research, public relations. That one of two partners shall have the final decision as to certain subdivisions of the enterprise, or even over the enterprise as a whole, is not inconsistent with fifty-fifty ownership. In fact, any other arrangement leads to overlapping authority, indecision, and to those things that offend common sense in committee management. This policy implies, of course, the frank exchange of views and necessitates the development of all the pertinent facts in any situation before a decision is made. Whether the command lies with two or ten thousand the rule is the same, authority should be apportioned logically according to the function being performed at a given time, rather than by position or title.

Foolish as it may seem, many enterprises, public as well as private, operate on the policy that no one can give instructions to those enjoying higher salary ratings. This arbitrary convention frequently delays logical changes in the methods of handling work pending payroll adjustments.

Even more unfortunate is the carry over into modern industrial organization of so much from the race's military past, without regard to the essential differences between the objectives of peace and war. Military efficiency, as Prime Minister Chamberlain recently expressed it, consists in "concentrating decisive force at the decisive point at the decisive moment." Battles have frequently been won by the weaker or numerically inferior side simply because the available troops have been so maneuvered as to achieve this result. Wars are frequently won or lost by such strategy rather than by the steady drive. Industry on the other hand strives for even performance. Peaks or depressions in industrial demand or output are to be avoided. The "supreme moments" of the battlefield have no place in industry. The sooner industry drops its militaristic attitudes, practices, and vernacular, the better prepared it will be for its own job.

To account for what is still arbitrary and dictatorial in American industry—for such common expressions as, "Do it because I tell you to"; "We have nothing to discuss"; and, "Who do you think is boss around here?"—one must recall that much in the tradition and the quality of present-day administration goes back to the industrial era following the Civil War. Then the "gang boss" was king, Chinese coolies built railroads in the West, and immigrants arriving on the last ship from Europe were in demand in industrial centers largely because they were supposed to be "cheap and docile" workers. This was the period in which the groundwork was laid for today's large scale enterprise. The techniques necessary for subduing a continent inhabited only by inhospitable Indians were best exercised by a domineering, he-man type of leader. But those days are gone, and the qualities then in demand are not highly rated today. The man who wants to be "the whole show" is more and more in disrepute.

In all branches of human activity, indeed, there is a growing recognition of the importance of special skills. The putt in golf, the fielding of grounders in baseball, or the service in tennis require very great skill in themselves, quite apart from their place in the game as a whole. So in industry, the choice of the appropriate fuel or steel are matters for experts equipped to make highly technical tests and decisions based on them. To displace "the hunch" and "the rule of thumb" there is developing the art and science of each play in the

ESSENTIALS OF CONTROL

total effort. There is growing need for a closer linking of authority and knowledge. Hence the whole emphasis of those seeking to improve the effectiveness of management has for some years been in the direction of procedures by which the greatest possible number of administrative acts can be performed by those individuals who, whatever their status in the organization, have the special knowledge required for reaching a wise decision on the special point involved. This is what is meant by functional management. It is true in industry as well as in other areas of modern life.

This recognition of the functional characteristics of all enterprise brings to the front the type of manager who surrounds himself with fact-finding facilities—not to detract from his dignity and importance, but to bring to him ready-made the materials that in themselves direct the largest possible number of decisions. Under this dispensation, control takes on the meaning of "developing and co-ordinating enthusiasms for commonly accepted purposes." In this connection it may be noted that the chief executives are relatively more important when management means maneuvers, and become far less important when management means processes, for the most part highly technical processes.

If leadership is to take on a less arbitrary character, ways must be found to discourage what appears to be a growing tendency to overestimate the top man in all organizations, whether it be the President of the Republic, the general manager of the industrial plant or the foreman of the road gang. Overrating leaders both stultifies and burdens them and, perhaps of even greater importance, detracts from the essential dignity and status of everybody below. The theory seems to be that there is in every organization, to quote a leader of thought in this field, "a supreme co-ordinating authority (which) operates throughout the whole structure of the organized body." This is nonsense. The picture of the hard-bitten Captain on the bridge of the Industrial Ship driving her through the storm to a safe haven, giving all orders, making all decisions, and hearing no other comment on his commands than, "Aye, aye, sir," while picturesque in a sentimental sort of way, actually was out of date about the time the square riggers were being broken up. There are a few square riggers still in service, but they are just as much a curiosity as the one-man-complete-control picture in industry. There are, of course, in any organization, dominant and subsidiary officials, but they are to be distinguished clearly from persons with arbitrary power. Authority—even policy—operates throughout an organization as does water flowing from springs originating at many points and located on different levels. It is further recognized that any employee—irrespective of rank—may be capable of a superlatively good performance on one function, and be ineffective to an equal degree on many others.

Except on rare occasions, industry operates under "The Illusion of Final Authority,"[1] not recognizing, as Mary P. Follett has pointed out, that authority even in the sense of military command must be functional today, and that functional authority is but the counterpart of a very definite functional responsibility. Early in our participation in the Great War, the newly appointed Quartermaster General U.S.A. (Robert E. Wood, now chairman of the board of Sears, Roebuck and Company), experiencing some difficulty in getting his department to function properly, called all the Divisional Q.M.'s to Washington. The meat of the conference was a ten-minute talk in which General Wood told his aides that they were falling down because they were depending on their authority rather than on their responsibility. "Just forget that you have any authority and we will get ahead with our task," said he. And this was in a military organization with a background of more than a century of relying on authority!

The capacity for genuine leadership implies a generous acceptance of functional responsibility at every level. This capacity is developed by encouraging in everyone the maximum of appropriate responsibility. Knowing how to do the task thus becomes the essence of democratic authority. Absentee ownership and ownership by those whose knowledge of the business is limited to the financial control both put a strain on sound management, whether it be of labor relations or any other phase of an enterprise. The maximum of feasible home rule is as wholesome for industrial as it is for political democracy.

Democracy is always a two-way stream and under modern organization, authority should stream up from those who command the local facts quite as freely as down from those who, because of position, are compelled to make final and inclusive decisions. "An executive decision is only a moment in process. The *growth* of a decision, the *accumulation* of authority, not the final step, is what we most need to study."[2] The leader should be constantly at pains to minimize his own job in order to emphasize the importance of others, especially of those in the organization whom he outranks.

Most people are benefited by periodically accounting for their stewardship of matters entrusted to their care. Similarly, anyone under the necessity for persuading others who are his equals in status or bargaining power has the best possible insurance against growing stupid, petulant and irresponsible. And these are the very defects which the organization of modern industry has tended to develop in its leadership.

In the political organization of this country, the doctrine of the separation of powers and the many principles and traditions which have stemmed from it have generally forestalled this danger. Industry needs the equivalent of this doctrine. No foreseeable regulatory compulsion exerted by government on industrial leaders will serve, because such pressure does not have the appearance of sufficient permanence to make industrial leaders believe that they must learn to work within the new dimensions which actually do give them adequate scope, while fixing new boundary lines. If it were possible for our leaders to believe that these changed dimensions were permanent, they would probably adapt themselves readily to the new frame. But so long as they feel that in one year or five years they will be able to go back to the old irresponsible ways, they are sure to do a lot of sulking and protesting during the one year or five years.

So we come finally to recognize that the democratic deference invoked in labor relations under the name, collective bargaining, is really a way of industrial life—a principle of very wide application. With the adoption of the democratic procedures of collective bargaining in the shops it is necessary that procedures of a like nature and spirit be established in managing the other phases of the business, such as sales, engineering, accounting. Good management requires that no one be arbitrary and that to be arbitrary before all the facts have been developed is especially to be deplored. At the same time good management—functional management—insists that when all parties at interest have been heard it is up to a single individual, not a committee, to decide what is to be done. But this individual should function like the Clerk of the Meeting provided for in the discipline of the Society of Friends (Quakers), who is present at, and if he desires, participates in, all discussions preliminary to taking action. When in his opinion the exchange of views has proceeded to the point where a decision is feasible, he outlines what he understands to be "the sense of the meeting." No exception being taken to it, this automatically becomes the program of action to which everybody is expected to adhere loyally.

Committees may serve a useful purpose in bringing to the discussion of a given situation a broader point of view than is normally possible to an individual; and they are an efficient mechanism for sorting out and developing future executives. They are important as discussion groups, especially when they are recruited to give advice on a stated and pressing problem. But when committees are not merely advisory, when they are permanent, instead of being temporarily set up for a specific purpose, they give rise to logrolling and to indecisive managerial control. At times, committees with authority are appointed because some functionary does not know what ought to be done, or, knowing it, wants someone else to assume responsibility for action. This is just one way of "passing the buck"—always a demoralizing practice. The army officer's rule of "handling the ball on the first bounce" is a good one.

While it is not easy to develop in an organization this capacity to settle moot questions without being arbitrary or resorting to force, there are practices which facilitate such a development, among which are:

1. An itemized written statement of objectives and techniques of management. The techniques so described should

ESSENTIALS OF CONTROL

be in more or less detail according to the size of the business in question. The start on any such program will of necessity be quite simple. But the recording of the details covering all operations, once thought out and determined, so that they will be available under all future circumstances, is fundamental to the conduct of the enterprise.

2. An organization and methods section of the organization, charged with responsibility for devising standard methods for the performance of all work and for outlining with precision the changes in the organization itself which altered conditions may require. Only through such an effort to harmonize the work and staff in the several parts of the same organization can anything approximating unity in action and objective be secured. The need for an agency of this type was clearly brought out during the war, when such agencies as the National Council for Defense, the Emergency Fleet Corporation, and the Q.M.C.'s Department not only grew rapidly but underwent over-the-week-end reorganization, sometimes one after another. The various parts of any organization must be kept in logical coordination.

3. An organization unit or an individual, according to the character and size of the business, whose first duty it is to maintain—to police, so to speak—the established routines, rather than to devise new routines. More trouble comes from failure to conform to existing procedures in administration and management than from lack of inspection of the product in course of manufacture. Yet it is only recently that this has been recognized as a function in administration and management comparable in importance to inspection in production. Higher-ups frequently issue instructions based on the assumption that something ordered to be done months back actually was done at that time. It is better to make sure that what you believe is being done is actual practice than to think up some improvement.

4. A flexible, itemized budget[3] in units corresponding to the executives responsible for its various items. Such a budget is essential not only for efficient management and control but for cooperation in administration between the representatives of ownership and labor. In spite of the fact that every individual in charge of work wants to have some

easily understood arithmetical measure of his success—or shortcomings—it is surprising how few are accorded this satisfaction. At times it almost seems as if there was a studied effort to keep those responsible for some subdivision of the total effort from knowing how results compare with the results being obtained elsewhere in the same establishment. This unnecessary pooling of the results of effort almost inevitably leads to injustice, since one man's shortcomings are averaged with another man's superior performance. Comparative statements of performance—this week with last week, or this month with last month, or this year with last year—have a stimulating effect, especially when they are sufficiently detailed to indicate the causes of progress or retrogression.

5. Establishment of other norms of performance, principally of a non-financial character, by which the effectiveness of individuals and functions can be measured.[4] A crew on a paper-making machine likes to know how its product is running in comparison with what was being done when it came on duty. It pays to buy the equipment to make it possible for artisans to know their relative worth. To give a gold-leaf layer in a bindery substantial reason to believe that she is as good as there is has a tonic effect, even on character. "A man's allegiance is not to himself eventually. All men who have done work, however humble, have realized that above the work itself and the pyrotechnics of personal expression in it, there has been the work of the world, and without having the thing to say or the words to say it they have known in the job that somehow men are never working for or living by themselves alone."[5]

6. The holding of meetings, at some of which management explains its objectives and the means proposed for achieving them, and at others the rank and file has ample opportunity to present suggestions for improving the conduct of the common enterprise. All such gatherings should be conducted with as little formality as the purpose permits. To hold too frequent meetings, or to allow those held to drag unduly, defeats their purpose. Meeting with employees should be the natural outcome of *esprit de corps* and of a democratic approach which has already been established.

ESSENTIALS OF CONTROL

It is a mistake to look upon the holding of meetings in itself as any hallmark of good organization.

With the recognition of collective bargaining, an entirely new era in the conduct of an industry is begun. No one is wise enough to attempt to forecast what the situation will be when collective bargaining is the rule throughout industry. But this much is certain: that no one in a position of authority and responsibility will remain possessed of all the privileges he considered advantageous before, and have in addition the advantages inherent in the new regime.

Before we finish this section on the whys and wherefores of management let us take a look at some of its more discussed practices just as we have already done for labor.

CHAPTER 8

SOME OF MANAGEMENT'S CONTROVERSIAL PRACTICES AND ATTITUDES

MANAGEMENT'S recurring responsibility "to meet the pay roll" often seems at odds with its responsibility to meet human needs. In addition to "balancing the budget," there is a growing demand today that industry "build men," and that there be more humanity in mass production.

Perhaps little is gained by continuing to point to the "inevitable conflict" between these goals of modern industry. Certainly as we step down from generalities into concrete practices and attitudes, the conflict loses some of its sharp edges. The outsider in close contact with even the bitterest strikes is impressed not by the sharpness of the struggle, but by the strength of the desire to get together and settle the issues at stake. No doubt this desire often arises from a desperate need for income and wages, but nevertheless it indicates the vitality of the bond which unites the two sides of almost any production enterprise.

Far more than in the divisive force of the profit motive, the cause of industrial controversy is to be found in the misuse of that managerial power and authority discussed in the last chapter. Probably the chief sources of friction are the use of official prerogatives for personal advantage and "shop politics." It is this type of mismanagement that often makes the defense of sound personnel techniques seem pharisaical and visionary. With few exceptions, only very small enterprises are so organized that the profit motive alone controls the executive staff and shapes their decisions. If there is a secret solidarity among the second line executives, it almost certainly prevents candor and eye-to-eye honesty with the chief. Though the subject is an extremely delicate one, cautious inquiry will disclose to the skeptic that this humiliating and hampering situation is so common as almost to be taken as a matter of course.

Intimate study of typical factories shows further that shop politics produce die-hard opposition to change. Such opposition irritates and dismays employees who offer suggestions for improving production practices. Under these circumstances, the foreman, even if he understands why a suggested idea is turned down, cannot state the real reason. Instead, he offers some pious fiction, or treats the suggestion with lofty scorn. If the worker concerned is conscious of the tangle of "politics" he is revolted by the disloyalty to the firm's interests; and if he is unaware of the situation, the foreman's attitude leaves him bewildered or contemptuous. In either case, there is undue and seemingly quite unnecessary strain on the bond of mutual interest in the welfare of the enterprise.

It is always easy to describe and appraise ideal techniques. Instead, let us attempt to consider industry as unions and management actually confront it, and the attitudes and practices developed under the stress of men's struggle for the prizes of life. But it is important to see clearly that controversy frequently arises from the industrial situation itself, rather than from the motives and practices of management; just as, conversely, unions are to be judged by their practices and accomplishments and not by the professions of their friends or foes. It may be added that when it becomes feasible for both groups to give credence and credit to the aims of the other, controversial practices will become a challenge to democratic disciplines instead of a source of exasperation and weakened morale.

Waste in industry is one of the evidences of the faulty functioning of the productive machinery. The Committee on the Elimination of Waste, did not attempt to define the basic causes of industrial waste.[1] Its task was to make a careful quantitative study of the degree to which waste is the fault of management, employees, and the public. The Committee found that about half the cost of waste was chargeable to management, and, with some variation among the industries studied, the other half was divided about equally between employees and the public. This finding as to responsibility for inefficiency has gone unchallenged for seventeen years. Since it is obvious that all the participants in industry have a stake in efficiency and share the losses of avoidable waste, it is reasonable to suppose that unions and management have an interest in methods which will eliminate waste. Yet it is equally unrealistic to deny that workers may fear and sometimes endeavor to block improvements in method.

Labor's attitude toward time study is an outstanding example of this fact, and it also illustrates how industrial controversy frequently arises from a difference between management's motives and its practices. It is now generally conceded that well-handled time study is a valuable technique, capable of resolving issues of long standing which have caused grave injustice, preventing rate cutting, and demanding a higher caliber of foremanship.

Put very briefly, well-handled time and motion study (process study) should be taken up only after a thorough study and reform of other shop practices. It is intended to establish operating standards of practice from the top down. But reliable studies for operating standards cannot be made until job standards are competently developed and the organization accustomed to their use.

When, after a period which must usually be reckoned in years, the plant is prepared for time and motion study, a range of considerations should be studied far broader than the mere techniques of observation and statistics. To the worker the "time study man" is the central figure in the improvement program. This representative of management is introducing to the employees a technique that has been so much misused that it is doubtful whether they have ever heard anything good of it. Perhaps, also, the workers as a group or as individuals are aware that petty deceits will now be disclosed; if so, the expert may have to convince them that they are expected to forego such advantages in the interests of a sound enterprise—and it is no mean feat of conversion. Qualities far beyond the skill of a mere timing job are needed, chief among them being a keen realization of management's commitments and the moral force and authority to insist that they be fully carried out. But the typical time study "expert" seldom possesses any such qualifications, or performs any such range of function. More often than not, his pay is well under $200 a month, and he rarely has the status even of a junior executive.

Critics state that time study, as practiced, is another example of how management takes all its economies out of the hide of labor. They hold that time and motion study accelerate the pernicious advance of specialization, whereby the skill of the artisan is reduced to a narrowing and stultifying routine. From the point of view of the job itself this is true. From that of the potential job holder, such specialization often makes it possible for a man of little skill to learn and hold a better position than otherwise would have been open to him. But the plight of skilled workers displaced by the subdivision of their craft into a series of quickly mastered routines is one of the most stubborn problems of the trend through specialization toward complete mechanization. Many critics of time and motion study question the wisdom of accelerating this trend.

Should industry hesitate to further the elimination of hand labor through fear of the necessary adjustments? And will a drift toward mechanization result in easier adjustment than would a sympathetic and thorough study of the whole problem? These questions are discussed elsewhere. Perhaps the utmost the union leader would concede—especially at the start—would be that the responsibility placed on those carrying out a time study obviously calls for cooperation at every stage of the task from the labor organizations—the ordained defenders of the worker's interests.

Enough has been said to explain the opposition to time and motion study as usually practiced. If detailed, aggressive research into waste elimination precedes such study, it will influence the morale of the whole enterprise. Such procedure demonstrates that management does not define economy as "what can be taken out of the hides of the workers," and that it subjects its own activities to scrutiny and its own members to the disciplines of effective operation. It is well known to all who have close contact with well-balanced economy programs that this clean-your-own-house-first policy is more than a strategic gesture made to impress workers. Determined effort so to plan shop operations as to reduce the necessity for sudden job changes and the causes of delays at the machines usually nets greater economies than the subsequent imposition of standard tasks on the workers. It will scarcely be disputed that idle plant equipment with wholly unproductive overhead costs for maintenance, taxes, and depreciation will soon wipe out savings from both sources.

Many kinds of waste resulting from current plant practice are plain to the workers in every department. For the most part, employees are cynical about such inefficiencies. Time study, launched in the midst of such conditions almost inevitably encounters furious if hidden opposition. The despicable secret time studies are a result of such situations. This practice overlooks the fact that high morale is essential to proper time study. No reasonably accurate production standards can be set, much less maintained, unless the management standards command respect. The intricate question of timing the pace of the worker without emotional tension calls for close rapport between observer and worker. When this is established, they share the adventure of joint discovery. But when the question of morale is not appreciated, or the authority complex dominates the scientific purpose, then the results of the study may be wholly unreliable.

The study and remedy of waste in addition to their practical value, show that time study is only one factor in efficient plant operation. The workers will not be found out of step in the desire for plant economies if management assumes a fair share of responsibility for both waste and its elimination. But improvements in efficiency threaten jobs. It is this threat to jobs that is feared and opposed—not the improvement itself. Too often plant executives coast along with no more than casual attention to economies until some acute situation calls for a cut in costs "all along the line." The ensuing drive for "efficiency" is almost certain to result in many dismissals. Obviously it is nearly impossible in these circumstances to obtain cooperation from the workers beyond mere outward obedience. Even in time of serious difficulty it will prove better economy to allay the fear of unmerited

MANAGEMENT'S CONTROVERSIAL PRACTICES

discharge by official assurance that workers will be "carried," if necessary, until vacancies occur through normal turnover. The official assurance will promote genuine cooperation in reducing costs and maintaining the economies effected. Even though this wave of economy comes during a period of expansion the reassurance should be given.

To give even a qualified assurance as to continuity of employment presupposes a number of things. There must be a continuous and painstaking concern for personnel, and this whether business is good or bad. There must be an aggressive sales policy having as a major objective the provision of steady work. No industry which accepts seasonal employment as an act of God and does nothing about it is efficiently organized. Through a statistical and business information section every effort must be made to anticipate squalls, so that the necessary readjustment will not have to be made under too much pressure. There is the classic example of a well-known Philadelphia concern which in 1907 and again in 1914 cut its force from 19,000 men working full time to less than 5000 working part time, and on both occasions it all happened within six calendar weeks! Even pretty crude business forecasting should have prevented any such holocaust.

It would be hazardous to suggest that the assurance that no one will lose his job as a result of economies is all that is needed to obtain from the staff wholehearted support of every effort toward the elimination of waste. But without such policies, only an iron hand can hold the gains which it fights through.

We have discussed the plight of a firm which lets itself drift into a critical situation. But normally it should never be necessary to carry superfluous employees. Continuous staff and line effort to eliminate waste and the installation of new machinery by gradual, planned steps will avoid not only the laxness which results in waste, but also the high cost of sudden change. Economical administration and management in the main depend upon routines and rhythms in the repetitive processes and upon careful thought on the part of those who carry broad managerial responsibility. Reckless change sweeps away the priceless advantages of such standards. This sort of snap action must not be confused with the change which is inaugurated after staff planning and preparation, and which is vital to a living industrial organism in an advancing economy.

Management must and should defend a policy of true economy. But if carried forward as here suggested, the techniques of improvement are consistent with the possibility of an industrial life which develops men and women of health and character. Such procedure does not seem an impossible dream, provided the owners and the unions (both with heavy stakes in its realization) urge it on those who set the policies. At present there is little evidence of such a trend.

There is, on the other hand, a decided trend toward regulating the speed of workers by means of conveyor devices, notably the assembly line. There are important manufacturing advantages in this. It is a stage toward increasingly complete mechanization. The expense of transporting heavy parts is greatly reduced, and all chance of error in transporting is eliminated. The device avoids the expense of setting and keeping individual records of piece rates by supplying an easily supervised pressure to hold each employee to the speed set for his task. Finally, controls of the cost and the rate of deliveries are greatly simplified.

These impressive advantages from the manufacturing viewpoint must not be forgotten in considering the publicized evils of conveyor work. It must also be borne in mind that many of the evils are not inherent in the device but are due to its misuse. Often the rate of speed is raised as the season advances without the knowledge of the workers, and without any increase in pay for increased output. It is the tradition of these workshops that the men be kept in ignorance of company plans. Is an indefinite lay-off just ahead? Will work and wages go on, or will workers and their families soon feel the pinch of off-season living standards? The plans of the executives are kept secret. Even the "bosses" do not know. The question may well be raised whether management has a moral right to this secret; even whether it is sound business policy. Excitement and uncertainty rise and fall with the tempo of the conveyor drive. In his *F.O.B. Detroit*, Wessel Smitter describes how, in one plant, rumors and nervous tension finally produced an hysteria during which the entire crew, "straw bosses" and "stool pigeons" included, smashed a great machine in a superstitious frenzy. As in the case of other controversial practices, final control of the abuse of the conveyor system must rest with informed local forces. Any reasonable regulation would probably receive common acceptance and support.

The stretch-out—a term implying the thought of "stretching out"* job assignments to the limit of a worker's strength or capacity and sometimes beyond—is a controversial scheme that, like conveyor-paced assembly lines, has so many advantages it cannot be checked by mere denunciation. Yet it too cries aloud for some sort of regulation. The economy possible through having men and women tend a constantly increasing number of machines is achieved only when machinery can be handled without unexpected demands upon the operator. Weaving will serve as an illustration, though the stretch-out is being applied to many operations in the textile and other industries. So long as the weavers have to be ready for short "peaks" of extra work, usually piecing up ends that break or "come down," they can do the other work required by loom operation in the time between "peaks" when they would otherwise be idle. But when research and improved standards reduce the frequency of breaks, so that the looms are run with relatively few stops, then the time of the weaver can be used with more economy if his skill is "stretched" to an increased number of looms, and the less skilled work is assigned to lower paid help.

Much of the opposition to the stretch-out has arisen when it has been installed without the research and improved standards which alone make it a genuine economy. Critics charge that in most cases the saving of the stretch-out has been specious rather than real, and that what is gained by overworking some employees is lost in the increased force required to free weavers from the incidental work formerly required of them. It is obvious that when the arbitrary introduction of such methods leads to the lessening of effort and loyalty, and even to strikes, any possible gains may easily be offset.

* This expression has no reference to a similar one used to describe certain wholly illicit practices formerly encountered in coal mining.

Given adequate preparation, the stretch-out has potentialities for economy, for using employees at their specialty, and for making the less skilled more useful than is otherwise possible. There are many examples to support this view.

But along with these advantages goes not only the abuse of the scheme, but also the problem of the highly skilled worker whose job is eliminated by the stretch-out. Is he to be demoted to a less skilled position, with lower rank and pay? Suppose there is no such position open—is he to be summarily dismissed? Abstract justice and labor policies based on it would keep him on the payroll without a wage cut. It is unlikely that the record includes many such instances. But along with this problem of the workers displaced by the stretch-out, the system itself raises insistent questions. Can a weaver paced by a mounting number of looms be looked upon as leading a rational working life? Certainly the union should establish adequate defenses for the mental and physical health of such a worker, or else some public agency should step in and put stern limits to the demands of the "stretch-out" on human nerves and energy.

Another controversial practice of management is the withholding of financial information. In this era of unstandardized accounting it would be naïve to believe that the balance sheet designed to meet none too exacting legal requirements would be informative as to those phases of an immediate and current situation upon which the ability to pay wages may depend. And normally the balance sheet is all that outsiders and workers have to go upon. It is a common practice to regard the operating situation of the company as a secret. And yet the conditions the books show, expressed in dollars and cents, are pertinent to almost every proposal or issue that arises between men and management. There is therefore much reason for the unions to insist that the books should be open to them or to their auditors, especially during negotiations when employers argue that they cannot afford to meet the demands of the workers.

The employer's defense of the closed books—or the locked ledger as in some concerns—is closely related to the traditional union policy that in one form or another it wants wages to be as high as the company can pay. The employer

MANAGEMENT'S CONTROVERSIAL PRACTICES 103

who is operating at a substantial profit improves his bargaining position by keeping that fact concealed until the contract is signed or the issue settled. There are times, too, when sales or financial policy may be crippled by letting operating conditions leak out. Yet no union can be expected to guarantee that there will be no "leaks" of what may be divulged to its entire membership.

Most people will grant that this secrecy is a substantial bar to mutual confidence. It indicates that the hatchets have not been buried so deeply but that a little superficial scratching would uncover them. Yet employers often seem justified in keeping their books closed in the absence of some formula which sets a limit to wage demands—a formula which does not mean the absorption of all the profits in wages and which leaves to labor some share of responsibility in a deficit situation. Fortunately the record shows that there are plants—here, there, at home, abroad—where this formula has been quite definitely developed.[2]

Two accelerating tendencies are evident. Enlightened concerns do make public their financial results allowing the effect on wages to be what they may and enlightened unions do demand a decent wage without too much regard to the profit and loss statement of the employing concern. Because a single concern in an industry cannot afford to pay a decent wage is not held to be an excuse for accepting less. On the other hand there are many instances of where union leadership has accepted temporary conditions of stress as warrant for accepting less.

Inherent in the task of supervision is the authority necessary to implement it. Management and union accept this as a matter of course. The foreman or assistant are tacitly or explicitly empowered to issue orders to their crew. They have a tendency to assume that this power is weakened, even destroyed, unless they can in their own departments both accept and reject individual workers. They may succeed in establishing a hold on their crew in some constructive way which avoids issues, but in the last analysis the authority of the "boss" rests on the power to hire and fire. This authority has the support of both theory and custom.

On the other hand, among the critical days in the lives

and fortunes of all but a favored few are the days of entering or leaving employment. Such a turn is always important; it becomes a crisis at a time of large-scale unemployment. The power to hire and fire is thus a power over personal destinies. When such power is vested in a whimsical or a prejudiced minor executive, the worker is close to despair; in a venal one, he is ripe for revolt.

Perhaps no competent executive in either factories or unions is unaware of this situation and its repercussions. Machinery for the prevention and remedy of individual injustices has been the first concern of organized workers. The problem has been attacked by management, too, through detaching the hiring and firing function from foremanship, the use of techniques of employee selection, through rating plans, and through the development of a variety of shop regulations. Measurement devices, sometimes dogmatic and often crude, have played a part only in isolated plants. These devices tend to centralize responsibility in a situation too vibrant with life and change for centralization; too fluid, too much influenced by changes in the environment for static classification. More constructive are the solutions developed through discussion by representatives of the various employment levels. One of their most effective achievements to date has been the joint union-management formulation of shop rules. By this method, the standards to which workers must conform are more fully understood because they are in a real sense self-imposed. Such solutions in which, whether organized or not, the spokesmen of conflicting viewpoints take part, not only settle practical questions but also serve as an educational exchange of information and point of view.

Lockouts, like strikes, must be looked upon as grave social disorders. The discipline of negotiations is threatened when either side presumes or is thought to presume on its advantage over the other. Yet it cannot be said that because the company initiates a lockout, the union is *prima facie* at fault, any more than the opposite conclusion is justified by a strike. A wicked eyelid may be responsible, or an overheard slur, rather than a general policy on one side or the other.

As has been indicated, it is unwholesome for either party to have unchecked power. The union leader who cannot rely on the employer to defend the firm's rights is often "on the hot seat," for his membership may soon expect him to overreach on their behalf. In that direction lies disaster, rather than stable relationships; yet in that direction he may be forced to go unless the firm's rights are upheld.

There come times in the course of negotiations when the lockout seems the only way in which the employer can convince the union leaders or the body of union membership that he has reached the limit of his concessions. As the union leader and the employer gain knowledge of the thinking, expression, and character of one another, they become better able to detect the difference between bluff and finality, to determine where real conviction lies. When that time comes, both the strike and the lockout are difficult to defend.

Many will remember the ineffectual "Shorty" in Owen Wister's novel, *The Virginian*. The foreman had delivered his cattle to market and was trying to maneuver his boys back to the Judge's ranch. But Trampas was working on contrary plans. " 'If there is going to be any gun play,' said Shorty, 'you can count on me.' " And the Virginian replied good naturedly, " 'Oh, go to bed with your gun play—this isn't a killing matter.' "

Testimony before the LaFollette Civil Liberties Committee revealed the private arsenals, hired thugs, spies, and company police assembled by employers. The extent of this arming came as a surprise even to many seasoned veterans of industrial strife. Most people had believed that the struggle for union recognition was more in the nature of a business matter, than "gun play."

We are less interested in the inappropriateness or social peril of the show of force by employers during strikes than in its waste and folly. Experience shows that such measures do not prevent bloodshed; they encourage violence. It would be difficult to cite a case where the opposite has been proved. Striking employees are alienated by a show of force as by no other kind of employer resistance. Rarely, if ever, have they regarded the decision to join the union as a breach of loyalty to the employer. Guns and tear gas are to the worker unwarranted indignities. It is not a killing matter—doesn't the boss know that much about us?

This rapid survey of controversial practices has not been an effort to portray villainy, but rather men and women with decent motives struggling over unsettled issues—adjustment to the disciplines of row on row of flashing machinery and to the problems of interrelated processes which are peculiarly urgent in this generation. Any charges here made or implied are inherent in the inevitable difficulties of such adjustments.

We may seem to express a belief that these problems are easily solved and that the profit seekers and those moved to defend human considerations can reach a ready agreement, if only they will. Most men, whatever their jobs, would welcome the success of both management and labor. We cannot claim that the processes here advocated lead toward any such happy Utopia. The most that can be claimed is that their trend is in the direction of sound and fruitful working relationships. They effect certain integrations and they isolate and define remaining areas of conflict, while giving practice and confidence in the disciplines of adjustment, research, and understanding. As illustrations of the areas in which these disciplines are needed for joint union-management determinations we discuss in the next four chapters: wages, hours, operating control, safety and health.

V. MATTERS FOR JOINT UNION-MANAGEMENT STUDY AND DETERMINATION

CHAPTER 9

WAGE SYSTEMS

"THE size and constancy of a man's pay envelope govern not only the satisfying of his physical needs but also his opportunity for social enjoyment and spiritual contentment." This is a labor leader's summary.

America has been the favored country of the modern world because the power of the average man to purchase that which he desires has been greater than in any other land. Chance has had little part in this. National resources and climate have helped a lot. But added to these advantages have been the energy, initiative, and perseverance that have enabled us to produce more goods. As a result, wages and other income here have been higher than anywhere else. This in turn has inspired still greater effort. This country's recent regression has not been caused by production in excess of its capacity to consume, but in a measure through the slackening of enterprise and action.

In this chapter are discussed some of the practices and principles which affect the earnings of the working man and woman and which have a direct bearing upon the relations between employer and employee.

Because a man's pay determines his share of the good things of life, it is easy to understand why he is constantly striving for better wages. On the other hand, to the manager wages cannot be separated from output because the amount done for a given wage determines the labor cost per unit of production. It is not difficult then to see why in a competitive market he opposes wage increases and constantly seeks ways and means of increasing the productiveness of each employee.

These opposing points of view, which involve not only

rates of pay but rates of production as well, often lead to controversy between employer and employee. Fortunately, it is possible through an analytical treatment of the problem of wage payments to separate much that is factual from the obviously controversial elements and thus to eliminate many of the initial causes of irritation.

Primary elements that can be settled on a factual basis include, for example, such points as the time required to do a job; the fatigue involved in operations; quality requirements; means of reducing exertion; defensible rewards for accomplishment; the importance of one job as compared with another; and working conditions which affect the well-being and therefore the production and earning power of employees. Inequalities in wage rates also may be thus eliminated.

Settlement of these problems largely on a factual basis, determined by joint union-management consideration and research, reduces collective bargaining about wages to such basic elements as general increases or decreases in rate, and the system to be used in remunerating workers. There is no one wage system or method of computing wages generally conceded to be the best. The goal is an adequate and assured annual income. Even among the unions there is a wide difference of view as to the form the wages should take under existing conditions. The fact that it is necessary to analyze work carefully as an aid to optimum production does not mean that one method of compensation is to be preferred to another. The kind of product to be turned out must necessarily influence the wage scheme. Perhaps a majority of workers today given free choice would prefer a daily wage with measured production. Variety and experimentation are highly desirable for the ultimate wage system is probably not yet born.

The amount of money in a worker's pay envelope is inevitably gauged, first or last, by the value of the work he has done. It is a fundamental American principle that the reward for services must depend upon value received. Yet so obvious a principle is often overlooked. On occasion a manager will gloat over the fact that there is no loss to him when a worker loses his "own time" because of delays or early quitting. On the other hand, workers have been known to boast of "soldiering" or purposely slowing down on a job. Actually the time lost by workers and not paid for directly is paid for indirectly by the company because the day or piece rates must be higher to provide the expected weekly wage. "Soldiering" may react on both the management and the worker through increasing labor costs that cannot be passed along to the buyer in higher prices, thus creating avoidable losses which may curtail plant activity.

Now in this chapter we are not concerned with theoretical economic principles so much as with a brief explanation of the various wage plans now in fairly common use in determining the pay an employee receives.

There are, in practice, three general plans of payment for services performed: time payments, when the employee is paid for the actual time he works; incentive payments, when the employee is paid for the number of units of product turned out or for the quality of the product; and salary payments, when the wage covers a specific period of employment —a week, a month, or a year.

Each of these general plans has many variations, but they will be considered here with reference to the principles involved and not in detail since many of the diverse "systems" are basically alike except in name.

Whatever the form of remuneration, the adjustment of the base wage is the first essential. If the payment is to be on a time basis, this base wage represents the total sum paid per unit of time worked. With an incentive plan, the base wage is the minimum guaranteed to the worker. When incentives are paid which require larger production the average payment to the worker must be appreciably more than for day work.

The base wage differs according to many factors, among them, the nature of the work, the skill required, and the length of time needed to attain this proficiency. In recent years increasing attention has been given to the technique of job evaluation or "salary administration," by which various types of jobs are compared with one another to determine their relative importance so that the base wage for each will take into account the degree of skill, responsibility, training, and other aspects of that job. This practice protects the base wage from the unbalancing effect of "market" influence and arbitrary promotion policies. Jobs are defined, rated against one another, and then "priced." The fixing of the rates for the different classes of work is not arbitrary; it calls for cooperation between management and union.

Under a pure time payment plan an employee is not usually held to any standard of performance in quantity or quality. His pay depends entirely on the number of hours he works. The amount of work performed is subject only to the inclination of the worker and the drive of the foreman. The results are seldom satisfactory to employee or to management. Production standards in various forms have been accepted by a number of unions working on a straight time basis. In an effort to avoid the bad features of piecework the Amalgamated Clothing Workers of America have worked out an effective system of production standards. Also the group attack on inefficiency of the B & O railroad workers, as a means of developing increased employment, is somewhat analogous.

A good deal of space could be used in discussing the ethics and effectiveness of the various forms of incentive wages in common use. While recognizing that there is widespread opposition to incentives among labor unions it is probably true that much of this is due to the shortsighted or unfair methods of application. Where morale is high and a good understanding exists between management and union members almost any wage system can be made to work. The argument for any incentive plan is that the worker has a chance to earn more than the base wage, and hence he takes a keener interest in his work, and derives greater satisfaction from it. In short, the worker gains benefits under the incentive plan without adding to the labor costs of the employer. For this reason attempts have been made to improve upon the ordinary time plan by periodically raising or lowering the hourly rate, on the basis of measured performance. If the measuring stick is effectiveness alone, that is, actual compared with standard output, the plan is known as a graded wage plan. If quality, versatility, dependability and skill as well as quantity are used as a sort of compound measure of performance, it is called measured day work. In both plans, the worker's hourly rate fluctuates down as well as up, as his performance rises and falls.

Sometimes, too, the effort is made to offset the monotony of the day's work by the use of non-financial incentives—an appeal to the worker's emotional "drives" such as his desire to excel his fellows, or to do a good day's work. Standards of performance and of quality as determined by routine tests are developed and complete records of individual or group production are kept. Posting the records in figures or curves gives a comparison of accomplishments and furnishes incentives to fair production of good quality. This plan is used effectively in the paper-making industry under the union wage scale.

Salary plans of payment are pretty much the same as time payment except that the period for which payment is made is longer. A salary designates a certain specific sum per week or per month or per year with an assumption (not always realized) of continued employment. In the past it has usually meant that the salaried person received preferential treatment as to vacations, sick leave, and so on, in return for which he was expected to contribute, without extra pay, any overtime required by peak loads and emergencies.

Incentive payment plans may be operated on an individual or on a group basis. The individual incentive is considered to have the greater effectiveness; but group incentives are better adapted to operations requiring team work.

All incentive plans, individual or group, may be classified according to the way incentive earnings are figured:

        1. Piecework
        2. Gain-sharing plans
        3. Empirical bonus plans
        4. Point plans.

In ordinary piecework the worker is paid for the number of units of work turned out without regard to the time worked. If his earnings are not permitted to fall below a stated sum, the plan is known as piecework with a guaranteed minimum. The latter offers the worker a measure of protection against factors beyond his control that might prevent him from "making out." In differential piecework the rate increases with the number of units. In this way the worker showing the largest accomplishment receives the highest rate per piece. From the standpoint of management, the underlying theory is that with increase in a worker's productivity there is a saving in machine time and overhead. From the standpoint of the worker, there is an award for superior achievement. Because it is so complicated, the plan is little used.

In the gain-sharing or premium plans the term "premium" sometimes is synonymous with bonus but usually represents the amount of saving over standard performance, which is shared by worker and management on a pre-arranged basis. When standards of past performance are used as yardsticks the plan is unfair to both parties because the productivity of some operations can be increased markedly without excessive effort, while in other operations only a small gain can be made.

Bonus plans are designed empirically either to give the operator a fixed bonus for reaching a definite task or to offer him rewards on a sliding scale, starting from an arbitrary point and increasing as the individual's production approaches task level. The theory underlying the first type is the powerful pull of the full bonus at task level; the second type encourages the worker, little by little, to task level. A bonus plan is frequently used in cases where specific quality requirements affect productivity.

The various types of "point systems" are simply modifications of bonus or premium plans. To give a new designation, a minute is called a "point." As generally used, a standard of production is set and the receipts above the standard are shared with indirect workers and foremen in the department. This division is often criticized by the direct worker.

When the methods of work have been previously standardized and the control of production developed, the point system is simply a special form of bonus although a complicated method of payment, which many of the workers fail to understand. Because of this and because the amount of work performed is rather vaguely designated, it is liable to abuse by an unfair employer.[1]

Although incentive plans vary widely in detail, they have at least three important features in common: (1) their effective use depends upon the establishment of operating standards, which represent the most suitable conditions under which an operation can be performed in a given plant; (2) they require standards of both quantity and quality in performance; and (3) the same performance standards can be used in establishing shop schedules and in controlling production.

Operating standards take into account the speed of the machine, the shape and size of tools; the motions and methods of the operator; the arrangement of supplies, parts and tools on the work bench; and the material used in fabrication. The best condition of each of these is determined by accepted research methods; failure to maintain these factors at standard may make it impossible for the operator to reach the expected level of production under any system of wages. Uncontrolled, they prove to be annoying variables the effect of which cannot be predicted. Moreover, the analysis of tasks and the development of operating standards are usually the real sources of the spectacular savings frequently credited to incentives.

But no matter how accurate and fair the standards of time, quality or process may be in themselves, unless they are used in planning the work throughout the plant, and in scheduling deliveries, there are bound to be irregularities and delays that are irksome to the worker, hold up delivery, and so result in loss of business.

If a firm is to make a profit in a competitive market, the cost of each product must be known. This, in turn, necessitates a knowledge of the amount of work performed in a given time by hand or machine. On the other hand, unless the worker has a measure of his productivity he has no protection against the driving foreman nor does he have the satisfaction of a day's work well performed.

Standards of performance may be expressed in terms of time per operation or in number of operations performed per hour or in points. In some cases, the standard is a measure of the work of an individual; in other cases, of group work, depending on the nature of the operation. In general, individual standards are preferable because they give each worker a measure as a person, instead of making him one of a "gang." Group standards have to be used where the accomplishment depends upon the united work of several people such as in an assembly or in a continuous process. In some industries quality or waste standards are more important than productivity; frequently good productivity depends on uniform quality as determined by tests or inspection.

Fundamental principles of fair remuneration have been obscured by over-emphasis on "wage systems" as such. As a matter of fact, the method of payment matters little as compared with the method of determining the standards upon which the wage is based. Whether the employee is simply paid for the time he works, or whether his wage is based on the amount or quality of the work he does in a certain time, the standard time required for each piece of work is the factor that counts. But the form of payments—day wage, piecework, bonus, or "points"—makes little difference to worker or employer, except insofar as the system used involves unfairness or guesswork.

There are good and bad ways of determining the standard of performance which plays so vital a part in the scheme of wage payment. A number of methods, still used by industry, belong under the heading "Poor": *past records,* as ordinarily used, represent a mixture of good and bad practice and fail to separate adequately different types of work; *judgment,* all too frequently, is a mere guess; *test runs* made by a first-class man, are inaccurate and unfair; *pocket stop watch,* used by the foreman, is bound to be unjust and irregular, since only fast times on a quick worker are snapped by the foreman who, in the nature of things, cannot handle time study or rate setting with satisfaction.

The sound methods of determining standards of performance are *motion study* and *time study,* or a combination of both. Some of labor's objections to the very phrase "time study" are discussed in another chapter. Here we are concerned with the techniques and the uses of this tool.

Shorn of emotion and controversy, motion study is simply the study of the best present method of performing a hand or machine operation through an analysis of the motions involved. It may be carried on with varying degrees of refinement. If the whole operation is not divided into a sufficient number of elements or parts, room for error creeps in. On the other hand motion study is frequently carried on with such a meticulous regard for detail as to make it properly applicable to a very small percentage of the world's work.

Time study consists in the timing of each of the several elements going to make up a given operation. It is useful in the scientific scheduling of work even more than in facilitating fair wage payment. In many classes of work involving repetitive operations, motion study is a valuable mechanism for reducing production cost and especially for making the worker's task easier and simpler. It is a mistake, however, to see time study too large in the whole management picture. There is a vast amount of organization work which should precede it. One effective industrial engineer never uses it, and another only after five years of preliminary work. But criticism of time study usually rests largely on a misunderstanding of how to make the studies and apply them. Properly made and utilized they are the most accurate and the fairest of all methods of fixing standards for wages and for production control.

The method of making time studies is so important that it is worth while to consider some of the essential principles:[2]

1. Time studies must always be made with the knowledge and cooperation of the union and the operative observed. Practiced secretly, they undermine morale and their results are worthless.

2. Tools and machines must be standardized in advance of, or in conjunction with, time analysis.

3. Methods of performing each operation and the quality of workmanship must be studied and recorded, as well as the times. Time studies which disregard methods are of little value.

4. Studies of the time elements of each operation must be divided into sufficiently small units to be utilized in various combinations.

5. The times which are alike for all jobs or which vary

with some other factor than time must be separated, in summarizing, from the repetitive elements. For example, set-up or get-ready time on each job must be considered separately from the times per piece.

6. The stop watch must be run continuously, and, in addition to the effective times, all delays should be recorded and described.

7. Enough operatives must be observed to obtain fair average time standards, and before utilizing the data continuous check studies of actual operation should be made.

These rules may seem elementary but it is a fact that most piece rates or other incentives today are set not by competent study but by guess or estimate. The abuses of method, committed in the name of time study, are many. Going operations are timed without regard to possible improvement of method; operations are broken down into elements and timed, and then all of the elements are not used; overall time studies are taken without analysis into units; arbitrary percentages for unavoidable delays and waits are added to carefully recorded elementary times.

But the fact that time study can be, and often is, badly used is no argument against the method itself. The stop watch, in fact, is one of the most effective tools for union-management cooperation, because it establishes facts that cannot be gainsaid. The workman, rather than the employer, is in most situations the first to appreciate the value of real time study, and he is also the first to gauge the correctness of its operation. As far back as 1916, cooperative time studies by a labor union and a manufacturers' association established standards acceptable to both parties.

In addition to managerial policies and the state of the labor market, wages are also affected by legislation and by union organization.

Minimum wage laws, both federal and state, have a direct influence upon the adjustments of the base wage. If the minimum is set too high, it may react on the wages of higher-paid skilled workers, especially in industries where the volume of sales is dependent on low selling prices. Further, the tendency of management is to discharge the least competent and to substitute fewer workers of a higher skill or improved machinery and equipment which would not be economical were "cheap labor" available.

If the standard is not too high, a minimum wage law is valuable in eliminating "sweat shop" competitors who grind their employees down to a stipend often below a subsistence level.

With the rapid growth of unionism in recent years the union wage scale has played an increasingly important role in determining wages and labor costs. The tendency of the average employer is to maintain as low a wage scale as possible and yet hold his men. Many employers, on the other hand, appreciate the fact that it is not only fair but good business policy to make possible to each worker his "maximum prosperity," using that phrase in Taylor's sense:

> Maximum prosperity for each employee means not only higher wages than are usually received by men of his class, but, of more importance still, it also means the development of each man to the state of his maximum efficiency, so that he may be able to do, generally speaking, the highest grade of work for which his natural abilities fit him, and, further, it means giving him, when possible, this class of work to do.[3]

The drive of the unions to raise the pay and reduce the working hours of their members has often had the cooperation of the employer. More and more the abler union leaders are using keen discrimination in making claims for wage increases and taking the long view of the profit position of the company and its ability to extend its busines and so to provide more and higher-paid employment through lower selling prices. The modern labor leader also realizes that to receive a good day's pay a man must do a good day's work and that increase in productivity has been the vital factor in this country's industrial supremacy and its relatively high wage scale.

Contrary to a belief commonly held, it is not the general practice of unions to demand uniformity in wages, thus retarding efficiency as well as preventing adequate reward to the energetic and highly skilled worker. Wage stipulations in contracts apply to minimum, never to maximum, amounts.

It is prevailing union practice to leave it to the skill of the employee and the judgment of management arrived at through conferences with the appropriate union committee as to how much above the minimum any one individual may be paid. The proper setting of minimum wages so as to accomplish the purposes outlined above requires intelligence, restraint, and experience in collective bargaining on both sides. Such arrangements do not follow any one pattern. Individuals and groups and situations vary too widely to make this possible.

The uniform wage scale required by some unions has on occasion prevented due reward to the energetic and highly skilled worker in those trades. While measured performance is not always desirable or practicable, the worker, through comparison of his work with standards of normal production, should have the satisfaction of work well done and the opportunity for advancement. Even without financial incentives, however, it is possible to maintain high production with satisfaction to the worker, and thus benefit industry by helping to take up the slack in employment through greater demand for the product at a lower price.

In addition to those considerations already discussed, there are others which affect wages. The payment of time and one-half for "overtime" work in excess of the regular daily or weekly hours because of union insistence has long been established practice for factory workers. In recent years it has been increasingly used for clerical workers, in lieu of "supper money." The Federal Wages and Hours Act now provides a legal basis for the payment of the overtime rate of time and a half for all hours in excess of the maximum legal hours per week. In a good many agreements between employer and union there is a further provision, fixing double time for work done on Sunday and on specified holidays.

Profit sharing is another wage scheme, varying widely in details and in effectiveness. Again and again attempts at profit sharing have met with little success or downright failure. On the other hand, there have been some conspicuously successful plans, most of them in relatively small concerns. One difficulty with profit sharing lies in the fact that the worker appreciates additions to his compensation when they appear but criticizes the management when, because of a business slump or other cause, the extra sum is not forthcoming. Usually, profit-sharing payments are made on an annual or quarterly basis—too remote from the regular routine to have any influence as an incentive.

Few workers understand accounting practice and the computation of profits is as a rule a complete mystery to the employee. He therefore believes that figures can be made to tell almost any story, and the lack of uniformity in American accounting practice adds to this confusion. Under these circumstances a profit-sharing plan has often proved to be a source of friction rather than a means to better industrial relations.

If it is to succeed, a profit-sharing scheme cannot be stereotyped. Its provisions must depend upon the nature, the practice, and the financial resources of the business. It must be initiated and carried on through genuine cooperation between the workers and the management. The workers must see the monthly statements of profit and have a voice in deciding on unusual expenditures which will tend to reduce profits temporarily in the expectation of increasing them at a later period. The distribution of profits must be made at least once a month, preferably weekly. When payments under the plan are interrupted, the worker must know the reason why and have an opportunity to offer suggestions for bettering the firm's condition. The best judgment appears to be that under existing conditions, and conceding the very best of intentions, the odds are all against the success of any profit-sharing scheme.

Another group of wage plans attempts to counteract one of the most serious weaknesses of modern industrial society —irregular employment and income. Seasonality of demand, business cycles, intense competition, technological change and poor management all contribute to this insecurity of the wage earner.

To offset it, annual wage plans have been tried over a period of years. Between irregular work at high hourly rates, as in the building trades, and stable employment throughout the year there can be only one choice. Some companies seek to sustain employee earning power by accumulating funds out of which unemployment benefits are paid, but the experience of the depression has proved that these funds become exhausted too readily to offer much protection against the ravages of a severe recession. In one "going" plan the employee is guaranteed a definite number of weeks' employment during the year, though with no guarantee as to his weekly earnings. In another, he is guaranteed fifty-two uniform weekly pay checks. Under a third scheme, his earnings are not permitted to drop below a stated minimum by letting him "borrow" time up to a fixed percentage, not infrequently 60 per cent, of his normal week's pay.

Pioneers in this difficult field deserve great commendation, but not too much should be expected from their efforts. Experience to date raises doubt as to whether annual wage plans can be extended over a wide area of business activity, for basic to their success is the stabilization of operations. This has been done on a limited scale by "ironing" out sales seasonality, or by "leveling" production and carrying large inventories for selling peaks. Both policies involve very onerous managerial tasks, and the second also requires unusual financial and storage facilities. Further, the outstanding plans for steady work and wages, are to be found today only in companies manufacturing or selling consumer's goods.

But because it has not been solved is no proof that the problem of a dependable yearly income for wage earners and their families is insoluble. From the worker's viewpoint, this is the chief factor in his health, happiness and well-being. From the standpoint of industry, steady purchasing power for the masses would open up a home market of almost limitless possibilities. Here is our economy's outstanding challenge to industrial statesmanship.

The question of wages has always been considered by the employing group as closely tied up with the question of hours. From earliest days it has been argued that any cut in hours should mean lessened wages. Now that we are down to the 40-44 hour week this direct relationship between hours and wages is admitted to be less obvious. Let's see what the factors are which have a bearing on hours.

CHAPTER 10

THE HOURS OF WORK

WE HAVE been concerned with the problem of hours only since we began to count them. In an agricultural economy and even in a guild society, neither craftsmen nor farmers punched clocks; they would no more have tolled up the time they had labored or complained about the fourteen-hour day than they would have questioned the rising and setting of the sun. The workday was defined by the immutable cycle of day and night; the dispensation of darkness brought an end to labor and the dawn brought its beginning once again. To this day laborers in the sugar fields of Louisiana work from "kin to kint" which means from the time they can see until they can't see—from dawn to dark.

Not until the coming of the industrial revolution, the introduction of indoor, factory labor, and the use of artificial light did the workman—though not his masters—begin to enumerate the dull and weary hours and to become all too conscious of their burden. Since then, as the proportion of the working population taken from farm work to business and industry has increased from a small fraction to a majority, the attention of millions and of society as a whole has been focused upon the question of the length of the working day and the working week. The drive by the labor movement, by governmental action, and by occasional public-spirited employers to shorten working hours has historically been based upon humanitarian considerations of health and well-being, supplemented by claims of greater efficiency. Periodically another argument has been urged: that if men work fewer hours, more men will have jobs.

For over a century after this campaign was launched, economists of the "classical" school have advised against attempts to curtail the freedom of employers to work their labor force for as long as the owners wished and the employees consented. These theorists believed that the unhampered play of competition for the "factors of production" (land, labor, capital and management) would result in a natural lowering of the hour-wheel as the productivity of the workers gradually increased and the labor required for production proportionately declined. Correlatively, they were convinced that "unnatural" intervention by government, or by the unions, to shorten the working period would only result in unemployment, pay cuts, or both. Now since this reasoning, slightly refurbished, still forms the backbone of the resistance to modern legislation and a support to employers who refuse collective bargaining with unions, it seems worth while to examine it in some detail.

Assume any industry, say these economists, to be operating under competitive conditions, with rent, interest, managerial profits, and labor costs held to a minimum. Then reduce the workday from ten to eight hours. What will occur? That, we are told, depends upon certain variables.

(a) If wage rates remain the same and no more men are hired, the unit labor cost of production will remain the same as before; as output will be reduced and some overhead costs will not be quickly adjusted to this diminished production, the capital cost per unit will be higher for a time. In any event, the labor force, though retaining the same rates of pay, will get a smaller aggregate wage for the new eight-hour day than they got for ten hours; the owners will receive a smaller total profit because of the reduced output; and the entire economy will suffer from higher prices and reduced production. The new effect then, say the classicists, will be a decline in the incomes and purchasing power of workers and employers, and of the total product of the industry.

(b) If wage rates remain the same, but more men are hired in order to keep up the level of production, the result would be simply a general reduction in pay: more men will be hired to work for a little less apiece, the product's price and quantity will remain as before, capital costs will change little, and purchasing power of all groups will be constant.

(c) If wage rates are boosted, so that the same number of men are receiving the same total wages for an eight-hour day as they received for ten hours, then unit labor costs of production will rise as output declines, and the result can only be an increase in price and a consequent slump in demand and in real wages. "Marginal" firms—those which had been just able to meet their costs—will be forced to take a loss and eventually to shut down. This will throw men out of work, lower the effective demand for other products, and, if enough such firms are closed, perhaps set in motion a cumulative decline.

(d) If, now, we assume that the industry whose hours are being cut maintains production by operating a} other shift, a speculative question is raised subject to factors of human engineering rather than of logic. Additional shifts might lower overhead-unit charges, permitting a continuous, intensive use of capital and reducing risks of obsolescence. If, in addition, wages per worker were reduced, the cost and price of the product would be cut, demand and output would rise, more workers would be needed to turn out the increased production, and the "real" wages of all labor (that is to say, its consuming power) would rise. However, the classicists assert, these same results could have been achieved by cutting wages and introducing the double shift, regardless of changes in hours.

These are the chief lines of reasoning of the traditional school. They are important because they have been advanced with great authority. They are plausible because they take account of costs, which are vital to management, and to production which is important to management, workers, and the consuming public. But the very perfection of this logic is a serious flaw. It is too watertight to be sound. As these arguments are worked, they treat the two animate factors of production—labor and management—as *fixed* elements of almost mechanical performance. Variants of human psychology and physiology which influence production are omitted, perhaps with intent, since they could only complicate the neat equations. In addition, the reasoning is built upon a doubtful assumption: namely, the prevalence in the labor market of persistent competition and equality of bargaining power. Let us look at these flaws more closely.

The economists' classic formula assumes that employers will constantly be goaded by competition to reduce the hours of the working day down to that minimum which is most efficient. And this competition among employers will be reinforced, presumably, by the continuous pressure of workers who will discriminate against employers who do not thus conduct their enterprise. For employers, it is said, will naturally want to set the most productive schedule, and since they are competing among themselves for labor, those who offer the best terms will have the first pick of the employables, thus elevating the whole level of working conditions. Therefore, the classicists feel safe in assuming that at any one point hours have already been set by these regulating factors at the lowest notch consistent with production costs. But actually there is no such beneficent competition for labor. The labor market is a buyers' market. Pools of reserve labor have divested workers of much of their bargaining strength, and for the last decade the persistence of large-scale unemployment has broken down any "natural" bargaining power the workers may possess, apart from their union organizations. Nor is it possible longer to consider this situation abnormal. Most economists have regarded full employment of the labor force as the norm from which there are occasional but brief departures. The opposite is nearer the truth. With this persistent surplus of laborers, it is futile to talk of an automatic regulation of hours by some efficient force called competition, acting in a field of equal bargaining power.

But the major flaw in the economists' thesis that union-management or state regulation of hours is either harmful or unnecessary proceeds from a sterile concept of the human element. For the argument fails to take account of the cardinal fact that hours affect workers' efficiency and hence costs, and that costs affect managements' skill in directing labor. It is obvious that the length of the workday will affect the alertness, the health, the carefulness, the efficiency of the man at the bench or the machine. And in so far as factual evidence exists, it supports this conclusion. There is a relation between hours of labor and accidents, for example. Over a period of years, the figures show that as the hours-per-man decline, accidents per man-hour decline; as hours-per-man rise, the accident curve follows.[1] That the tragic element of fatigue lies behind this relationship is plain. Workers who are not worn down by oppressive hours retain their alertness and caution; workers who are dulled by long working days or nights become careless and clumsy. Accidents are costly to employers and to society in general. It is apparent from the available evidence that there lies here a rich field for union-management cooperation in the interest of greater production and reduced cost.

There is a similar correlation between man-hours and sickness, although the data on this are not nearly so complete or so accessible. The U. S. Public Health Service figures, however, show that the sickness index among American male workers was at 85 in 1932 when hours were 38 per week, dropped to 71 by the end of the year and fell to 66 as the work week slipped to 35 hours in 1934. Then while hours rose to 37 in 1935, sickness climbed back to 74. Throughout 1936 sickness followed hours upward until in 1937 as hours stood at 40 a week, sickness had reached 90.[2] The statistics are meager, and need to be cautiously interpreted, but they indicate a close correlation between hours above 35 and sickness rate.

The grave significance of such data is underscored by the knowledge that the least medical care goes to those who need it most, that those who work the longest hours are customarily the lowest paid, and that those who suffer the greatest fatigue and the greatest susceptibility to illness can least afford medical attention. Among relief families in recent years disabling sickness was 45 per cent higher than among families with comfortable living standards, and 73 per cent higher among families whose incomes remained in well-to-do brackets. A notable study conducted by the California State Medical Association, showed that over 40 per cent of all urban whites needing care in families with incomes up to $2,000, more than 50 per cent of the sub-$1,000 group, and over 56 per cent of the sub-$500 stratum were receiving no medical care at all.

But if long hours can lower workers' efficiency, can shorter hours improve it? It is no paradox to assert that in many instances men produce more in a short shift than in a longer one. The record of British war industries provided elaborate proof:

In the general enthusiasm of the first months of the War many have been in favour of a complete suspension of the provisions of the Factory Acts which limited working hours, and in consequence very long hours were often worked. But instead of increasing output, an extension of the working day, by the excessive fatigue which it caused, its detrimental reaction on health, and consequent irregularity of attendance, actually diminished output, in the case of men no less than of women and children. A restriction of hours was not only good sentiment, but also good business, and the policy of the munition factories was accordingly revised.[3]

Everyone is familiar with one of America's most notable experiments in shorter hours—when U. S. Steel went from its traditional 10- and 12-hour basis to 8 and 10 hours. The new shifts proved a practical success to the astonishment of the management and to the gratification of the engineers and social workers who had foreseen it. But there are scores of cases quite as definite as this. The National Industrial Conference Board made a survey in 1929 of 94 plants which had switched from the 5½- or 6-day week to the 5-day week. The tabulations revealed that nearly 70 per cent had experienced either no drop in output or an actual increase. This rise in man-hour efficiency they credited to operating economies from eliminating the overhead involved in starting, stopping, and cleaning machinery for the uneconomic "short Saturday"; elimination of absences and low vitality among laborers on Saturday; opportunity to use Saturday morning to overhaul and repair machinery; maintenance of greater good will and better health among employees, with less "soldiering" and fewer accidents.[4]

Of course, where the speed of work is determined largely by the pace of the machine itself, the individual is not free to step up his hourly output to cover his shorter workday or work week. But even here other economies can come into effect—all those cited above, plus managerial savings

THE HOURS OF WORK

that will differ in detail from plant to plant but which are common to nearly all.

The historical work-week in the hosiery industry under union agreements was 48 hours up to the adoption of the Hosiery Code under NRA, when the 40-hour work-week was adopted. The experience in the reduction of 8 hours per week in the total working week proved conclusively that those employees on handwork operations, or such operations as were to a large extent handwork, were able in a short period of time to increase their hourly output so that total output for the 40-hour week netted virtually the previous total on the 48-hour basis. In those operations in which the work was governed by the speed and tempo of machinery, the same experience did not result. While there was some increase in hourly output, due to the efforts of individuals to meet their previous production standards, this could only be accomplished to a small extent on machine operation. Management, technique, however, entered into the picture also and a large number of hosiery manufacturers in an effort to keep down their overhead costs, turned their attention to the improvement of existing machinery and the proper repair and maintenance of machinery, to the extent that combination of increased machine efficiency plus increased man efficiency reached virtually the same production level in 40 hours work per week as had existed under the 48-hour week.[5]

This statement clearly shows that the employer, like the worker, is not a mechanical, but a human and variable factor. Circumstances alter his efficiency too, and hence the productivity of those working under his direction. The causes underlying this observation that shorter hours may prod employers into greater efficiency and so counteract any increase in costs is well expressed by Beatrice and Sidney Webb:

... The enforcement of the Common Rule on all establishments concentrates the pressure of competition on the brains of the employer, and keeps them always on the stretch. "Mankind," says Emerson, "is as lazy as it dares to be," and so long as an employer can meet the pressure of the wholesale trader, or of foreign competition, by nibbling at wages or "cribbing time," he is not likely to undertake the "intolerable toil of thought," that would be required to discover a genuine improvement in the productive process, or even, as Babbage candidly admits, to introduce improvements that have already been invented. Hence the mere existence of a Common Rule, by debarring the hard-pressed employer from the most obvious source of relief, positively drives him to other means of lowering the cost of production.[6]

There is another facet, too, to managerial economies which is brought out by the Webbs:

> From the point of view of the economist, concerned to secure the highest efficiency of the national industry, it must be counted to the credit of the Device of the Common Rule (standard hours and rates of pay) that it compels the employer, in his choice of men to fill vacancies, to be always striving, since he cannot get a "cheap hand," to exact, for the price that he has to pay, greater strength and skill, a higher standard of sobriety and regular attendance, and a superior capacity for responsibility and initiative.
>
> But the rigid enforcement of the Device of the Common Rule does more than act as a perpetual stimulus to the selection of the fittest men for employment. The fact that the employer's mind is constantly intent on getting the best possible workmen silently and imperceptibly reacts on the wage-earners. The young workman, knowing that he cannot secure a preference for employment by offering to put up with worse conditions than the standard, seeks to commend himself by a good character, technical skill and general intelligence. There is, accordingly, under a Common Rule, not only a constant selection of the most efficient candidates, but also a positive stimulus to the whole class to become ever more efficient.[7]

The literature of business economics abounds in specific examples of economies discovered or explored by managers faced with rising costs or falling prices. Such efforts on the part of executives were particularly noticeable in the years of the post-war depression when, with prices drastically flattened, managers were forced to find ways to increase the workers' productivity; that they were successful is apparent when one notes that from 1899 to 1914 the factory laborer's output went up only 8 per cent—whereas in but three years, 1920-23, it shot forward by 23 per cent. What was accomplished then under the menace of lowered prices has been and still can be accomplished under the stimulus of shortened hours, which places the same challenge before management to do its job well.

In general, then, it is safe to say that within a significant margin, shorter hours mean increased efficiency to the worker and the employer, and a lower production cost. Reduction of hours therefore does not call for reduction in wages, and under favorable circumstances should mean an increase of workers' incomes. Further, in some areas of American industry, where exhausting workdays are still the rule, the reduction of hours will mean improvement in the education, intelligence, and health of the working people, with consequent increase in their productivity.

But granted the desirability of regulating maximum hours, in the interest of production, there remains the question: who is to regulate them?

Historically the unions have taken this as their own prerogative, and have opposed or been lukewarm to state and federal legislation on hours of labor. The unions have been successful through collective bargaining in gaining for their members, and also for the unorganized, steady improvement in the length of the day or week.

The passing of years and recent events have almost completely reversed labor's attitude. The union movement is now found solidly supporting the Wages and Hours Act and the various state hours laws. Needless to say, labor will continue to regulate hours by collective bargaining in particular firms and industries; but it is equally sure that the unions have come to realize that state-wide and nation-wide standards are essential to put a floor under even their best contract terms, and to prevent cutthroat competition of other firms and regions from undermining their own local achievements.

Another regulator of hours often called upon by popular writers is "enlightened self-interest." Some cases are to be found where employers have taken the initiative in shortening the workday or work week. But the majority of employers have approached the question in neither a farsighted nor a humanitarian manner. Certainly, the primary impetus given to hours revision has only infrequently come from them; and the day-to-day necessities of industrial enterprise being what they are, there is no reason why workers should look to employers for such leadership; the initiative must logically come from the group which is most concerned with working hours, aided and directed by sociologists, economists, engineers and labor specialists.

"Organized public opinion," too, has been urged often to take over the campaign. And it is true that those corporations most in the public eye are usually more scrupulous in their formation of labor policies than are the concerns which can exploit their workers with little fear of publicity. Yet, for all that, public opinion is a pretty awkward and undependable weapon with which to hunt down exploiters of labor. Even the experienced Consumers' League finally abandoned its White Lists through which it strove to lift and stabilize working conditions by public pressure. Today the League concentrates its energies upon legislative safeguards, fighting for minimum wage and maximum hour laws, and the right of labor to organize.

Action by separate states has the obvious advantage of reaching intra-state industries which fall outside federal statutes. It has the disadvantage of competitive pressures from other states; that is, the attempt of one state to raise its working standards may be sabotaged by the slackened requirements of a neighboring state eager to entice migrant industries within its borders. Further, to get 48 states to pass adequate and fairly uniform measures is a formidable task. After half a century of striving by many groups, only 25 states have passed minimum wage laws; those with restrictions on hours for other than children and women are even fewer.

Consequently, the need for a basic federal statute to set nation-wide standards has long been recognized, and finally has been met with the passage in 1938 of the Fair Labor Standards Act, popularly known as the Wages and Hours Act. This legislation stipulates a minimum wage of 25 cents an hour and a maximum of 44 hours a week for those enterprises engaged in interstate commerce or the production of goods for interstate commerce. After the Act has been in force one year, the wage is to be lifted at 30 cents, and hours dropped to 42. After two years (1940), the hours will be

THE HOURS OF WORK

reduced to 40, and in 1945 a 40-cent minimum wage will be the rule for all covered industries. Though the Act is national in scope, it excludes certain large groups—executives, administrators, professional workers, retailers, outside salesmen, farmers, agricultural processers and canners, and government employees. Exemptions, too, are possible for "learners, apprentices, and handicapped workers"; and the provision that all overtime work will be paid at time-and-a-half rates can be waived for industries "found by the Administrator to be of a seasonal nature." On the other hand, industry committees are set up by the Administrator, their members representing employers, labor, and the public, and these committees can recommend to the Wages and Hours Division that maximum hours be lowered, or minimum wages be raised, beyond the statutory limits of the Act, so long as these changes do not substantially curtail employment.

Of the functioning of the Act—which is even now under the threat of amendment—it is difficult at this time to say anything final. It has been estimated that in 1938 some twelve and one-half million persons have been covered by it, 300,000 were being paid less than the wage minimum and 1,380,000 were working more than maximum hours—a harsh commentary upon the American standard of living, since the Act requires a minimum wage of only $11 a week ($572 for a full work year of 52 weeks) and a work week limited to 44 hours. But of these 300,000, it is impossible to reckon how many may have been discharged because their firms could not meet even these standards. Estimates range from 25,000 to 75,000. The Wages and Hours Administration has cited a convincing number of cases in which employers have shut down their plants and blamed it on the Act when subsequent investigation revealed that the shut down was a regular seasonal occurrence. This misstatement of facts has been so frequent and has involved such numbers as to throw into question any estimates by newspapers and critics (in and out of Congress) as to the unemployment created by the wage-hour rules.[8]

Yet the issue must be faced squarely: if the Act does cause some plants to close down, if some employers are unable to make adjustments or economies to offset the cost of 25-cent labor for 44 hours a week—or the slightly increased wage and somewhat shortened hours provided for—then is the Act justifiable? Its sponsors think so. They claim that even if some workers are not worth employing under the new conditions, they are worth a great deal more than that, potentially, to society, and if necessary society must give them public employment and train them until they command more than this bare minimum. Also, the friends of the Act argue, a worker's value and his wage have a circular relationship: it may be true to say that he gets little because he is worth little; but it is equally, and more importantly, true that he is worth little because he gets little. A laborer living in a slum on an inadequate diet, devitalized by long hours and pauperized by an income inadequate for physical or mental health, will not be productive enough to earn higher wages or better hours; not until he is paid enough and given short enough hours to gain or to recover his true efficiency will he be worth any more. That, presumably, is the underlying aim of the Act: to require employers to consider their labor not as an item of fixed quality, but as a factor with real possibilities of development.

The new Act is a controversial measure, for in it are focused the issues involved in the question of hours. The long record of attempts to "interfere" with the working day and working week culminates in this national ceiling upon hours. In the evolution of the Act, this country will be making a significant experiment in which the theories and arguments, the aspirations and the forebodings of a century will be tested on a nation-wide scale.

The impression gains ground that the rather restricted conception of hours control embodied in the Wages and Hours Act must presently yield to one in which certain long-time factors—now all but ignored—will have a place.[9] Of course at a time when the idea of the possibility of plenty for all is battling for recognition and when an advancing technology has barely scratched the surface in its effect on production, the idea that leisure rather than work may prove to be the ultimate problem will receive scant attention. But with unemployment rated an all but insoluble problem in every developed country—except as preparations for war may ease it temporarily—certainly in any such discussion as this it should be pointed out that many of the considerations which lead us to shorten the working day and week and even the working year have a bearing on what the working life should be. When we come to place a ceiling on the length of the working life, where should we begin? Should young people postpone wage earning to permit lengthened education and training? Should retirement begin earlier than is now customary? What should be the pattern of the working life as a whole in relation to the increased freedom from toil made possible by man's increasing conquest of his world? This is the lengthening vista of the question of hours of work.

CHAPTER II

OPERATING CONTROL

THE year-in and year-out support for rational wages and hours for the workers and a satisfactory return on the capital investment is dependent on the regularization of operations within the plant and this in turn is dependent on farsighted market research and balanced sales effort. Without a continuing evaluation of the changes in demand and a selective sales policy, effective shop operation is usually impossible. Further, the development of the cordial, cooperative type of environment both in the field, and in the shop, required for the regularization of operations is a matter of slow growth. It requires consistency and fair dealing for its cultivation and an intense regard for detail. These are severe requirements. That they are difficult of realization accounts for the fact that industrial enterprises vary so widely in their techniques and effectiveness, and is a principal factor in engendering the bitterness which usually attends discussions of hours and wages.

The development of an increasingly scientific control of industrial operations has been one of the major factors responsible for the great industrial progress of the last fifty years. The growth in the application of science to industry has been so gradual that its profound influence upon business has scarcely been realized even by industrial executives to whose notable success it has contributed. On the other hand, one of the reasons for the depression has been the failure to extend this development into the broader field of industry as a whole.[1]

Fifty years ago increase in the size of American corporations was in full swing, but the methods of management were crude. Sales were made by high pressure and extravagant advertising claims, with no thought of coordinating sales with production capacity. Orders were dumped into the shop to be filled by the superintendent and foremen, as best they could. The workers waited for materials and tools and the shipments waited until the goods came through.

A measure of order in this chaos resulted largely through the developments initiated by Frederick W. Taylor. Starting as foreman of a machine shop, he tried to eliminate the constant friction between the management and the men through painstaking analyses of jobs, standardization of equipment and fairer methods of wage payment. He simplified foremanship by sub-dividing and re-assigning its duties such as the routing of the work through the shop, studying out the best methods of doing work, teaching the operative where required, inspecting the work at its various stages, providing for the necessary repairs to and upkeep of equipment, and so on. He found that the principal sources of trouble were the lack of planning, unsystematic control of materials and tools, failure to define what constituted a day's work, and insufficient training of the workers. Taylor defined Scientific Management[2] as development in the direction of truly scientific method, including the scientific selection of the workman, his scientific education and development and the intimate friendly cooperation between the management and the men. This latter has logically developed—largely since Taylor's time—into the union-management cooperative movement. "Until after the beginning of the present century there were no published or extensive developments of method in manufacturing that could be termed scientific other than those with which Taylor was associated as the master mind."[3]

Taylor arrived on the scene of American industry when it was an unbelievably rough and tumble affair with low wages and long hours the rule. He opposed to these high wages and shorter hours. He knew almost nothing about economics and, although kindly and considerate in his relations with all kinds of people, he died when it was still only the occasional business man who in any way sensed the constructive function possible for labor unions and collective bargaining. Taylor made no contribution to this phase of industry. But nevertheless his was the genius that took the chaos of his day and in its stead gave us those beginnings of an ordered industry in the absence of which organized labor would have difficulty in playing a constructive part today.

In the early days of Scientific Management in many instances dictatorial managements picked up the bare bones of Taylor's ideas and in the absence of any restraints, such as are provided by labor unions, instituted a system of virtual tyranny and called it the Taylor System.

Today the fundamental principles of control as developed by Taylor and other management specialists are generally accepted in the manufacturing divisions of most industrial plants. Even in these, however, there is great opportunity for improvement which will tend to reduce production costs further, make the work flow more smoothly and permit the payment of higher annual wages. There is still a general lack of appreciation on the part of business executives, even in many of the best-operated companies, of the importance of a scientific approach to all business problems including general policies and management of sales. Such an approach takes into account the factors controlling both long-term income and the regularity of employment, and is "surely superseding the old idea that the head of a business is a czar to give imperialistic orders to all of his subordinate officers and men. The successful executive today instead of a captain of industry judging himself on his quick decisions based on his personal judgment is one who thoroughly analyzes, through his executives, each problem that arises and bases his decisions on this factual analysis."[4]

In a comprehensive analysis of operating control[5] Harlow S. Person summarized the general principles of Scientific Management as research, standardization, control, and cooperation. Thus viewed, operating control is not simply the planning of the work in an establishment. Its function is much broader. It includes the financial relations which affect the extent and direction of business development; the shaping of policies covering the selection and volume of products to be made or sold; the management of sales; and, above all, it must cover the proper coordination of finance, sales, and production. The phases of operation control with which we are chiefly concerned in this chapter are those which most directly affect both the management and the workers; that is, control of production and sales. Production control affects the everyday work in the shop, while sales control is equally important in its relation to volume and continuity of operation.

Production control means planning the work throughout an establishment so that it will flow smoothly, thus avoiding delays and the aggravating waiting for work. This involves, when satisfactorily performed, the best possible distribution of production throughout the year, the scheduling of orders—not only to please the customer, but to make the best use of equipment and personnel—the systematic distribution of materials and parts to the proper machines and workplaces, the maintenance of materials and supplies so as to avoid excessive inventories and yet have them on hand when needed, the routing of the work to the proper machines or workmen, and the sequence of packing and shipping to fill orders on scheduled time.

To illustrate more clearly the importance of production control and to show the deficiencies that exist in many establishments, let us see how manufacturing orders are made up and sent into the factory. The initiation of the order, that is the selling, will be discussed later. The general principles are common to all industry.

It is necessary to separate orders that come in direct from the customer and orders that are made for stock, that is for future sale. Most plants have both of these types. Customers' orders must be filled on specified dates. Stock orders have more leeway and one of the most important duties of control is to handle stock orders, and the manufacture of materials and parts so that production can go forward at a reasonably even rate throughout the year.

But if goods are to be completed at a given date—and this applies both to customers' orders and to stock orders— it is essential for the planning department to know the time required for each phase of manufacture and to be sure that with the equipment and the available operatives the work can be done in the required time. All materials and parts must be on hand before putting a manufacturing order in process. It is here that many otherwise well-organized plants are at loose ends.

In a case of a forge shop in a plant manufacturing large complicated machinery, it was found that the work laid out for one group of the machines would require forty working days instead of the twenty-five called for by the order. In other words, the carrying out of the schedule was a physical impossibility. Furthermore, the production beyond this group of machines was blocked and men had to be laid off. This plant's difficulties were remedied by basing the manufacturing schedule on the actual times required to perform the operations.

Even using standard times, machine equipment is of course relatively inelastic. But in a book plant it was found that by teaching employees one or more optional lines of work nearly every emergency could be met by the regular force. The neglect of careful analysis in planning work raises hob with the operatives in the plant. It leads to "speeding up" on the one hand and "soldiering" on the other. It prevents delivery of orders on time and results in congestion of work and materials in the shop.

Even in such a relatively simple manufacture as shoes, the same inadequate control is to be found. Of the vast number of shoe factories, only a few can be said to plan their work properly. The usual practice is to make up for each day a "day sheet" calling for the production of a uniform number of pairs. Yet the time on certain operations varies greatly in different styles. In the fancy stitching on women's shoes, for example, the time on one style may be thirty-five times the time on another simpler style. In one shoe factory, forty fancy stitchers were employed. One week they had only enough work to keep twenty of them busy. The next week, with the same number of pairs of shoes turned out, there was enough work for sixty fancy stitchers. Some years ago the style in men's clothing demanded a sharp point to the lapel of the coat—known as a "peak" lapel. This feature required considerable skill in the making—more skill than was available. The output of some shops was cut 25 per cent. Yet, notwithstanding such style vagaries it is possible with proper adjustment of the sequence of orders and knowledge and utilization of the time required on each operation to spread the work and to have enough workers in all departments without constant layoffs and rehiring.[6]

In a few industries, such as garment factories making a uniform product, the problem is solved by "straight-line" production, with machinery arranged in lines so that the parts of the garments may progress in consecutive operations.[7] The usual method is to perform identical operations on a group of similar machines, then bundle the parts and redistribute them to the next set of operators. In the straight-line plan the machines are placed in cross rows of one to four machines, depending upon the work required on a single piece of the garment. These individual machines and short rows of machines are ranged in a line so that the cut pieces start at one end, and the completed garment comes out at the other. The plan is most useful where there are few changes in style and in design, and it succeeds only when the work is planned ahead to fit the capacity of the machines.

In shoe manufacture a similar plan, using a conveyor, is sometimes followed. Here again the method is best adapted to staple lines of shoes and the work must be carefully planned ahead or the conveyor will be stalled. Any such production scheme is similar to assembly work, the most notable example of which is to be found in automobile plants. There work in process is carried forward on a conveyor and the various operations are performed by men at stationary points along the line. The finished cars roll off the end of the conveyor under their own power.

All planned production obviously calls for the determination and use of standard times for performing the necessary operations. This is as essential for control of production and hence of employment as it is for setting piece rates or incentives. Management is too apt to think only of the bad effects of irregular work on the employee; in reality it represents a heavy loss to both employer and worker.

Control of inventories is another factor which is important to production control. Unless raw materials are on hand ready for use when they are needed and unless parts are ready to make up the finished article, there is delay. Excessive or unbalanced inventories must be avoided. With improper inventory or purchasing control one frequently finds a shortage of certain parts, requiring shut downs, and a quantity of other parts sufficient to last for years. A further disadvantage of such unplanned operations is that unfinished product piles up in the workrooms so as to get on everybody's nerves and block efficiency.

But it is evident that in spite of expert production control, there will be irregular employment unless the sales control is equally effective. Everyone looks forward to the day when employment throughout the year will be more nearly uniform, when the pay envelope from week to week will represent full-time work. A few firms with the cooperation of the employees have reached the goal. The accomplishment is possible, however, only with scientific management of both production and sales. The necessity for production control has been illustrated. But unless there are enough orders for the finished goods, with deliveries distributed equally throughout the year or with inventories of stock or advance orders to be made up ahead of time, work cannot be regularized. In cases where uniform wages are paid from week to week throughout the year, operating control, including both sales and production, must be developed to a high degree in order to insure steady work through each day and week by week.[8] Nothing is more demoralizing than to have a scheme of this kind started and then have it collapse for want of planning.

Sales control is thus essential to production control. Yet in the majority of plants proper planning of sales is rarely undertaken. In department store merchandising, on the other hand, while the selling and service departments are apt to be much inferior to similar operations in the factory, the control of sales, purchases and inventories has been developed to a high degree of effectiveness during recent years.

The control of sale involves a thorough standardization of policies and methods. Formerly the "crack" salesman was the man with the high-pressure, superficial, "hot air" talk. Advertising was designed for the ignorant reader who accepted alluring statements without question. Today, in most fields, the salesman must know his product and sell through constructive explanation of values. Advertising is reaching a higher plane and the truth is more and more considered essential. So much is good. But this is not "control." Control means thorough analysis and budgeting of prospective sales. The salesman must be given a territory he can cover effectively. He must have standard volumes of goods or "quota" to sell at different periods. He must aim particularly to sell the quantity and lines of goods that correspond to productive capacity and personnel and at the same time result in the largest profit. The goal of the whole selling plan must be to distribute production over the year.[9]

The task of achieving an operating control that will result in continuous employment is great and one that must be pursued constantly year after year. It involves not merely the individual establishment, but also each industry and the relationship of competing industries. It involves policies of pricing and of product development, the proper adjustment of wage levels, the organization of executive control and cooperation between workers and management.

In the final analysis, operating control goes far beyond a satisfactory production control. In the sense in which the phrase is used here, operating control is a goal, rather than an achievement. The factors entering into it are: coordination of sales, production and finance in a finely planned and adjusted organization. Such a goal is possible only through full utilization of the skills and knowledge of union and management.[8]

CHAPTER 12

SAFETY AND HEALTH IN INDUSTRY

THE health and safety of industrial workers are matters directly affecting the volume and the quality of output. And in addition to the interest of organized labor in efficient production, industrial health and safety are of immediate personal interest to every worker. This is one of the areas of modern industry in which both management and labor have an obvious stake; and, as this chapter will show, it is one of the areas in which progress depends on intelligent cooperation between employers and employees.

Long after other industrial nations bestirred themselves to deal with industrial accidents and occupational disease, this country still paid little attention to statistics showing the undue proportion of sickness among wage earners, and took for granted the tragic rule that a man must die for every mile of railroad track laid down, and for every floor erected in a skyscraper.

American industry has always enjoyed a world-wide reputation for recklessness, and this is borne out by the accident figures which, even after years of "safety first" campaigns, still show both frequency and severity rates double those of Great Britain, France and Germany.

One of the earliest estimates of the number of accidents in American industry was made by Frederick L. Hoffman, statistician of the Prudential Life Insurance Company, who, in 1908, stated that between 30,000 and 35,000 American workmen were killed annually.[1] Further he estimated that about two million were injured each year, more or less seriously. Another Prudential statistician estimated that in 1919 about 23,000 workers were killed, about 575,000 disabled for four weeks or more, and about 2.4 million less seriously injured.[2] According to the National Safety Council, of 98,000 accidental deaths in this country in 1929, 20,000 occurred in industry. The estimate for 1936 was about 18,000 accidental deaths in industry, and about 1.5 lost-time injuries.

The worst "killers and mutilators," as Carroll M. Daugherty, professor of economics at the University of Pittsburgh, describes them, have always been the mines (coal and metal), building and construction, iron and steel, outside electrical work, railways (steam and electric), fisheries, stevedoring and navigation.[3] In these occupations, production has taken a shocking toll of life and limb. But, as Mr. Daugherty points out,

Most people are not impressed by large numbers, nor are they aroused by the steady sniping that means death on the industrial front. . . . It takes a major spectacular disaster or a graphic method of presenting statistical material to bring home the physical risks of industry. The few coal miners that are killed each day by falling roofs, for example, attract no headlines compared to those who die *en masse* because of explosions, yet the total number of the former far exceeds that of the latter. Perhaps the significance of the estimates . . . will become clearer if it is borne in mind that during the period when the United States was in the World War, more American workers were killed in peaceful production at home than American soldiers in France. Every two weeks as many men give up their lives in industry as sank with the "Titanic" in the greatest peacetime ocean disaster. During the one hundred and fifty years of independent national existence, the industrial casualties of this country have outnumbered by fifteen times all those killed or injured in all the wars in which the United States took part. Here someone loses his life in industry (on the average) about every nine minutes, and someone is less seriously hurt about every four seconds.[4]

The high cost of industrial accidents represents one of the major items of preventable waste in American industry. The available figures leave out of account what the worker and his family must pay in physical pain, anxiety, fear, discouragement, shattered hopes, broken standard of living. These are items that cannot be reduced to dollars and cents. But the direct and indirect financial costs of industrial accidents, as computed by W. H. Heinrich of the Travelers Insurance

146 ORGANIZED LABOR AND PRODUCTION

Company add up to the staggering total of $5,010,000,000 annually.[5] The actual wage loss of the injured workers is another yardstick for measuring the high cost of industrial accidents. The National Safety Council in 1934 figured that the annual wage loss for death and injury as amounting to $460,000,000.

The movement to cut down the high toll of industrial accidents started in Europe, partly out of humanitarian impulses, partly as an outgrowth of class conflicts. But although Great Britain enacted workmen's compensation laws in 1897, the safety movement gained little ground here until 1905. Then the "safety first" campaign spread rapidly, because of its humanitarian appeal, as an aspect of good management, and because of the passage of mandatory legislation, wiping out the old rules of "voluntary assumption of risk," "contributory negligence," and "negligence of a fellow servant," and compelling the employer to assume at least a share of the financial cost of industrial injury and death.

Research by a few large corporations had uncovered the high cost of accidents to industry. Studies by the Committee on Safety and Production of the American Engineering Council showed that accident rates could be reduced even in a period of increasing production. From its founding in 1907, accident prevention was one of the outstanding interests of the Association of Iron and Steel Electrical Engineers, which in 1912 established the National Safety Council.

The labor unions were apathetic in the early agitation for safety, engaged as they were in the struggle to survive. From the start however they played an active part in the struggle to have workmen's compensation laws enacted. As a matter of fact when employers first thought to enlist the interest of the workers in safety the campaign partook of the psychology which later became associated with the drive for company unions. In certain instances the workers felt that the move to do away with particularly obnoxious abuses was inspired by a desire to stop workmen's compensation legislation rather than because of any interest in the workers.

Launched by large industries, the safety movement at first reached only a small proportion of the wage earners; and social workers, state labor departments, and the American

SAFETY AND HEALTH IN INDUSTRY 147

Association for Labor Legislation formed the spearhead of agitation for compulsory compensation laws. This campaign envisaged the problem of industrial safety as something more than a matter of efficient management, and as properly in the domain of public policy. The first workmen's compensation act in this country was a federal measure passed in 1908, covering certain classes of federal employees. In 1910, New York followed with a limited law, and in 1914 enacted a general law. Then came a succession of such laws, until today only one state, Mississippi, has no such legislation on its statute books. The forty-seven state laws differ widely in coverage, compensation scales and administration. But each requires contributions from the employer to a compensation fund, the contributions being scaled in proportion to the employer's accident rate. Once the employer was faced with financial responsibility for accidents occurring in his plant, the "safety first" campaign leaped forward. It was obviously cheaper to prevent accidents than to pay out compensation.

With the enactment of workmen's compensation laws, the first place the employer looked for ways to reduce the accident rate was in the equipment of the plant. Dangerous machinery was safeguarded, even machines which, it had been held, would be "too costly" or "impossible" to make safe. Illumination was improved, passageways cleared, transmission equipment put in better repair and its safe use studied, wet and oily floors cleaned up, and so on. It was found that much could be accomplished toward reducing the accident hazards in old plants; even more could be done when the safety factor was kept in mind in laying out new plants or installing new equipment. Sometimes special personal equipment must be provided, such as goggles, asbestos gloves or boots, acidproof garments, in order to protect the worker from injury. Such things almost always call for special training of the worker, and for "check ups" by management or the union to be sure they are not put aside for the sake of speed or because their use is "a bother."

But it was early realized that the human factor is even more important than mechanical factors in reducing accident hazards. Management took the lead, first in better personnel selection, then in giving new workers more adequate training in the special requirements of their jobs. "Safety education," it was found, must be continuous, keeping before the supervisory force and the workers the value of accident prevention, underscoring the high cost of preventable accidents to the worker, his family, and the industry, teaching the "safe way" to go about the plant, to use or to move tools, material and equipment.

It was found that rivalry speeded up the safety campaign. Competitive records between departments, among the several plants of one company or in an entire industry, with medals or other rewards for outstanding safety achievement helped. These safety efforts have succeeded or proved disappointing almost exactly in proportion as they have been the joint effort of management and workers, with genuine cooperation between the two groups.

As the safety movement gained ground, safety methods improved. These included better mechanical safeguards, including both equipment and inspection, more exact location of hazards, better record keeping, better training methods, more effective ways of enlisting the interest and cooperation of labor. The gains are not uniform throughout industry, but scarcely a shop or plant could be found today which has not felt the effects of the safety movement. In many enterprises, safety now receives equal emphasis with other production problems as one of industry's major responsibilities. In such plants, the safety engineer is a highly trained and highly paid executive, and his department is as carefully staffed and as thoroughly "backed" as is accounting or sales.

The movement for industrial safety is likely to be advanced in the future by appropriate use of psychiatry. Studies have discovered that a large number of the accidents happen to a relatively small number of people. People who have accidents are likely to be repeaters. People who have minor accidents are more likely to have major accidents than are others. People who have accidents in the factory are likely to be those who have accidents in the home or driving an automobile or walking on the street.

In other words, there is such a thing as the "accident habit," which is separate and distinct from the degree of risk with which a person is surrounded. It is something that often is found in the make-up or personality of the accident-sufferer, regardless of the peril of his environment. Of course, some surroundings are much more dangerous than others, and everything possible should be done to make them safe. But in any factory or street or office or home, no matter how safe, some people are much more likely to have accidents than others.

Mere warnings or injunctions to be careful are not sufficient to protect those who have the accident habit. Nevertheless something may be done to help them, if they are discovered before anything serious has happened and are given special attention. Even a recognition on their part that they are peculiarly susceptible may help them to avoid taking unnecessary chances. Wherever the help of a physician who is a specialist in psychiatry may be obtained, there is a chance of getting rid of the habit entirely. This subject is still in the early stages of study, but great promise lies in possible future discovery of ways of dealing with it effectively on a large scale.

The Safety Codes of the American Standards Association represent the pooling of opinion and experience in furthering the safety of industrial workers. About sixty of these codes have been drawn up and are widely used, not only by industrial and safety engineers, but as the basis for public legislation and regulation.

While American accident records still compare unfavorably with the records of other industrial nations, the results of the safety effort are encouraging. The National Safety Council figures for 1938 are substantially below the estimates of three decades ago. In 1938 there were 16,500 deaths, 1,350,000 severe injuries, as compared with 30,000 deaths, and 2,000,000 injuries in 1908. The Council estimates that since 1913, when organized safety work was first attempted on a large scale in American industry, the lives of 285,000 workers have been saved, and perhaps 27 million injuries prevented. But beside any such statement one must set the conclusion of safety engineers that from 90 to 98 per cent of industrial accidents are preventable. Stronger legislation, better law enforcement, more efficient management, including more effective cooperation between employers and labor are still needed. With the advent of union-management cooperation the way appears to be open for a more spontaneous and wholehearted support of safety work by both men and management.

Americans were slow to admit that industry was responsible for accidental injury to the workers, but much slower to admit responsibility for sickness which, far less dramatic than injury, is also less closely linked up with the job.

Some diseases, though not always regarded as occupational, occur much more frequently in certain occupations than in the general population. Steel workers, for example, have an abnormally high death rate from pneumonia; and tuberculosis is frequent among textile workers. Other diseases are directly caused by poisons or harmful materials used in industry. Thus lead poisoning is the great plague of the storage battery men, of refining, smelting, painting, and pottery making. The dreadful "phossy jaw," the eating away of the jaw bone, still sometimes occurs among workers who use phosphorous. Workers who inhale zinc fumes in brass foundries suffer "brass chills," and mercury used in making felt hats produces "hatters' shakes." From time to time the press reports the death of another of the twenty-one doomed workers who contracted radium poisoning in painting watch dials for aviators during the World War.

Today, twenty-three states have provided more or less adequately for compensation for occupational diseases. This has fundamentally changed the attitude of employers, labor, physicians, the courts, and the public toward the problem, and toward the duty of industry to prevent sickness so far as possible, and to provide medical care when prevention fails.

Industrial medicine is now one of the recognized medical specialties. It is a specialty which differs in several ways from ordinary medicine. One of the most striking is the great emphasis on preventive medical care, because the environment of the individual worker is far less under his direct control than is the environment of the non-industrial worker. A worker can protect himself against accident hazards to some extent, but he cannot ward off the hazards of

SAFETY AND HEALTH IN INDUSTRY 151

dangerous dusts or poisonous fumes and gases. He cannot control the air he breathes, and it is polluted air that causes most of the poisoning and all of the dust diseases found in industry.

Many other factors in the industrial environment constitute health hazards. Heat, for example, makes a man breathe more rapidly, even pant, and this means that he draws in more of the dust or poison than if he breathes normally. Heat covers the skin with sweat and flushes the surface blood vessels, encouraging the action of poisons that attack the skin. Long hours increase the daily dose of poison or dust. Heavy work is another factor, for not only does it make a man breathe deeply, but it is a strain on his heart. During the World War, the Germans found that the soldiers who developed acute heart failure on forced marches were not the white collar men, but the miners and steel mill men whose hearts had already been overstrained. Another factor which makes a worker an easy victim of unwholesome dust, heat and fumes is low wages, with all that this implies—poor housing, poor food, too little of the things that make life worth living. This is especially true of the dust diseases, many of the victims of which develop tuberculosis.

The prevention of industrial disease means first, control of dangerous dusts and gases, by means of (a) a closed system with no escape; if this is impossible then (b) exhausts to draw off the fumes at the point of escape or, in the case of dust, wetting down; if that is impossible, then (c) protecting the worker by a mask or helmet which feeds him fresh air through a pipe.

Second, prevention means a careful selection of personnel and close supervision during employment. Those who already have some organic disease, and youthful workers, especially young girls, must not be exposed to dusts or poisons, no matter what protection is afforded. There will always be some over-susceptibles among the ones selected as healthy, and these must be detected and transferred or dismissed before exposure has gone on long enough to do any real harm. This means regular medical examination for all those employed on work dangerous to health.

Third, prevention means explaining to the employee the

nature of the dangers he faces, the best ways to avoid these dangers, and the warning symptoms he must look out for and report. It is a great mistake to try to keep workers in ignorance, to pursue a policy of secrecy with regard to these facts, for a sensible person usually recognizes danger and, if nobody deals frankly with him, he naturally develops mounting suspicion and resentment toward the enterprise of which he is a part. Moreover, such secrecy requires so much evasion not only on the part of the foreman but also on the part of the doctor that the physician loses the confidence of his patients who regard him as simply a company tool.

There are several systems of medical care now provided by industry. They may be classed as poor, fair, and excellent. The poorest system is the one which was almost universally used in mining and in the heavy industries some twenty-five years ago, and which, a recent study by the Bureau of Co-operative Medicine reveals, is still in force in coal mining in the organized as well as the unorganized fields. Under this system, the cost of medical care is borne by the miner, whose wages are "docked" $1.30 to $2.00 a month for this purpose. No accounting of these funds is made. The doctor is hired and paid by the company, and is regarded as a company employee. Testimony before the Senate Civil Liberties Committee indicated that a large percentage of the medical fees collected by some mine operators goes, not to the doctor or the hospital, but into the treasury of the coal company. The study by the Bureau of Co-operative Medicine, covering four coal-producing states, made clear the urgent need for medical care for coal miners and their families, and the utter inadequacy of the service provided, including the failure to provide any preventive care in this most hazardous of all industrial occupations.

The majority of large industrial establishments do much better than the mines. They cover the costs of the medical department and are careful to select competent doctors who deserve and gain the confidence of the workers; they insist on pre-employment medical examination; they see that surgical cases and cases of illness which are brought to their attention receive adequate care; but as a rule the doctor has

SAFETY AND HEALTH IN INDUSTRY

little knowledge of actual conditions in the plant, and nothing to say about them.

Finally, there is an increasing number of large concerns which furnish effective preventive health service, including periodic medical examinations and health advice, sickness benefits, and visiting nurse service. Such a set-up is usually beyond the means of the small establishment, and small establishments employ a large proportion of American wage earners. Here the employer, at the best, provides a first-aid room, a nurse on duty, and a physician on call. This arrangement sometimes works very well, but even this is considered too expensive for the majority of small factories, and then the problem is one that can be dealt with only through a group plan, or through the public health service.

A manufacturers association is now engaged in making a study as to what is being done generally to safeguard the health of industrial workers and more particularly what can be done for the employees in smaller plants. Dr. Victor G. Heiser, author of "An American Doctor's Odyssey," is conducting this inquiry.

As with the safety movement, unions have played a less vigorous part in the industrial health movement than might have been expected, though there are notable exceptions to this generalization. One of the outstanding examples of union health services to its members is in the program of one of the needle trade unions, the nine New York City locals of which voted in 1919 to establish and maintain a Union Health Center for the benefit of their 45,000 members. Complete medical and dental services were provided in a union-owned building, under a staff of full-time doctors, dentists, and nurses. Other unions were gradually permitted to make use of the Union Health Service at a modest fee, and in 1928 it was endorsed by the Central Trades and Labor Council of New York City.

In Cincinnati and Chicago, locals of the Amalgamated Clothing Workers have organized health services, stressing preventive work through regular health examinations and education.

Some unions have organized or co-operated with health services dealing with the special hazards of their industry.

For example, the United Auto Workers established a clinic in Detroit to study the health effects of the speed-up in the plants. Tunnel workers and "sandhogs" in New York have at various times assisted the State Labor Department in studies of silicosis, one of the special hazards of the men who drive new subway tunnels through the solid granite of Manhattan Island.

While the last twenty-five years have seen much progress in the country in securing compensation for the employee who is the victim of industrial accident or disease, much effort will be required to mend the inadequacies of existing laws, and to improve their administration. According to an estimate made by the Chief of the Division of Accident Statistics of the U. S. Bureau of Labor Statistics, not more than 40 per cent of the gainfully employed workers are actually protected by laws providing compensation for industrial accidents. No state law covers all employments.[6] Farmers, domestic workers, and casual workers are usually excluded. In many states, small employers (those with from one to sixteen workers) are outside the scope of the compensation law; and other exclusions, in some states, are relief workers, home workers, clerical workers, teachers, those vending or delivering newspapers, aviators, employments not for gain (churches, charitable organizations, hospitals, schools and colleges, and so on). Compensation for industrial disease is a much newer principle in this country. By April, 1939, 23 states had such measures, and the Federal Employment Compensation, and Longshoremen and Harbor Workers Compensation Acts had provisions protecting workers against all or some kinds of occupational diseases.[7] Nine state laws and the two federal measures cover all occupational diseases. The broad Wisconsin law, for instance, defines "injury" as "mental or physical harm to an employee caused by accident or disease." The remaining fourteen states provide compensation only for such occupational diseases as are listed in their laws. Some states also specify the occupation or industry in which the disease must originate if it is to be compensated under the law. The number of diseases listed varies from ten in New Jersey, to thirty-one in Michigan and Rhode Island, and thirty-eight in Arkansas. In some states,

SAFETY AND HEALTH IN INDUSTRY

the individual diseases are defined, in others, as in Pennsylvania, broad groups are listed.

It is increasingly recognized that back of all efforts to cut down the hazards of industrial accident and disease, lies the more fundamental problem of the worker's general health and well-being. Scientific studies today buttress the conclusions of good common sense that the most efficient worker is the healthy, unworried worker. The man who is dulled and slowed down by fatigue is more prone to accident than is the man who is fresh and alert. The discovery that accident frequency is markedly higher near the end of the working day, that accidents are more frequent where employees work long hours than where they work a shorter day and week is only statistical proof of what all experienced workmen know. The worker's situation outside the plant—his nutrition, housing, and medical care, which are as a rule directly related to his wage; his "state of mind," which also depends in large part on his wages and his job prospects, contribute to his efficiency as a worker, and also to his "proneness" to accident or illness.

So it appears that health and safety are subjects peculiarly adapted to cooperative effort as between employers and unions—just as are the matter of wages and hours and some of the techniques, like time study, through which production is controlled. But across the path to any outstanding accomplishment as to better industrial relations stands the challenge of the wholly unsolved problem of unemployment. Just at a time when the technicians tell us that for the first time in world history there can be enough to satisfy the legitimate needs of everybody this major dislocation makes it difficult to cash in on the opportunity. Unless we can cope with unemployment the reign of law and order in industry and other things we value are gravely threatened.

On top of this comes the realization that electric power development is in its infancy but advancing with giant strides. Desirable as it is that the work of the world be done by other than human labor it would appear that this new factor is in the way of aggravating an already critical unemployment situation. In the next two chapters are discussions of these fateful questions.

VI. TWO MAKE-OR-BREAK FACTORS

CHAPTER 13

THE IMPACT OF TECHNOLOGY ON EMPLOYMENT

THAT social change and modern technology go forward hand in hand and with increasing swiftness can be illustrated in a thousand ways, as for instance by the countless social and economic effects of the internal combustion engine. One need only point to the vast growth of the automobile industry with its endless ramifications into road building, petroleum, steel, rubber, cotton, glass, real estate, and other areas to see what a world of changes and what a changed world we have as a result of this single invention.

Other illustrations equally dramatic can be found in the upsurge of the new chemical processes which include changes in food and food habits, new and more efficient fuels, synthetic fibers, synthetic rubber and plastics; and in the whole field of communication—telephone, telegraph, radio, and television.

Treated alone, each of these technological milestones could be and often is regarded as the basic development of modern civilization, and so we speak of the machine age, the age of the auto or of the radio.

Such classification, however, leaves out technology—the ingenuity of the human mind—which not only makes such inventions possible but which uses them separately or combined in a thousand intricate steps toward further invention and further progress. Ours is not merely a machine age or an automobile age. Rather it is an age of technology and technological progress in which radio, the gasoline engine, the photoelectric cell are but a few outstanding examples of achievement.

No longer do we depend solely on the genius of the individual to snatch inventions out of thin air, so to speak. While the individual inventor is still productive, technology relies chiefly upon organized institutional investigation and research as the most efficient agency for further development. Its source of growth lies in the actual operations in shops and factories which are analyzed and refined in experimental laboratories.

The growth of technological development 'is not only dynamic but it is also compounded. An improved tool is used to build a better machine, which in turn is used further to improve the tool in order to build a still better machine. Technological development is not necessarily mechanical; it also comes through non-mechanical means, such as the better ordering of operations or the application of industrial psychology. Among the more familiar steps of modern technological advancement are these:

Mechanical steps
1. Improved tools, hand or machine, including specialized single purpose machines
2. New or improved chemical processes
3. Automatic attachments for new or old machines
4. Improved machine assembly
5. Increased speed of machines
6. More effective control of machinery
7. Better adaptation of machine units to their several processes
8. Better materials for the construction of machines, improving their performance and prolonging their life
9. Better and more easily workable materials for the manufacture of products of better quality and greater durability

Non-mechanical steps
1. More effective utilization of mechanical power
2. Economy of time and energy of operatives
3. More effective flow of work within plant and between plants

4. Incentive to greater efficiency on the part of workers and management
5. Health and safety devices

The method of technology is to produce more and better things with decreasing human effort. By developing natural resources, by creating, if need be, its own raw materials, by utilizing the inheritance laid up by all the sciences through all the ages, technology, it would seem, has reached the stage when it can compensate man, its creator, with a world of plenty such as was never dreamed of in any previous civilization.

But technology and its application to industry do not operate in a vacuum. Though exerting a tremendous influence on individual and social behavior, including industry and trade, technology is nevertheless the product of human endeavor devised and used primarily as a means to an end. In a capitalistic economy based upon the profit motive, the functioning of technology is determined primarily not by its capacity to produce more goods and services to satisfy more human wants, but rather by its effectiveness in producing profits.

A perfect competitive system with unhampered operations of the law of supply and demand would make technology yield the largest profits only when utilized to satisfy a maximum of human wants. But the growing concentration of economic power in the hands of a few large corporations and the control which these corporations exercise over consumption, capital formation, the price structure, and the supply of some of the most important basic commodities no longer make it certain that a reduction in labor cost brought about by a labor-saving device will result in a reduced price with an increase in demand and hence in production.

Profits can often be maintained through the adjustment of total production to the exigencies of the demand within the confines of a rigid price structure. Under these circumstances, it is no longer necessary to operate steel plants, for example, at their maximum capacity; or to utilize all the available supply of labor and invested as well as uninvested capital. Every reduction in labor requirements as a result of technological improvements, whether of the tangible type (new processes of operation, improved machinery), or of the intangible type (rationalization of production, consolidations, mergers) will increase the supply of available labor in relation to the demand and must therefore result in technological displacement of workers. By the same token, every reduction in plant and capital requirements (improved plant layouts, the elimination of wasteful operations, better control instruments) must of necessity lead also to a technological displacement of capital as well as of labor.

The tens of thousands of steel workers whose jobs are being eliminated by the continuous hot-strip mills find little consolation in the arguments of orthodox economists that "permanent technological unemployment is impossible." Nor will the contention that in the long run technology creates more employment than it displaces prove of much solace to the union whose function it is to protect the interests and jobs of steel workers, or to the communities where the old hand mills are now being dismantled or abandoned. So long as a break-even point can be reached and profits made with plants operated only at 50 or 60 per cent of capacity, or operated only a part of the year, idle labor and idle capital will continue to be technologically unemployed, the orthodox economists to the contrary notwithstanding.

The argument that permanent technological unemployment is impossible is based largely on deductive reasoning and briefly runs as follows: labor-saving devices make it possible either to produce a larger quantity of goods with the same expenditures of labor time, or the same amount of goods with a reduction in labor requirements. The reduced labor cost per unit of output is automatically followed by a corresponding reduction in the price of the product. This will increase the demand for the particular product affected by the technological change, if its demand is sufficiently elastic, or the increase in consumption will increase the production of other goods and services. It is further argued that it makes no appreciable difference whether the benefits of the increased labor productivity caused by labor-saving devices are turned over to the workers in terms of higher total earnings or to employers in terms of higher profits. Sooner or later, directly or indirectly, the money saved through reduced labor costs will be plowed back into greater production and therefore bring about increased employment. The same type of argument is also applicable to reductions in labor cost resulting from consolidation and mergers, to rationalization of operations, and even to speed-ups and cuts in piece rates paid to workers.

Nowhere in these arguments is there any indication as to the length of time elapsing between the introduction of a labor-saving device accomplished by immediate labor displacement and its culmination in the re-employment of these or other workers through price reductions and the subsequent increase in demand. Further, most economists will admit that in actual practice, a general increase in labor productivity is not followed automatically by a reduction in price, and it is therefore likely that a considerable period of unemployment will intervene before all the displaced workers find re-employment.

There is no doubt that in a rapidly expanding economy characteristic of a growing population, expanding frontiers, or an increasing foreign trade, there may be a continuing shortage of labor, in which case the workers displaced by labor-saving devices in one industry promptly find re-employment in this or another industry. This was probably true of the United States in the 1800's and through the first decade of the present century.

The same condition may obtain at rare intervals when a revolutionary invention such as the steam engine or the automobile suddenly opens up new vistas of economic activity. The effects of the automobile on economic and social development have not yet been fully realized or evaluated. It is likely that much of the current technological unemployment is due to the fact that no such far-reaching innovation has occurred in the United States since the automobile, in spite of the vast utilization of labor- and capital-saving types of invention since the World War.

While there seems to be no check in the labor-saving type of technological progress, the revolutionary type of invention which creates employment cannot be relied upon permanently as a correcting factor. The rapid application of

164 ORGANIZED LABOR AND PRODUCTION

technological improvements to newer fields even tends to neutralize the employment-expanding tendency of these inventions. For example, the total volume of unemployment since 1929 has not been affected by the ten-year increase in employment in radio or air conditioning, both of the employment-expanding type.

Technological progress therefore has two effects: First: displacement of labor, and sometimes of capital, at the points where the new technology is applied. Second: the cumulative effect of technological development under present conditions of capital and price control by large corporations, which prevents the automatic adjustment of supply and demand, with a consequent diminution of economic activity and of employment generally. This is especially serious because the mean income and especially that part which goes to the mass of the people is reduced; hence the purchasing power of consumers generally is not sufficient to make effective demand for all the goods which the new technology is geared to produce.

In setting the stage for the monopoly or the Temporary National Economic Committee investigation into the causes of "idle factories and idle men," Isador Lubin, Commissioner of Labor Statistics in the Department of Labor presented what may be regarded as an inventory of economic conditions in the United States since 1929. The rate of growth of the population in the United States, he said, has been steadily declining for some time. The population of the United States grew from 23,000,000 people in 1850 to approximately 127,000,000 in 1935. It doubled between 1850 and 1880, but during the next 30 years, 1880 to 1910, it increased by only 80 per cent. From 1900 to 1920, the average annual rate of increase was 1 2/3 per cent and from 1920 to 1935 only slightly over 1 per cent. By 1960, it has been estimated there will be in the United States only 10 per cent more people than in 1940.

Next, he showed the tremendous cumulative losses in the total national income, in employment and pay rolls, in farm income, and in returns on capital investment which the country has suffered since the beginning of the depression in 1929. Citing the uneven distribution of consumers' income in the United States as shown in the National Resources Committee study, Commissioner Lubin emphasized the fact that American industry, geared to mass production, cannot continue full operation by relying on the demand of that small portion of the population which enjoys annual incomes of $5,000 or more. On the other hand, he said, the 5,000,000 non-relief, wage-earning families with incomes averaging less than $1,250 a year are not able to increase their demand for the goods and services which American industry and trade are capable of producing. Nor can industry and trade depend for their market on the millions wholly dependent on relief or on those who are partly employed and are compelled to apply for relief to supplement their meager earnings.

Finally, to indicate the gains to American industry in a higher standard of living, particularly among lower-paid factory and "white collar" employees, Commissioner Lubin proceeded to calculate the probable effects of an arbitrarily selected $2.25 a day increase in the consumer income of the 5,200,000 wage earners whose annual incomes in 1935-36 averaged less than $1,250.

. . . if this amount were made available to families now earning $1,250 or less, the story would run something like this: they would buy $800,000,000 worth of food more than they buy now; they would increase their purchase of clothing by $416,000,000; they would increase their purchase of housing or rents by $613,000,000; they would spend $213,000,000 more on fuel, light, and refrigeration; they would spend $385,000,000 more on transportation, automobiles, etc.; they would spend $73,000,000 more on personal care; they would spend $234,000,000 more on recreation; they would spend $208,000,000 more on medical care . . .

Now it should be borne in mind that these estimates cover the effects of the change of income of only a limited number of our population, only 5,200,000 families out of 25,000,000 non-relief families . . . I might go a step further and say that if there were moderate increases in the income of all families or single individuals receiving less than $2,500, you could reasonably expect that most of our surplus capacity would run far short of the demands by the population of this country.

Briefly, the fairly widely held solution presented by Commissioner Lubin for the unemployment problem and the present economic impasse is first, a higher standard of living for the large masses of the population, coupled with more and more production and second, some equitable distribution of the produced income to absorb the increasing quantities of goods and services made available by larger production. He failed, however, to indicate the ways and means by which this highly desirable increase in the income and standard of living of the lower-paid groups of wage earners and salaried employees could be accomplished, and he did not show how a more equitable distribution of the national income could be secured and maintained. A higher standard of living—even maintenance of the standard to which we have become accustomed—cannot be achieved without full use of the new technology. Yet the new technology has been so used as to defeat its potentialities. The problem is, how to employ it so that we may have the benefits without offsetting losses.

Intensive studies undertaken during the present depression have made it clear that there is no overnight solution for the problem of unemployment which, if not caused by, is inextricably bound up with technological progress. Numberless panaceas and short cuts are offered as sure roads to the millennium. These range from good old "rugged individualism" to the Townsend plan, technocracy, and totalitarianism, of both the fascist and communist brands. Most of these cure-alls either claim too much or involve the sacrifice of all our individual liberties and democratic institutions—a ruinous price to pay for anything, and especially for the dubious results of an uncharted experiment.

While a final solution of the unemployment problem must be left to the future, forces already set in motion by the government, by industry, and by organized labor, may, if properly directed stave off the hardships resulting from further displacement of men and women by labor-saving machinery. Among these are: unemployment insurance; old-age pensions; public works projects; minimum wage and maximum hour laws; dismissal compensation; the timing of the introduction of technological improvements to coincide with increased activity; and public examples, as in the T.V.A., of passing on to consumers the benefits of technology.

The objective of increased purchasing power for the masses has been in the forefront of the government's economic program since 1933. The social-security legislation, the AAA, PWA, WPA, the various housing laws, the Fair Labor Standards Act and NRA were all devised primarily for this purpose. Some of these efforts—notably NRA—unfortunately were permitted to develop opposite tendencies. Though very little has been accomplished toward an immediate solution of the unemployment problem (the total number of unemployed is still above the 10,000,000 mark) much has been done to alleviate the difficulties of the jobless and to keep social and economic conditions from becoming worse. And the foundations have been laid for future betterment. During the 1937-38 depression, the payments of unemployment-insurance benefits and the work relief program of the WPA supplied enough purchasing power to the unemployed to prevent a repetition of the 1929-32 collapse in trade and industrial activity.

Responsible industrial leadership more and more recognizes the need to protect workers against technology's encroachment upon their jobs. At the 1934 convention of the American Management Association one industrialist described the step-by-step procedure of his company in spreading the introduction of labor-saving devices over a period of years without causing any appreciable labor displacement. The program included the training of workers, foremen, and management in the new methods of operation, the adjustment of pay schedules to protect the earning capacity of those affected by the change, and the timing of major technological changes to correspond with periods of increased production, thus avoiding the need to discharge permanent employees.

The growing demand by organized labor for a dismissal wage for workers displaced by technological improvements, and the growing acceptance by employers of the principle of severance compensation express a recognition of such displacement of labor as a legitimate cost of industrial progress, to be included among the other *bona fide* expenses of production. The advantages of such recognition may prove to be far-reaching. First, it makes it possible to tackle technological unemployment at the point of incidence. When each plant or each industry holds itself responsible for the technological unemployment it creates, solutions will be developed covering the particular conditions of the various enterprises.

Management has made notable progress in developing research departments, cost-accounting systems, forecasts of demand, and so on. When a new machine or change in operation is contemplated, management calculates in detail the possible gains and losses involved in the proposed change. If a machine is to be rendered obsolete, the cost is estimated and the necessary adjustments made in the balance sheet. The problem of displaced (obsolescent) skills may not prove so simple and may not be so easily blueprinted as that of a displaced machine or even of a displaced plant. But in view of management's handling of technological problems, this, too, seems soluble, especially when management has the active assistance of both organized labor and government.

The present tendency is for union agreements to recognize specifically the rights of employers to change methods of production and to install labor-saving machinery, provided the new conditions of work are fixed by further collective bargaining with the union. These are the terms generally found in agreements of the International Pressmen's Union, for example, or in those of the Textile Workers' Organizing Committee.

Other agreements are more specific. For instance, the contract between the American Communication Association of the CIO and RCA Communications, Inc., has a section devoted to mechanization which provides that:

(1) Whenever, because of mechanization, a reduction in the number of employees is contemplated, the company shall endeavor to agree with the union upon an equitable solution before dismissing or reclassifying employees.

(2) The union and the directly affected employees shall be notified at least six months in advance of proposed mechanization changes and such employees shall be allowed an opportunity to acquire such additional knowledge and skill as may be necessary for retaining employment in a dif-

ferent classification. During these six months, no new employee shall be added to the regular staff.

(3) Dismissals made necessary in mechanization shall be made in the reverse order of seniority.

(4) An employee dismissed because of mechanization shall be given preference over a period of one year for re-employment when a vacancy occurs for which he is qualified.

(5) If, because of mechanization, any employee is released or dismissed from employment, he shall be given severance pay, as specified in the agreement.

In industries where the problem of adjustment to technological changes has become more acute and therefore calls for more radical measures, organized labor has time and again evinced its readiness to join with management and the government in a common effort to solve the difficulties.

The Railroad Brotherhoods and the Railroad Shop Craft unions in and out of the A. F. of L. are intensely interested in the problem of railroad reorganization, which is bound to affect the jobs of many of their members. Under the railroad reorganization bill, pending in Congress at this writing, no consolidation or merger of railroads can be executed without definite plans submitted by the railroads to take care of workers whose jobs may be eliminated by the reorganization.

The Appalachian Agreement between the United Mine Workers and the bituminous-coal producers provides for a joint commission consisting of an equal number of representatives of the coal miners and of management to study and to deal with the problems of mechanization in the industry. The Steel Workers Organizing Committee's pamphlet, already mentioned, suggests how production problems, including the introduction of labor-saving devices, can be handled jointly by representatives of the union and of management of the plant. The Amalgamated Clothing Workers has a special research department to cooperate with employers in studying the marketing problems of the men's clothing industry with a view to its stabilization.

The American Federation of Hosiery Workers has taken the position that labor should not only share the benefits of technology but, when the situation arises, should be willing to share the costs of the industry's adjustment to new production methods. This union has therefore agreed to accept a temporary reduction in wage rates and the hazard of technological unemployment for some of its members in order to enable northern hosiery manufacturers to install up-to-date machinery to compete with the more completely mechanized southern plants.

Technological developments as they affect individual plants and industries frequently present special problems. But even the acute conditions found in railroading and coal mining are encountered elsewhere throughout industry in less drastic form. It becomes more and more apparent that just as no single plant can be prosperous in a sick industry, no single industry can in the long run be prosperous in a total social economy burdened with widespread unemployment. Even the railroad problem discouraging as it now seems, might be worked out without loss of jobs or capital investment if the distribution of the national income were such as to give purchasing power to the masses whose demand would then offer the railroads more goods and more passengers to haul.

No sane person wants to go back to the days of spinning wheels, wooden plows and candles. There is no need to continue the century-old debate on technological unemployment to prove the accomplishments of technology and its still larger possibilities for human welfare. At the same time, all the attacks of literature on the workings of technology in a free competitive economy will not disprove the fact that with a large reserve of unemployed workers, additional labor-saving devices cause additional unemployment.

The unemployment generally resulting from the impact of the new technology (as distinguished from individual plant layoffs resulting from the installation of a particular machine) is economic in nature: that is, it results from the conditions developed by private industry to utilize the new technology to the greatest profit advantage. Seeing the savings ahead as measured by past technology, industry has organized new enterprises, capitalized promotional expenses and promotional profits, capitalized temporary advantages through stock dividends, and so on, and then has found it necessary to maintain high prices in order to support the elaborate capital structure. The high prices have reduced the amount of the product that can be bought by the consumer dollar, and the new equipment has not been able to realize its potential productivity.

If a price ceiling is reached, a ceiling that brings about a real drop in sales, the employer turns to cost reductions. His capital he regards as a fixed cost; his materials are fixed costs in the sense that their prices are determined by their producers, also on a high and fixed price basis; therefore he sees labor cost as the only flexible item. Organized labor is finally modifying this habit of arbitrarily handling labor cost as the one possible economy. And the new wage-hour law is helping to drive this thought home.

Granting that people are beginning to see the involved elements of technological unemployment and that many useful steps have been taken both by the employers and the unions to meet the situation, it must be admitted that a solution of the problem is not in sight. A bold public program involving two parallel moves seems essential:

1. Maintenance, and in some instances, increase of wages
2. Simultaneous reductions in prices

This program can be only at the expense of capital as capital is now organized, for it means low interest rates, which the volume of savings justifies; no inflated capital structure; no over-investment; no unloading of over-investment securities on the market. But it will leave reasonable profit for reasonable service rendered.

There is the need for a bold plan in the handling of top-heavy capital structure. Perhaps the most effective course by which to put our capital structure on a better basis in the future would be to discourage forced saving and investment, either by prohibiting the further issue of new securities except in exchange for cash investment; or by discouraging, through a carefully devised mode of heavy taxation, the issue of securities based only on earnings, actual or prospective. Existing excessive capitalization could then be dealt with by deliberate steps, in the full acceptance of the fact that to deal

172 ORGANIZED LABOR AND PRODUCTION

with it effectively is one of the most important elements of our present problem.

This real attack upon technological unemployment calls for a nation-wide spirit of cooperation. Pressure groups—employer and labor alike—must temper self-interest with public interest. Technological unemployment is accelerated by every unwise or unsocial move of a pressure group, every move that succeeds in crystallizing a selfish group advantage. All such moves force acceleration of machine installations to compete with the new obstacles, and thus complicate the problem still further.

Today very little is known of how technology really operates in a complex economic society in which monopoly and near-monopoly control in some industries exist side by side with practically unrestricted competition in other industries. Are the effects of technological development similar in all industries at all times? Are these effects the same in all stages of the country's economic growth, or do they change as the country reaches what may be called a stage of economic maturity? These and similar questions offer a fertile and instructive field of research worthy of the best efforts of the industrial engineer, the labor leader, and the government economist. Only further study and cooperation will pave the way to a permanent solution of the paradox of millions of needy unemployed in a land of potential plenty for all.

And now as probably adding to our discomfiture comes the realization that electric power—hardly a half-century old—is permeating the fabric and the mechanism of industry, and with every advance is removing the need for human labor. The next chapter reviews the situation.

CHAPTER 14

ELECTRICITY AND HUMAN LABOR

DEVELOPMENT in the mechanical arts due to the use of electricity, especially since the turn of the century, may well rate with the discovery of the principle of the wheel as one of those master innovations by which the race moves forward at double quick into new territory and to higher levels of accomplishment. To plan intelligently for the future of the world's work, one must therefore seek to understand the deeper implications of an electrically motivated industry. The significance of the shift from mechanical to electrical power is qualitative as well as quantitative. Of course, only the first elementary developments in this drama have been made in the less than half century since electricity made its inconspicuous entry into industry. Yet one can already see the beginnings of fundamental changes in the material, and more especially in the human, factors involved.

A nineteenth-century savant made the prediction that within one hundred years education would become the passion of the race. One is tempted to make some such sweeping generalization about electricity. The dullest imagination kindles to the elusive quality of electric energy and to the romance of its development at the hands of Fariday, Kelvin, Edison and many others. To the mass of mankind struggling through ages of unrespited yearning for the satisfaction of the most meager human wants, what a release is promised through electricity's magic! To seek the fulfillment of this promise may also become a passionate pilgrimage.

Myriad have been the steps, some of them short and others thousand-league strides, by which electricity has in a little over forty years become the unchallenged ruler of the world's workshop. The story of the development of the utilization of electricity, both in detail and in reach, is quite unlike what happened in the case of mechanical power, beginning with Watt's invention of the steam engine about the middle of the eighteenth century. "Electricity in industry serves as a sort of universal lever for mechanization, automatization, and rationalization of production, completely transforming the conditions of industrial enterprises."[1]

The application of electricity to industrial operations may be said to have passed through four important phases:

1. Its use on processes not readily feasible for mechanical power
2. The substitution of the individual electric motor for belt-driven mechanical power on machines
3. The development of delicacy of control and of distant control
4. The "penetration" of the machine itself by electricity.

The first applications of electricity to industry were chiefly in the operation of traveling cranes and other handling mechanisms in machine shops, and to mine elevators. Men now living well remember the time when ponderous loads were lifted and moved by block and tackle and by similar hand-operated appliances. The weight and size of the moving parts required in cranes and mine elevators limited if they did not prohibit the use of mechanical power. One of the authors of this book in 1895 while serving his apprenticeship as a machinist worked in a shop equipped with an electric crane while candles were still the principal source of light for night work.

The next stage in the application of electricity to industry has often been described as the "lengthening of the driving belt." Mechanical power was invariably carried to the individual machine by means of a line shaft, which might be hundreds of feet in length, and from which the energy was drawn off by a leather belt, sometimes revolving at great speed. These belts at appropriate tensions caused the driving wheels of the machines to revolve. When the individual electric motor drive was provided for each individual machine, the electric wire running from the power plant superseded the combination of line shaft and driving belt. Mechanical considerations put limits to the length and power carrying capacity of these devices, but there are practically no limits to the length of an electric wire or to the power it can transmit. This was socially, economically and mechanically a master move in the development of modern industry. No longer was it necessary to assemble men, materials and machinery immediately adjacent to the steam plant—a condition which brought about the gruesome living and working conditions associated with the early stages of the industrial revolution. As a specially designed steam plant no longer anchors an individual enterprise, so the far-flung electric supply gives industry a new mobility—a potential threat to human values, but, if controlled, a promise of human progress.

As so frequently happens, the move to equip each machine with a motor of its own was carried too far. Today we have the "Drive Right" movement, advocating the grouping of machines about a short motor-operated line shaft. It has been discovered, for instance, that ten machines of a certain kind each requiring a 10 H.P. motor or a total of 100 H.P. when operated individually, can, when grouped, be operated from a motor-driven line shaft using a 30 H.P. motor. A great economy in electric service results.

Electricity gives a delicacy of control not feasible under mechanical power. For instance, "the starting and stopping of lathes is reduced to decimal fractions of a second. On revolving lathes, screw threading machines, automata, etc., when it is necessary to effect quick changes in the direction and speed of revolution, the switch control renders it possible to pass in less than a second from a speed of 1500 revolutions per minute in one direction to a similar speed in the opposite direction."[2] This means the elimination of jostling, of wear, and reduced capacity, unavoidable in mechanical transmission. Under this electrical dispensation the necessity for fly wheels is usually obviated.

Furthermore, the ease with which electricity—a uniform "fluid" commodity—is transported means that mechanisms even if large and complicated can be readily operated and controlled even at great distances. It is no longer necessary for the operator of a mechanical contrivance to be virtually on top of it. He may be quite out of sight, even in another building, or if need be hundreds of miles away. There are numerous instances of power released under controlled conditions doing work thousands of miles away, as for instance when President Roosevelt started the gigantic Boulder Dam power plant with an impulse originating across the continent in the White House at Washington, D. C.

Distant electric control effected by pushing buttons and pulling levers is aided by devices such as those installed for visualizing the operation of the Panama Canal locks. In a control cabin, situated on the center wall of each set of locks, there is a miniature reproduction by which the man in charge can see at any given moment the positions of the gates, the operating valves, water levels, and even the chains which protect the works against damage by passing boats. It would be quite feasible, of course, to assemble these control cabins at one point many miles away. In recent years comparable devices have found widely diversified application, both in light and heavy industry. The beginnings of wireless operation of distant control have been made. "The motor, the transmission mechanism and the working machine, under the influence of the steam techniques, were becoming more and more specialized and separated from one another. Upon the new electrical basis they are, on the one hand, becoming even more separated, separated sometimes for hundreds, and in the near future for thousands of miles. Yet, on the other hand, they are beginning to overcome this separation, being merged into one organic whole."[3]

Perhaps the most spectacular demonstration of electricity's power to change qualitatively the whole face of industry, lies in fact that it has "penetrated" machines in such a way that they become pulsating electrical devices endowed with an almost human intelligence and adaptability. Required energy is dispatched automatically to the myriad centers of work, almost as nervous energy is distributed without thought throughout the human body. Thus wires become the arteries and current the life blood of modern industry. As long as mechanical power was introduced, for instance, into paper-making machines at a single point and transmitted from that point by gears, cams, belts and other mechanical devices, a definite limit was set both to the length of these machines and to the speed with which they could be operated. Additional size or greater speed meant racking the machine to pieces. Presto! the makers break the modern machine into say seven distinct and, from a mechanical standpoint, entirely separate sections each motivated by its own electric motor but each so synchronized with the others that at a given instant of time each section and each part moves harmoniously with all the others.

Some of these developments have carried the utilization of electricity within the machine to the point where it is easy to believe that anything is possible. Take, for instance, the making of paper bags, the wrapping of gum, soap, and candy bars, and the perforating of postage stamps, all of which come close to the everyday life of everyone. Under the general term of "register control," electricity has taken over these processes, with the result that unheard of speeds and marvelous accuracy are attained.

The phototube or "electric eye" is the master of the system, waited upon by a retinue of other tubes, relays, motors, generators, and accessories to the end that, while increasing production fourfold, the operator is relieved of eye strain and of mental and physical fatigue. Small marks between printed designs on the roll of paper or cellophane are checked with lightning speed by the "electric eye" to see that the cuts occur at exactly these points and not through the design. Other tubes amplify the signal to cause the web to move ahead or back and to change the speed.

When the mark indicates to the "electric eye" that creepage has taken place, the web is re-positioned, corresponding to *resetting* a watch, and at the same time the speed is changed to counter the tendency, corresponding to *regulating* the watch. Thus equipped, machines make bags, 600 or more a minute; wrap gum, involving twelve operations, two packages a second; perforate stamps 300 holes a minute. Devices of this general type are rapidly influencing the design of large-scale machinery. For instance, each "bobbin" on some types of modern rayon machines is driven by an individual motor, and revolves up to ten thousand times a minute. Acres of such machinery are all but free from human supervision.

178 ORGANIZED LABOR AND PRODUCTION

A master illustration of the way in which electricity is supplanting human labor is the placing of twenty million tons of concrete in the Grand Coulee Dam on the Columbia River —the largest structure ever built by man! By means of electrically operated devices, under push-button control by one operator, water, cement, sand and gravel of each size, in quantities appropriate to the mix required, are automatically weighed out for each batch and delivered to one of four 4-yard mixers, graphic records of all components and the consistency of each batch being automatically recorded.

Mixers deliver their charges into 4-yard, bottom-dumping buckets, which are hauled away—four buckets to the car— by 10-ton Diesel-electric locomotives. This process goes on hour after hour, day after day, month after month and even year after year with monotonous uniformity.

Such developments in the use of electricity have been paralleled by an equally remarkable series influencing its generation and transmission. From the original low voltage independent "lighting plants," of our boyhood the industry has passed to large-scale central stations inter-connected over vast areas with "coast to coast" service technically feasible. Coincident with this extension in the area covered by a unified industrial electric service there have gone on reductions in cost resulting from breath-taking new "efficiencies that back in 1905 listed 500 degrees Fahrenheit as the maximum steam temperature compared with 950 F. today, and 180 pounds as the maximum steam pressure contrasted with today's 1800 pounds." Time marches on!

Electricity is coming to be so generally recognized as the universal lever that we increasingly use electrical standards wherewith to measure and contrast national industrial efficiencies. Thus the percentage of industry conducted electrically—as contrasted with mechanically—was early in the present decade: 75 per cent in the United States; 70 per cent in Germany; 61 per cent in England. Similarly the load factors (i.e. the efficiency with which electrical facilities are utilized) were: 35 per cent for United States; 25 per cent for Germany; 21 per cent for England.

Long before the beginnings of recorded history man used mechanical devices and indeed operated some of them, such as sail boats and irrigation wheels in a limited manner with natural power. But it is only since the last decade of the nineteenth century with the first use of electric transmission lines of a size to carry adequate power from the generating station to the factory that there has dawned the prospect of illimitable artificial energy applicable to an unlimited variety of uses. First used as an extension of man's muscular effort, electric power now bids fair largely to supersede physical human effort and other forms of natural power in the performance of the work of the world. Indeed in one industry, the manufacture of electricity, whether by coal or falling water, human labor has actually disappeared, all necessary operations except repairs being energized and controlled by electricity, directed by the human mind.[4] Rexford Tugwell in his *Industrial Discipline* feels this change to be so imminent that he suggests that we acquire rapidly the discipline of adjustment so as to be able to make the pressing transitions into a social order in which income is divorced from physical effort and even, perhaps, from employment!

In an industry where electrical power is taking the place of human muscles and where in increasing numbers the jobs are to watch, regulate and control electrically motivated mechanical appliances, the characteristics of desirable employees are necessarily quite different from those in demand when practically all workers were essentially prime movers. Walter Polokov expressed "the labor specifications for any really modern industry in these terms: 1, sustained attention; 2, correct perception; and 3, quick reaction."[5] This formula appears to be as applicable to a modern factory or mill worker as it is to a chauffeur, and especially to an executive. These qualifications call not only for mental power but more particularly for nervous poise and intelligent coordination.

The control boards of the new Atlantic clippers house 48 different registering devices—recent bombing planes even more. The large photographing telescope on Mt. Wilson has fourteen different adjustments to be made at varying intervals. It is difficult to find individuals so well organized that their nerves and muscles can be depended upon for the right reactions in the proper sequence. The more modern an industry the more widely and completely is the work mechanically and electrically organized to respond to these control centers. In view of the unifying influence of electricity, both the importance and complexity of industrial tasks to be operated from a single control center are likely to increase, making ever greater demands on the attention, perceptions and reactions of employees. The question has already been raised as to whether a wage system based on rewarding human beings for units of physical effort will be well adapted to compensating for services which have little or nothing to do with man as a prime mover. Further, it seems clear that the advance of the electric power age will tend to aggravate the effect of the natural law of the survival of the fittest by making only the most competent useful in industry. If present tendencies continue, a growing percentage of all industrial jobs will require the type of trained and able technician above described. Hence an increasing need through education and wise social legislation to seek to improve constantly the average ability of our people.

No discussion of the characteristics of the power age would be complete without some reference to the relationship between an impending unified power supply and the public order. It is obvious that in time of war large-scale central generating stations and the high-powered transmission lines leading from them are vulnerable points in any nation's defense. It should be equally obvious that if we cannot organize our industry so as to avoid the use of force in the settlement of industrial disputes, we cannot safely avail ourselves of the economies and convenience that go with a unified power supply. The results of temporary interruptions in the electric service of large metropolitan areas, such as those due to storms, suggest the demoralization which might be the outcome of studied attacks on vital centers.

It is largely due to the efficiencies resulting from the wider use of electricity, to its unifying influence and to a growing realization that its application to industry is still in a primary stage that people begin to vision the conquest of poverty and instead of vast areas of need, a conditioned plenty for all. Such a future, of course, depends upon changes in the economic structure of society to take advantage of the opportunity of the power age. Among important groups—educators, scientists, businessmen and labor leaders—one can trace the beginnings of a differentiation between those who work in channels largely determined by precedent and privilege, and those who are already visualizing new levels of human progress and guiding their research and their efforts toward these goals.

As early as 1908, Simon N. Patten at the Wharton School in Philadelphia was discussing methodology in economics in the terms "genetic" and "structural." The genetic approach to the solution of a problem involved inquiry into origins, evolution under the influence of forces beyond man's control, and finally, the probable trends. The structural approach, on the other hand, involved: the assumption that man has a considerable degree of control over his development; the examination of current practices and institutions as causal factors; and the need of modifying them to achieve desired results. Patten called attention to the fact that early society had a deficit economy, was restricted in the solution of problems by this limitation and could only roughly guide trends. He held that modern society has a surplus economy and wide liberty for positive controlling action looking toward predetermined results, and *calculated* surpluses.[6]

In recent years American businessmen have more and more utilized this structural approach, notably in the quota system in sales operations. They first decide how many units they want to sell and then make all necessary arrangements to accomplish the desired result. On other occasions when purchases have fallen off, a sales price at which it is thought the public will enter the market again is determined, and both the product and manufacturing methods modified so that the product can be turned out profitably at the new figure.

In the growing literature of planning we find the same distinctions being made, especially in the attack on social and economic problems. This time the contrasting adjectives are "genetic" and "teleological" to be interpreted about as follows:

The genetic approach implies prognosis or forecast of the future, based primarily on a projection of historic or past trends. Past trends are used as guides to future policy of control. But as governmental "interventionism" modifies more and more the trends in economic activity as reflected in market phenomena, as was the case in the Soviet Union during 1927-28, the genetic approach to planning yields more and more to the teleological approach. This is also called the "directive" approach, in which broad objectives are formulated to be achieved within a given period of time as, for instance, in Russia's Five-Year Plan. In this case the productive resources of the country are consciously guided toward the attainment of the goal set.

Surface indications often make it seem that such techniques can be put into operation only under an autocratic or dictatorial form of government. But democracy rightly envisioned suffers under no such handicap. In fact, there are many critical problems faced by this country, the answers to which could not be obtained except through the democratic process. For instance, the ablest of dictators would probably be defeated in establishing soil erosion control on our six million farms or in re-establishing the balance in our gravely depleted ground water reserves. These are tasks only for a democratic people, but a democratic people who after heart searchings have cast off such debilitating appendages as pork-barrel legislation and monkey-gland politics.

We who are interested primarily in industry cannot realize the possibilities of a more effective industry to provide a better life for all until employer-owners, abandoning the defenseless tenets of the overlord, and organized workers responding appropriately, together set a high "structural" or "teleological" goal and then drive enthusiastically, confidently and democratically for its accomplishment. The factor of electricity must be increasingly reckoned with in any such planning.

With the as yet unsolved problem of unemployment and the unappreciated role of electricity behind us we can proceed to discuss the measures through which we believe a better industry can be brought about. Before all the others comes, of course, collective bargaining.

VII. TOWARD SOLUTIONS

CHAPTER 15

THE CURRENT PRACTICES OF COLLECTIVE BARGAINING

THE prospect of impending collective bargaining ordinarily arouses fond hopes in employees for job security and increased wages, and excites employers' fears of interference and domination. Attitudes toward collective bargaining have been expressed, therefore, principally in contrasting terms of unbridled praise and vitriolic denunciation. More objective appraisals are properly being made as collective bargaining finds wider usage and since it has been adopted as an essential part of national labor policy. Such appraisals are not solely in terms of black and white. In the complete picture there are plenty of gray shades, and even tints of mauve and periwinkle. They will be discerned in this discussion of current practices.

Fundamentally and ideally, collective bargaining is a process under which employees actively participate, as equals, with employers in fixing the terms and conditions of their employment. Such participation of employees, through representatives of their own choosing, is visualized as the way to secure their genuine consent to the conditions under which they work, and, therefore, to minimize the risk of disturbed conditions including strikes. It has been declared, in effect, that individual bargaining tends toward the imposition of terms by employers rather than their acceptance by employees, and breeds a dissatisfaction that frequently erupts into a more or less serious labor dispute. The National Labor Relations Act approves collective bargaining through labor unions as the process by which employees can most effectively participate in determining conditions of work, and accepts the written labor agreement as a device which embodies the understanding of the parties.

In determining whether collective bargaining has a fair chance of meeting the difficult objectives set for it, one must carefully distinguish between a labor agreement made as an incident of the period of organization from one that is negotiated after union status is assured. The president of one company recently stated, "Well, we've done it; we've signed up with the CIO. But don't forget this is the flow in the labor movement, and when the ebb tide comes shortly we'll see to it that we have enough employees with us so we can kick out the union." On the other hand, in the same case, the union visualized the agreement as a "foot in the door," giving it an opportunity to secure sufficient strength so that it would not be flotsam when the ebb came along.

Why was the union so insistent upon becoming the sole collective bargaining representatives of these particular employees? It happened that their employer paid less than the union scale and undersold "union manufacturers" on the market. In collective bargaining with companies that had already recognized the union, the employers sought either a substantial wage cut or preferably the organization of their "chiseling competitor" so that he would be forced to pay the "standard rate." When the union finally secured a tenuous status in the plant of the "chiseling competitor," the so-called collective bargaining that ensued was principally a tactical struggle. In such cases, the actual "sitting down around a table to negotiate" has frequently been preceded by employer-initiated increases of wage rates and improvement of conditions "to keep the union out." Then comes the inevitable insistence on concessions necessary "to keep the union in" the plant, and for "improved conditions" under the agreement to show returns for the dues that are expected. The real issue in such organizational collective bargaining is whether there shall be genuine collective bargaining in the plant. It is not realistic to appraise the economic possibilities of collective bargaining from the results that are achieved in such situations which may be more aptly described as "collective arguing."

It cannot be assumed that organizational collective bargaining is always accompanied by belligerency on the part of employers. In numerous instances, management has sincerely and in good faith taken the position that "it is up to the union to sell itself to our employees and to show management what it can do. We're neutral but open-minded in the whole matter." While there is much to commend in such a position, it may become a highly impractical policy upon which to operate a plant. Inevitably the union is forced to adopt policies that are not unpopular with any minority group, if the union is to "hold its members." Union officers are required to become followers rather than leaders since they have had little or no opportunity to undertake educational work respecting the limits of collective bargaining.

Certain typical situations develop. Under an agreement, recognizing the union as spokesman for its members only, a sit-down strike of one department recently occurred in violation of the agreement, and in protest against the meager results attained by incumbent union officials. A check-up revealed that virtually every employee in the department had just resigned from the union. In this anomalous situation the union was held responsible by management for an "unlawful stoppage" of a department in which the union no longer had any members. Management soon determined that it could not be entirely "neutral" under such circumstances. It suggested that the union had originally secured an agreement with the company by virtue of the membership of certain employees. They could not equitably secure the benefits of the agreement and then evade their contractual obligations merely by resigning from the union. For very practical reasons, management saw that the union must have power and status if it is to be held responsible. It was agreed, at the insistence of the company, that the jobs held by union members when the contract was signed were to be considered as union jobs throughout the term of the contract.

Employees should be free from all coercion in designating their representatives for collective bargaining. However, once a union is chosen as the employees' representative and enters into an agreement with the employer, the union must be given sufficient status to insure that its members meet their obligations. This does not inevitably mean the closed shop or the check-off, although these devices have been often used and more frequently sought by unions. Their advantages and disadvantages need a more careful analysis than is ordinarily given them by the usual snap-judgment opinion or wholly emotional point of view.

The recognition of a union for collective bargaining implies not that the employer has taken a position of neutrality, but that he has accepted the principle that individual bargaining will be supplanted by collective bargaining as the procedure by which conditions or labor will be determined. This is a fundamental step. Management then has the right to expect the union, as representative of its employees, not only to comply fully with the terms of the agreement, but to cooperate in achieving efficient plant operation. But if the union is to "do a job," it has the right to expect management to refrain from all undermining activities and to cooperate in all reasonable ways in developing a union of real status in the plant. For many employers, who have gone far in even tolerating a union, it is difficult to see how they benefit from having a strong union. Yet, experience shows that it is the weak union, struggling for its existence, that takes unreasonable positions based upon the will to survive.

In the creation of collective bargaining on a mutually satisfactory basis, the employer must realize that a code of civil rights for the employees will inevitably develop. On the other hand, the employees and their union representatives must realize that the determination of wages and conditions of work is an economic function and not an arbitrary process dependent upon the exercise of sheer power. Sound attitudes in these two particulars are the *sine qua non* of genuine collective bargaining.[1]

The demand for civil rights, or for a so-called system of industrial jurisprudence, involves building a system of rules to govern employee status. Such rules supplant the arbitrary will of the employer in such matters. The civil rights objective assumes greater importance when jobs are relatively scarce and hence more precious. Under individual bargaining, the employer has an unquestioned right to make selections for discharge, layoff, or promotion on any basis he desires. Under collective bargaining, there is a mutual agreement upon rules designed to protect the individual's right to work. Some have considered such rules as the beginning of an industrial common law defining what to the worker amounts to a property right in his job.

It is significant that in new industries labor agreements chiefly stress the protection of employees from unjustified discharge and the designation of seniority rules to govern layoffs and promotions. Work-sharing programs, policies relating to protection of workers in the face of technological change, and restrictions upon entrance to a trade are other examples of the subjects that are covered in the industrial common law; nor can these matters be disposed of by the simple statement that they constitute unwarranted interference with management prerogative.

The development of civil rights in industry for employees need not be oppressive to the employer. Consider the matter of discharge. One well-established collective agreement provides: "The employer shall have the free exercise of the right to employ or discharge any worker in accordance with the necessity of his or its business, provided in the case of a discharge from employment, such discharge is in good faith and for just cause." In the operation of the clause management has recognized discharge to be, not an essential proof of authority, but a distasteful responsibility that must sometimes be met to insure efficient plant operation. Experience has shown management and the union that poor workmanship falls into two categories. The occasional careless mistake of a good workman represents one problem. A single instance of such poor workmanship usually represents nothing more than human imperfection and calls for discussion, warnings, or training—but scarcely discharge. Surely representatives of management would protest if the board of directors "fired" them for an isolated, careless mistake in purchasing raw materials or in pricing. But if management representatives made too serious, or too many, careless mistakes, they would expect to be replaced. A similar standard can be applied to workmen. The other kind of poor workmanship involves an apparent lack of ability to meet minimum standards of efficiency. If blame must be placed for such inefficiency, it usually must be shouldered by management since poor selection or poor training is almost always at the root of the trouble. The first requirement in this situation is a cooperative effort by the union and management to develop the employee by retraining rather than to deny him a reasonable chance to make good. Only after the failure of such efforts will the step to discharge be taken—and, then reluctantly, with attention to the selection standards of the company that permitted the man to be taken on. The working out of such civil rights, of which the discharge question has been considered as an example, need not restrict management efficiency but may even increase it. Such rules eliminate the fear of capricious discharge as a "tool" of management.

Just as the employer assumes an obligation under collective bargaining to cooperate in the establishment of equitable civil rights for employees, the established union faces the responsibility for bringing sound economic judgment to its participation in the cost-determining process.

In a few instances, unions have been sufficiently strong to enable them to exact terms of employment that were beyond a company's continuing ability to pay. Collective bargaining can then become the opposite kind of a unilateral determination from that which is effective in individual bargaining —the employer has the choice of taking or leaving the contract offered by the union. Genuine collective bargaining, however, implies a relative equality of bargaining power between the parties. Certain strong unions, honestly desirous of making collective bargaining work, have on occasions been impelled to assist in the formation or reorganization of strong associations of employers so that the bargaining might be between equals. Such a program is not illogical.

Prior to 1933, the collective agreement was rather generally viewed by unions as the all-sufficient means of providing against all the economic insecurities faced by employees. This point-of-view engendered a measure of labor opposition to social legislation and probably influenced the fixing of wage levels without regard to the predictable effects upon employment, production, and consumption. Some labor leaders, in effect, said, "We don't need laws providing unemployment or sickness benefits. If we can sit around a table with employers, and bargain, we'll get the workers a wage

COLLECTIVE BARGAINING

sufficient to enable them to provide their own fund for such contingencies." Such a policy might conceivably produce results for union members if bargaining were to be restricted to a few crafts representing a small percentage of the total employees in a plant, or in industries where labor costs form a small part of the total manufacturing costs. It cannot be applied to employees organized on an industrial basis where bargaining involves the total wage bill.

In many industries, labor unions have come to realize that collective bargaining has limitations as well as possibilities. They have heard the protests of workers who have become unemployed at high rates, and have experienced the power of authority that lies in the market for goods. "What the traffic will bear" without causing unemployment becomes very important in collective bargaining. There are not many situations where continuous gains to labor represent merely a diversion of excess profits and have no compelling effect upon the needed flow of capital into an industry or upon prices and the volume of goods purchased by consumers. Moreover, the very spread of membership in the labor movement has led to a growing recognition that the position of a relatively small number of skilled workers is less crucial to the national economy than the improvement of the real wages of labor generally. And by real wages is meant the compensation which pays the worker's personal bills in and out of season.

As the concept of the "all-sufficiency" of pure and simple collective bargaining is becoming obsolete, the objectives of labor unions are being extended to so-called "industrial stabilization" ventures, social legislation and increased political activity. The approach to collective bargaining is from new directions. Most labor unions are realizing that the widespread use of collective bargaining requires much more than a series of restrictive measures, set up in one industry after another, if there is to be an improvement in the real wages of labor generally. Labor is the principal consumer, and its real wage depends upon the prices it must pay for commodities. There are significant indications in the programs of numerous unions that collective bargaining can develop to the point where the maintenance and improvement of labor standards will be based upon programs that decrease costs and prices to the consumer without jeopardizing the status and security of employees. Development of this type of collective bargaining requires:

1. A wider opportunity for participation of union employee representatives in matters of plant and business management, as well as in industry economics. One large company, engaged in genuine collective bargaining with an established union, is even now discussing the practicability of seating the president of the union on the company board of directors. Such active participation in management affairs can naturally come only after the organization phase is over and after the development of a comprehensive educational program for both employers and employees. To have this step necessarily mean very much it would probably be necessary to effect fundamental changes in current concepts as to the responsibilities of directors.

2. Provisions for assistance to employees who may be displaced, temporarily or permanently, by programs to reduce cost.

So far, attention has been centered upon that phase of collective bargaining concerned with the establishment of the contract terms and the development of the basic principles that are to govern relations between a company and the union. Negotiations on these matters are usually conducted yearly, or at longer intervals, by national officials and top-flight executives. It has been the history of the making of agreements between trade-unions and employers that their conclusion has been postponed now by one side and now by the other, almost to the hour when they are to go into effect —either side or both hoping for some last minute advantage. Perhaps as we become more accustomed to collective bargaining agreements in this country we shall move toward the Swedish practice, which is to have all the details arranged and the documents signed six months in advance of the effective date. Thus neither side takes advantage of last minute pressure.

Although agreement making is an extremely important function, genuine collective bargaining is not confined to "sitting around a table" to work out an agreement every year or so. On the contrary, collective bargaining is also a continuous process by which contract provisions are applied to day-by-day problems. The administration of the agreement must be largely in the hands of shop stewards or of a shop committee for the union and of operating executives for the management. Theirs is often a difficult task, concerned with the application of principles and the maintenance of plant morale. The best agreement can "bog down" through inept handling within the shop, and in many cases this is still the least worked-out aspect of collective bargaining. Nevertheless, union educational programs for shop committeemen are showing results. There is a responsibility on the part of management to undertake similar educational work among its representatives. It would be helpful if there were more general recognition of the fact that the company personnel department not only assumes new duties under collective bargaining but that to execute them satisfactorily, quite new techniques may be required. It is surprising, indeed, to hear of personnel departments being scrapped with the coming of collective bargaining relationships. Their objectives may frequently be in need of revision, but such departments can become an invaluable staff department to assist in the administration of agreements.

Even expecting a competent administration within the shop, agreements ordinarily provide for the possibility that certain differences of opinion will not be reconciled. Such cases are ordinarily referred first to negotiation of union officials and top-flight executives, and, if still unsettled, to a board of arbitration or to an impartial umpire for a "final and binding decision." Grievances must be settled as expeditiously as possible if they are not to be nurtured into an urge for precipitate action. Since the labor agreement invariably outlaws strikes and lockouts during its term, the hearing before an impartial umpire or arbitration board provides the means through which unadjusted grievances—real or imaginary—may be aired and settled.

In the settlement of a particularly embittered strike it was agreed that the employment status of a number of discharged workers would be decided by an arbitrator. The company claimed that the employees were wholly unacceptable because of their alleged improper conduct during the strike; the union sought their reinstatement, claiming that the men were being victimized for their active support of the strike. The arbitrator considered each case individually. The arbitrator soon discovered that the workers' alleged activities on the picket line could not be separated from the company's practices prior to the strike. Mr. Brown, for example, was accused of having thrown a brick through a window of the plant. In questioning Mr. Brown, the arbitrator saw in him an average law-abiding, useful citizen, middle aged, and by no means militant or aggressive. Brown was a conscientious worker and a good one with a long service record in the plant. But he had a grievance he could not forget. The company had a system of fining employees for infractions of company rules or work standards. He did not argue the question of his blame when he was fined $35 within one week, but he did resent deeply that the foreman had arbitrarily imposed the fine, acting as judge, jury, and prosecuting attorney, and had ruled that the money must be paid by such a time or he would be discharged. The arbitrator was astonished to learn that this incident had occurred "seven years ago." During all that time, Brown had been unable to secure redress. He was unable to appeal the ruling of his foreman. The arbitrator immediately recognized that the lack of proper procedures for handling grievances was not only poor management but represented an unsocial policy, which seriously affected morale in the plant. The company forthwith started the development of a proper personnel program and requested the umpire named in the agreement with the union to accept for hearing every case, even minor ones, not adjusted through negotiation to the mutual satisfaction of both parties.

The impartial chairman, or arbitrator, having the approval of both sides and whose compensation is shared on a 50-50 basis is more and more frequently provided for in union contracts. Continuously engaged in the same industry, sometimes through a period of years, such an official gains an expertness not possible for an arbitrator brought in only at long intervals and to settle isolated disputes. Such an official is well advised to resist getting in on too many of the petty details of shop administration. The necessity for too much arbitration is an indication either of faulty management or too little statesmanship on the part of the union leadership or both. The impartial chairman is useful where both sides want the same thing.

In industries where impartial arbitrative machinery has been developed, there is seldom any problem about "wildcat" strikes or lockouts during the term of an agreement. Acting to reconcile the rights and interests of both parties as defined by the agreement, and giving a fair and informal hearing, the umpire is, in a sense, a more civilized substitute for the ancient weapons of "economic warfare." Not only does the record show a virtually one hundred per cent compliance with decisions of the various impartial officials but also that the plan can be an effective aid to the development of proper personnel relations under collective bargaining.

The indications are clear that the terms of employment in American industry will be fixed to an increasing extent through the process of collective bargaining. While experience with genuine collective bargaining in this country is limited, it is broad enough to point the way along which "collective bargaining can be made to work." There is an important stake in the effort to effectuate collective bargaining. As long as the primary objective of the labor movement is the securing of collective bargaining rights, there is assurance that employees conceive their interests to be best protected by a continuance of the present form of economy. The collective agreement recognizes the employer-employee relationship, and is adapted to a wage system under which employees are paid by employers from the proceeds of the sale of goods and to a production system where capital investment depends upon profits. There are cogent reasons, indeed, why "making collective bargaining work" is a major task for those who eschew the "isms."

What has been said here as to collective bargaining was applicable to the relatively small number of situations where it was being practiced before we even had a Wagner Act. Now let us see wherein that legislation has affected the situation. Why did the government intervene in an area heretofore reserved for private initiative and private negotiations?

CHAPTER 16

THE WAGNER ACT

THE National Labor Relations Act is a law the full effect of which cannot be estimated by its apparent impact on the current industrial scene. Those who would understand its significance must come equipped with some knowledge of the past relationships between government and industry in the United States. In imagination they must go back fifty years to those pitched battles by which workers and employers then settled their difficulties. They must recapture a sense of the barbaric violence of the tempers engaged and the weapons used in those battles. They must decide whether that was a reasonable way to settle differences between men and management, and, if the answer is negative, they must consider whether that pattern of industrial warfare has not nevertheless so persisted over the course of the past half century that its original evils are still apparent in modern labor relationships.

Only on the supposition that these evils persist can there be justification in invoking such a remedy as the National Labor Relations Act. If employers have always recognized the right of their workers to join together for the purpose of choosing representatives for collective bargaining, then the Act has no place in American industry. But if employers in the great majority of cases have refused that right, and if such refusal has been a major cause of the bitter strife by which industry has been plagued, then a remedy for these old, recurrent evils was clearly indicated.

This book has already recounted some of the struggles between workers and employers during past decades when no holds were barred, and when the public sat impassively by, deploring the strife, occasionally quelling it by armed

THE WAGNER ACT

force, but in general taking no part other than that of impatient spectator.

Except in railroad labor relations, and temporarily during the World War through the activities of the War Labor Board, the government made no effective intervention during these past fifty years of profound industrial readjustments. That fact must underlie all thinking about the National Labor Relations Act as a remedial law. A dynamic law, such as this one, is a component of past forces. Today's newspaper story about it cannot be read with the same instantaneous comprehension as can the account of a fire. What went before is determinative. For that reason, let us recapitulate briefly the past role of government in labor disputes.

The violence which has accompanied labor disputes was described dramatically by Stuart Chase, writing of a strike in 1877:[1]

> In Pittsburgh as a result of a 10 per cent wage cut and a speed-up order on the Pennsylvania, the State troops were finally beleaguered in a railroad roundhouse. The strikers bombarded them with two pieces of captured artillery. Making a breach in their walls, they attacked in force, only to be cut down by the concentrated fire of the troops. Next the besiegers sent cars of oil-soaked coke down the tracks toward the roundhouse, and finally they set it on fire. The troops retreated with heavy losses across the Allegheny River to Claremont, twelve miles away. Two roundhouses, 1600 cars, and 125 locomotives were destroyed.
> In Reading the whole Sixteenth Regiment—largely composed of Irish workers—went over to the strikers, following a violent battle in the streets. In St. Louis a committee of strikers took possession of the city government for a week. They were finally dislodged by a combined force of infantry, cavalry, and artillery. In Chicago there was a pitched battle between federal troops and strikers at the Halstead Street viaduct.

This sort of government intervention, naked strength pitted against mob outlawry, was the low point from which American labor relations had to begin an upward climb. That the ascent has been slow appears from recurrences of such episodes as late as 1921 when federal troops deployed in battle line against coal miners on a West Virginia mountain.

Indeed, every call on the militia for strike duty is a reversion to brute force and a setback for rational relations between free men. In spite of decades of proof that the two great parties in industry could not, or would not, get together in civilized negotiation, the government could think of no other remedies than to use suppressive measures during the heat of battle and, afterwards, to appoint commissions for the compilation of reports on the causes of the trouble.

Thus, the government began to use injunctions in situations where troops were too stringent a palliative for industrial trouble. It has been estimated that between 1894 and 1931, the federal courts issued more than 500 injunctions in labor disputes. During the railway shopmen's strike of 1922 scores of federal injunctions restrained the activities of the striking employees. Attorney-General Palmer used the injunction in the bituminous coal strike in 1919, ordering the United Mine Workers to rescind their strike order.

Since President McKinley in 1898 appointed his commission to seek causes of labor disputes, there have been other ably conducted investigations along similar lines. Countless witnesses have been heard, and the savage tale of a tooth-and-claw relationship laid bare. But the reports have had no more than a passing effect on public opinion and never resulted in curative legislation.

In the light of present government attempts to deal with the causes instead of the results of labor strife, it is interesting to discover in these old reports that the clue to a better relationship was always pointed out, even though it was not followed.

The findings of each commission define, as a basic cause of disputes, the workers' desire for employer recognition of their organizations. For example, the report of the special commission in the Colorado coal strike of 1912 stated that: "the struggle in Colorado was primarily a struggle against arbitrary power in which the question of wages was secondary as an immediate issue."

Here, twenty-eight years ago, was stated the distinction between labor disputes arising from the employers' refusal to recognize the right to organize, and disputes over wages, hours and working conditions. But that distinction was disregarded.

The right to join a labor organization without employer interference or threats was a deeply felt need in generations of workers. The exercise of that right precedes any possibility of collective bargaining between worker and employer representatives. To establish the right, workers were willing to risk their lives in conflict with their employers, even when employers enlisted the aid of public authority. But for decades, strikes for the right to organize were not recognized as essential to the later course of peaceful bargaining. Militia and injunctions were used against such strikers without concurrent inquiry which would have made clear that the workers were merely seeking to sustain rights which in common sense and in law were already theirs. The government applied itself to settling disputes only at strike stage, without attempting to prevent strikes through the establishment of bargaining equality between the contestants.

Whatever the beneficial results of the industrial revolution —and they were many—it brought in its wake a great many kinds of inequality, bearing particularly upon the worker. It left him unequal in financial resources, industrial and economic knowledge, and bargaining experience, as contrasted with the employer device known as the corporation, which represents a pooling of financial and other resources.

Industry appreciates the difference between individualism and union. It can fully assess the meaning of Chief Justice Taft's decision in the American Steel Foundries case[2] in 1921, when, speaking for the Court, he said:

". . . Union was essential to give laborers an opportunity to deal on equality with their employer. . . . The strike became a lawful instrument in a lawful economic struggle or competition between employer and employees as to the share or division between them of the *joint product* (italics supplied) of labor and capital."

That employers appreciate the value of associating for business purposes is attested by the approximately 7000 trade associations of all kinds, 1000 of which are international in character.

But industrial relations in this country before 1933 were

200 ORGANIZED LABOR AND PRODUCTION

based largely on the essential inequality between employers and their employees. Employers were free to organize and choose representatives, such as local managers and superintendents, to establish the wages and conditions under which employees must work. The employees, for the most part, were denied the right to join unions and through them bargain with management. Many of the most serious strikes of the past had been caused by the earnest desire of workers for union representation and a corresponding employer resolve that they should not have it. To remove this cause of dispute, and to promote the collective negotiation which follows upon legitimate worker organization, it seemed necessary to outlaw unfair methods of defeating worker organization and to establish a procedure for the secret election of employee representatives.

These two concepts, well grounded in past experience, were behind the government's moves, beginning with NRA, to deal with the causes of industrial unrest as a means to a hopeful new relationship.

Contrary to common report, the new labor law was not suddenly dashed off in a "midnight draft" during the early fervid days of the Roosevelt administration. Two years of active and full experience under the labor clauses of the NRA were drawn upon, as well as the thought and experience of hundreds of labor leaders, experts on labor problems, statesmen, and industrialists throughout the United States. Extensive hearings preceded the passage of the bill in House and Senate, and the public debate on it extended to the press, the pulpit and the radio of the country. The vigor with which the principles of the Act were discussed attests their fundamenal importance, comparable, indeed, to those embodied in the Bill of Rights in that they attempted to restate human rights in consonance with the new industrial imperatives of the modern machine age.

The courts, Congress reasoned, had for decades stated that the rights of labor to organize and bargain were just and legal. But for lack of the practical application of this ruling, the industrial relations of this highly industrialized nation were marked by costly warfare between those who, in common sense, should have been pooling their energy and thought for mutual betterment. In its 1935 report, the Senate Committee on Education and Labor estimated that industrial strife was causing an annual loss of one billion dollars, an index of the severe strains on interstate commerce, industrial production, on the security of the wage earner and on the quality of American citizenship itself.

Congress placed hope in genuine collective bargaining as a corrective of many of these evils. If the unwillingness of some employers was the only barrier to adopting that principle, Congress proposed that their reluctance be overridden for the sake of the common good. To that end the National Labor Relations Act, after full hearing and debate, was enacted.

In essence it is a simple law. It forbids to employers those practices which experience shows prevented the submission of disputes to peaceful negotiation, including discharge for union activity, domination of worker organizations and refusal to bargain.

Its simplicity has not saved it from being misunderstood. Many people who believe in collective bargaining still have difficulty in comprehending the procedure established to protect it. This is not surprising. The law is still new and for most of its first two years it was under a cloud of suspected unconstitutionality. After the Supreme Court of the United States upheld its validity, on April 12, 1937, industry was called upon to make fundamental changes in its dealings with employees. No less fundamental was the change which the public was asked to make, almost overnight, in its attitude toward the rights of the worker in the industrial relationship. That shift could not be made quickly; it is still in process. A waste product thrown off in the heat of effecting that change is a set of misconceptions about this simple law.

Most frequent is the charge that the law is one-sided because it does not extend its protection to employers. Yet the employers have always been free to organize and use their common strength. They scarcely need protection for rights which have never been questioned, in principle or in practice. The allegation of "one-sidedness" probably arises out of the fact that union adherents are permitted to bid for members among the workers while under the Act employers may not try to influence their workers one way or the other.

Again, the labor law is held inadequate because it does not punish workers who resort to violence or threats against fellow employees during strikes. Such criticism of the Labor Act overlooks the fact that such misdemeanors and crimes as breach of the peace, assault, and so on are properly the province of the police power of the state rather than the labor law.

Such is the atmosphere of controversy surrounding this law and its administration that debate on its provisions is almost endless. Of more practical moment are the results it has achieved.

Congress in passing the Act held that its protection of the rights of workers to organize would remove the cause of strikes called to force those rights upon unwilling employers. Four years of operations under the Act seem to justify this expectation. The number of strikes to protect organization has fallen off relatively since the validation of the Act. Concurrently there has been a strong tendency for workers to appeal to the protection of the Act rather than to use the strike weapon.

Much point has been made of the fact that the year 1937, eighteen months after the passage of the Labor Act, was one of the worst strike years in our history. But in considering such criticism, several important points should be borne in mind. A significant cause of unrest in 1937 was the dishonor in which some employers and their associations held the Labor Act. Many denounced it as unconstitutional, enjoined the Board from operating, disobeyed Board orders, and persisted in the very practices the Act prohibited. Labor, discouraged, returned to its traditional weapons.

It must be recalled also that the Act sanctioned no Board intervention in strikes involving solely issues of wages, hours and working conditions.

The record shows that in the year and more following validation of the Act strikes in the United States, whatever their cause, have decreased in numbers, intensity and duration. In comparison with 1937, the number of working days wasted due to strikes (the most accurate reflection of the effect of industrial strife) decreased more than 65 per cent in 1938, the first full year after the constitutionality of the Act was established. Other factors of course contributed to this sharp decline in unemployment caused by strikes. But that the Labor Board deserves some recognition for this accomplishment is possible of demonstration. Whereas before 1937 workers turned twice as often to the self-help of the strike as to the Board, in 1938 they turned to the peaceful device of the Board three times as often as they resorted to their own economic weapons. This tendency is most marked when we note that strikes in those industries which fall under the jurisdiction of the Board decreased about 50 per cent from 1937 to 1938 as compared with a 29 per cent decrease in strikes in industries over which the Board has no jurisdiction.

In something less than four years after its passage on July 5, 1935, the Act was invoked in 142 strikes, involving 368,865 workers.[3] Seventy-five per cent of these strikes were settled by the Board, and 235,684 strikers were reinstated. In addition, action by the Board averted 693 threatened strikes involving 175,054 workers.

On the whole the performance of the Labor Act should be judged in relation to the transition it was called upon to effect. In 1935, employers generally rejected the aspirations of labor to deal with them through union representatives. Congress assigned the Labor Board the tremendous task of making employers change their attitude 180 degrees to an acceptance of collective bargaining as sound public policy. Resistance was inevitable, cries of resentment to be expected. The record, however, does not disclose undue hardship on employers.

The Board has handled more than 20,000 cases in its first four years of existence. Only 7.9 per cent of the American Federation of Labor and 8.1 per cent of the Congress of Industrial Organizations cases had to go clear through the procedure of charge, complaint, hearing, and final Board decision and order. The remaining 92.1 per cent A. F. of L. and 91.9 per cent CIO cases were closed in an intermediate step. 53.5 per cent of the A. F. of L. cases, and 53.8 per cent CIO cases were settled by mutual agreement among the workers, the employer, and the Board. The A. F. of L. withdrew 23.9 per cent of its charges, and the CIO withdrew 26.1 per cent of its cases. The Board dismissed 13.4 per cent of the A. F. of L.'s cases and 10.9 per cent of the CIO's. The remaining one per cent or so were variously disposed of.

The test of the Act's effectiveness does not lie in the vigor of partisan cheers or complaints which for four years have confused the public. If the original intention to protect the procedure of collective bargaining were wise, then the Act is sound and effective. For there is no doubt that under its protection industrial wage earners have largely escaped from the perils which attempts to organize formerly entailed. Five million workers have brought to the Board their complaints and their petitions for elections. Thousands of workers, discharged for union activity, have obtained reinstatement and hundreds of thousands of dollars in back pay for the periods of their layoffs. Employees have sought and secured the disestablishment of dominated company unions, some of these in the country's largest plants. More than 600,000 workers have cast votes for representatives in 2000 Board elections, in which 90 per cent of all eligibles have taken the trouble to vote. On this fact the Chairman of the Labor Board, J. Warren Madden, has commented: "The value of this education in democracy cannot be overemphasized."

A concern for the imponderable effects of the Act on American life has characterized many of Chairman Madden's statements. To the Senate Committee on Education and Labor he said on April 18, 1939:

A large proportion of the millions of newly organized workers are enjoying for the first time those civil liberties which organization often helps to secure—the right of free speech, the right of free assembly, the right of adequate protection against organized lawlessness. Civil liberties have become a living reality in many communities where they were not previously enjoyed.

On several earlier occasions Chairman Madden had defined, as he conceived them, the alternatives confronting Congress in 1935 when it was debating the National Labor Relations Act: on the one hand to impose fiat regulation over wage scales and conditions of employment; on the other, to run the risks inherent in self-determination, in the faith that free labor and free employers will reach reasonable adjustments. Government might hope that necessary pressures would be applied at the bargaining table rather than on the picket line, but beyond encouragement of the bargaining procedure government would not go. Chairman Madden presented his analysis of these alternatives to the Senate Committee:

This was the choice to be made in a world and time in which the trend was, almost without exception, toward surrendering liberties to government in return for bounties, or yielding them unwillingly to the superior force of government. The proposal of Senator Wagner and his associates was directly counter to this trend. They proposed that the millions of American workers who would come within the protection of the Act should be trusted to determine for themselves and through their own chosen leaders what they wanted in the way of terms of employment, and to bargain rationally with their employers about those terms. They saw nothing in the history of American workmen and their leaders to indicate that they could not be so trusted. They saw in that history courage, patience, self-reliance and self-restraint in the face of impossible and irrational legal impediments. They also saw some racketeering and other criminality, but probably in a proportion as small as in any other element of our population. They proposed to create a new liberty in a world where the old liberties were being taken away. They proposed to have instead of more government, more liberty.

The Congress and the President concurred in these proposals and the National Labor Relations Act was passed . . . Recorded history will show that at that critical time America and its government and the leaders of American labor moved definitely against the trend of the world, and dared to confer upon millions of Americans more freedom and more democracy than they had ever before enjoyed.

The effective date of the National Labor Relations Act was April 12, 1937, when the Supreme Court dispelled the cloud of suspected unconstitutionality by upholding Board procedure, jurisdiction and fact finding in the first five cases coming before the Court for review. During the next two years, 14 additional National Labor Relations Board cases reached the United States Supreme Court for final adjudication. The Board was upheld in full or in large part in 11 of these. It was upheld in part in one and reversed completely in only two cases. The various Circuit Courts of Appeals have sustained the Board in full or with modification in 39 cases and decided against it in 13. The Board also obtained 154 consent decrees in the Circuit Courts.

The term "quasi-judicial" as applied to administrative agencies such as the Labor Board is somewhat misleading. As an administrator it proceeds to investigate and hear cases. In its role as decision maker, however, the term "quasi" has no application since the Board in fact becomes a lower court subject to review by the Circuit Court of Appeals. While its findings of fact in principle are binding on the review Court, the latter in practice determines whether or not substantial evidence supports the Board's conclusions.

Thus arbitrary or capricious rulings are subject to reversal. The Board is further impelled to judicious care through realization that its decisions are precedent-making in a new field of labor law. Already many, if not most, of the important areas of the Act's jurisdiction and interpretation have been marked out by Supreme Court decisions on Board rulings.[4] Briefly, they are as follows:

In *Jones & Laughlin Steel Corporation* case the Board's procedural provisions were held not to offend against constitutional requirements, and, affirmatively, were considered to afford adequate opportunity to secure judicial protection against arbitrary action.

In *Associated Press* case the Court held that the Act does not abridge freedom of speech or press by requiring reinstatement of an employee unfairly discharged.

In *Friedman-Harry Marks* case the Court granted jurisdiction over a manufacturing concern which, although small, engages in interstate commerce.

In *Santa Cruz Fruit Packing Company* case the Court granted jurisdiction even though all raw materials originated within the state and less than 40 per cent of the finished product was shipped across the state line.

In *Pennsylvania Greyhound Lines* case the Court sustained an order of the Board requiring disestablishment of unions found to be under employer control.

In *Mackay Radio & Telegraph Company* case the Court sustained the Board's position that strikers retain their employee status even though the strike was not the result of an unfair labor practice.

In *Fansteel Metallurgical Corporation* case the Court refused to uphold reinstatement of employees who had been discharged for participating in a sit-down strike.

In *Consolidated Edison* case the Court struck down that part of the Board's ruling which invalidated a contract made with a union for its members only, and where the union had not been made a party to the proceedings.

Other important issues such as the requirement of a written contract where employer and union are in agreement on terms, have not been passed upon at this writing by the Supreme Court.

The Labor Board under NLRA was not commissioned by Congress to organize workers into unions. There can be no doubt, however, that Congress in the preamble to the Act approved of labor organization as the means toward the end of stable industrial relations through collective bargaining. And there seems no doubt that the effect of the Act has been to promote organization, and written contracts between unions and employers.

When the Labor Act was passed in 1935 there were about 3,500,000 workers in organized unions. Today the number has increased to an estimated 8,000,000. That this was due in large measure to government protection of the right to organize cannot be questioned.

Studies of the percentage of organized workers to the total gainfully employed show that in 1881, the first year for which data are available, there were 105,000 union members out of 17,985,000 employed, or 0.6 per cent. The ratio fluctuated for four decades but never reached as high as seven per cent until the government as an emergency measure guaranteed worker self-determination through the War Labor Board. The highest percentage was in 1920 when 5,048,000 workers, or 12.1 per cent of the gainfully employed, were union members. Once this protection was withdrawn the percentage rapidly fell off. In 1933 it was less than seven per cent, practically back to pre-war level. The years of

Labor Board operation have brought organization to an all-time high both in numbers (8,000,000), and in percentage to those gainfully employed (14.7 per cent).

As had been hoped by those who drafted the Labor Act, this has resulted in an even greater increase in the proportion of employers and employees covered by the known and renewable terms of written trade agreements. Upon this point we have the evidence of the U. S. Bureau of Labor Statistics which in November 1937 stated:

> In less than five years the picture of employer-employee relations has markedly changed. By expanding first in industries only partially organized and then to the mass production industries, collective bargaining through trade union agreements has grown to the point where it has now become the accepted procedure in establishing wages, hours and working conditions in a considerable part of American industry.

By April 1939 Chairman Madden was able to tell the Senate Labor Committee:

> Another profound factor in the decrease in industrial strife has been the making of thousands of agreements following upon the acceptance by employers of the principles of collective bargaining. These agreements have been made not only in the newly organized industries like iron and steel, automobile, rubber, flat glass, petroleum, electrical equipment, textile, and maritime. New agreements have been made by old and powerful unions, like the International Association of Machinists which now has more than 4,000 agreements, half of which represent agreements made for the first time or renewed in 1938, and many of which cover thousands of freshly organized workers in the aircraft, automobile repair, and office equipment industries; or like the Brotherhood of Teamsters which recently signed an agreement with seventeen truck companies operating in twelve States extending from Kentucky to Nebraska.

> These thousands of new agreements almost uniformly contain "no strike, no lockout" clauses, and thus represent additional insurance against industrial disputes. These provisions for the adjustment of disputes and grievances are the statutory mechanisms whereby the two great groups in industry, employers and employees, are learning the art of living together within the framework of an industrial democracy in the same way that our

citizens generally have learned the art of living together in a political democracy.

The numbers and stability of trade agreements indicate that the transition from general employer belligerence toward worker organization is shifting to employer acceptance of the bargaining procedure. Evidence of that drift is convincing, despite the very vocal protests of some employers who would halt the process by weakening the Labor Act.

Whether or not the Act will be allowed to function unimpaired is by no means clear, nor can it be until both Act and Board escape the hazards of being made political footballs.

Never in its four years has the Board been spared harassment. For its first eighteen months scores of injunctions crippled its activities. At the same time a large organized body of corporation lawyers denounced the Act as unconstitutional and advised their clients to ignore or defy it. Next a wave of strikes and sit-downs, in some measure the result of a cavalier rejection of the Act's principles, caused a misinformed public belief that the National Labor Relations Board was somehow at fault. Then appeared an assortment of proposals to amend the Act into a shadow of its original stature. All of these factors have been a deterrent to labor organization. Injunctions, the cries of unconstitutionality, refusals to comply with Board orders, dilatory tactics of employer lawyers and attempts to amend—each such attack on the National Labor Relations Act has discouraged workers in some degree from exercising their rights under the law.

At the same time the current labor situation has made the Board's work more difficult as well as more useful. In trying to act impartially it has ruffled the feathers of both organizations. If the A. F. of L. condemns the Board for invalidating collusive contracts, the CIO denounces the Board's doctrine of craft representation. Yet no Labor Board can know the security of doing a job without interruption so long as these internal difficulties continue. Proposed amendments which may yet wreck the Act stem from attempts to rig the law to suit a special organizing technique, and, further, give vast encouragement to a highly vocal minority of employer interest which hopes that eventually there may be no such thing as governmental intervention on behalf of labor's right to organize.

From the viewpoint of this book, the success of such efforts to devitalize the Act would be disastrous. For it is evident that in the American scene—tormented as it has been by powerful opposition to collective bargaining—the active principles of the National Labor Relations Law are needed to protect the free functioning of organized labor. This, in turn, is an underlying necessity for the maintenance of decent labor standards and, beyond that minimum, for the proper cooperation of men and management in effectively handling production problems.

When labor is organized it is in a position to act cohesively and effectively. If the employer is cooperative, this strength of organization can be directed toward improving methods and maintaining and increasing production.

Further consideration of these problems must take into account the fortunes of the National Labor Relations Act, for the continuing application of that law is basic to any advance in the relation of men and management from picket-line antagonists to cooperators. As the organized workers are permitted to take an attitude of cooperative interest, more and more will their full aptitudes be available for the common undertaking.

CHAPTER 17

TAPPING LABOR'S BRAINS[1]

THE substantial safeguards afforded labor unions by the Wagner Act may well mean the gradual introduction of democratic techniques into industry, thus bringing into the play the heads as well as the hands of the workers.[2] Because they are thus protected in their right to organize, the workers, for the first time in industrial history, can participate in the thinking which in the end makes or breaks all human institutions. This new freedom is bound to be stimulating to our political democracy.

Not many years ago the English economist, Marshall, stated that more than half the brain power of the world lies with the working classes and bemoaned the fact that so little use is being made of this resource. In the Navy ships used to be rated according to the thickness of the bulkhead which separates the quarters assigned to junior and senior officers. If there was an interested and friendly association between the two groups the bulkhead was said to be "thin." Where the senior officers were formal and stood on the prerogatives of rank the bulkhead was "thick." The thickness of a figurative bulkhead between men and management has thwarted the improvements which the workers, in intimate contact with the process of manufacture, might have contributed to industry.

Suggestion systems, which it was hoped would afford a means of communication, came into quite general vogue during the twenties,[3] although the Suggestion Box was a feature of "model" plants as early as 1910. There is a record of a set of such boxes—one for each department—which were regularly shown to the visitors to a famous factory and into which, over the years, not a single suggestion was ever dropped. On the whole, suggestion systems have not been profitable. And with reason. Foremen have always discouraged the use of the "suggestion box" or its equivalent on the theory that some employee might make a real contribution to the efficiency of the department, in which case the foreman might be asked the embarrassing question, "Why the heck didn't *you* think of that?" Then there is a tradition that to have direct dealings between an employee and the management above the foreman is "not done." Shop management and discipline have always been modeled on military lines: the boss gave the orders to department superintendents who transmitted them to the foreman, who transmitted them to the workers—and they were carried out. It was as unthinkable for an individual employee to go direct to the boss with a suggestion or a criticism as for a buck private to lay before the commanding general a possible change in tactics.

If these conventions were flouted on occasion by an employee with a valuable contribution, and if the suggestion were adopted, there was as a rule no adequate provision for a reward or for fair recognition. And there is no deterrent to cooperation so effective as unworthy recognition of successful effort. In brief, management has not been prepared to utilize the potentialities of the labor force in improving its methods. The individual was not strong enough to buck the tradition. Backed by an organization, the worker might get through this "bulkhead." But now modern technology seems to be setting up a new barrier.

Significant as the contributions of technology are to industrial development, the work of the technicians—engineers, chemists, designers, inventors and scientists—sometimes seems so spotlighted that the total picture is not brought into focus. You see a piece of machinery weighing many tons revolving hundreds—possibly thousands—of times a minute; an electric eye sorting beans or cigars for color or imperfections; adjustments accurate to 1/10,000th of an inch; steel sheets passing a given point in the line of manufacture at 15 miles per hour; soap in a whirling vat 150 tons at a mix—surely these accomplishments and thousands like them represent no mean performance. To the layman in the shop and out of it such inventions are so amazing that they distract attention from the great human drama of which they are only a part. But such feats are obviously the accomplishments of highly trained specialists, men whose success is based on their concentration on a single line, frequently a narrow one, and who therefore have neither interest nor facility in the broader tasks of management.

The employer of ten or ten thousand will admit that his technical problems are on the way to solution as soon as they are recognized. But the human problem—of give and take, of keeping the big things big and the little things little, of making another persons interests your own, of loyalty in the face of injustice, of doing your own task and a bit more when the other fellow falls down, of making all hands see the landfall through the murky weather, of resisting when you are tempted to make the day's routine dominant in your own life and that of others, of the use of good common sense —here are the real problems in all enterprise, for everyone in the organization, from the bottom to the top. Anything contributing to the solution of this complex adds stature to the contributor—whether he be top-boss or lowly private. The triumphs of technology threaten to dwarf the importance of personality. But industry's master problem will always be human.

More effective democracy is the mainspring of American progress. This means the adoption of more democratic political techniques—merit systems, short ballots, and so on—but even more important is the development in industry of the maximum democracy consistent with effective control. Political democracy cannot grow to full stature under the pressures of industrial autocracy.

In simpler days, when most Americans were ruggedly individualistic pioneers and farmers, democracy meant political democracy. But since our national life has grown more complex, since more and more of us have become corporation employees—industrial and commercial—opportunity for the average citizen to practice political democracy has diminished. A decreasing percentage of those eligible to vote now exercise the franchise. This is only one indication of the remoteness of political responsibilities today. Only through re-education can such an indifferent electorate be brought back to the hearty participation in public affairs that characterized the early days of the Republic.

Modern psychology shows that the most effective teaching is in the area of the pupil's interest. For most Americans, the workplace, after the home, is the center of major interest. Hence, to build up in the individual an understanding of democracy, a devotion to it, and facility in its practices, industry is the most promising field of endeavor. Democratic techniques and loyalties acquired in industry may be counted on to carry over into political fields, where such safeguards are sorely needed today. There is little hope of interesting the average man in political ideas and practices when his political experiences are largely confined to voting at widely spaced elections. By contrast, his contacts with industry fill every hour in the working day.

When the early union contracts were being signed, workers often expressed a desire to cooperate with management in "improving the business." These proffers were discouraged by management on the theory that "head work" was the prerogative of white collar folk. Though there has been some change in this attitude, even today there is all too much emphasis on the traditional barriers between management and men. And this in spite of the fact that during the last fifty years Scientific Management has made it clear that only through close cooperation between workers and employers can maximum production be secured.

Now, as management and labor through strong labor unions become more nearly equal in bargaining power, they can either wage war to gain the spoils of production restriction and scarcity prices, or they can together devise improved production practices that increase the social income. The second course is more in keeping with the potential age of plenty. Further, it opens up vast opportunities for democratic experience. For organized workers to come face to face with management's problems will have both an educational and sobering influence, just as management will be both educated and sobered by insight into the problems of unions. Power, wherever it lies, cannot in the long run be disassociated from responsibility. If the labor movement fails to develop an adequate sense of responsibility for output, the alternative will be increasing tension and bitterness over "wages, hours and working conditions," reducing the opportunity for constructive accommodation and community of interest between management and union.

Speaking generally, the developing attitude of industry toward its personnel may be divided into four phases:

I. Paternalistic and un-unionized.
II. The struggle for unionization ending in recognition, collective bargaining and a written contract.
III. A gradual strengthening in contractual relations and continued efforts toward improvement in "hours, wages and working conditions."
IV. The beginnings of labor-management collaboration for greater gross productivity in which both may share, thereby affording organized labor the fullest status and widest hearing consistent with unified direction and control of the enterprise.

During the first three of these phases—especially I and II—a decidedly militaristic type of leadership is dominant. Only as American industry enters the fourth stage—represented today by a few spearhead enterprises—will there be demand for labor leaders who are production conscious and who are ready and able to cooperate with management in furthering the common enterprise.

The leadership of unions still battling for recognition must necessarily be of a more rugged type than that of unions whose standing is accepted. To conduct successful strikes—and strikes involve picketing, the financing of large numbers of people out of work, maintenance of morale, court proceedings—calls for nerve, brawn, endurance and intense concentration on immediate issues. These are the qualities of the battlefield. On the employer's side periods of strife call for the same type of leadership. But given real recognition, the first evidence of which is a written contract, a union is free to choose leaders with characteristics appropriate to peace rather than war, to the practice of justice rather than of force. With the acceptance of collective bargaining as a necessary part of the modern scheme of things, leaders of labor in this country as in England, and especially as in Sweden, will manifest a growing solicitude for the national welfare as including the welfare of workers, in contrast to the current narrower conception of what constitutes labor's interests.

If the workers—the organized workers—are to have a more important part within the frame of the production process, labor's interest must be allowed to express itself in activity at all levels such as:

1. At the individual workplace
2. In the operation of the plant as a whole
3. In the local labor market
4. Throughout a given industry
5. Throughout the national industrial scene.

Given the growing interdependence of all industry, labor-management cooperation under a single employer is too limited a field. Cooperation confined to a single shop or even to a single enterprise may easily work to labor's disadvantage, and quite likely to a cutting down in the amount of employment available to the participating group. The important management problems of today and tomorrow are on the two higher levels: the intra-industry level, among concerns within the same industry; and the inter-industry level, among major industries; and between government and industry.

On a problem of national scope, for instance, it would be inspiring to see the whole organized labor movement cooperating with the organized employers—and the electrical industry—in an industry-wide investigation of the highly significant, and as yet unexplained, idiosyncrasies of the industrial load curve—the measure of the use of power, hour by hour, within a given industrial district as well as in the individual plant.

The labor of every individual in industry, whatever his status, must more and more be seen as a part of the total environment—political, social and economic as well as local, national and international. The organization of labor is increasingly directed to this end. The realization that what finally gets into the pay envelope is influenced by considerations over which the individual employer may have little control, is giving labor an entirely new attitude toward employers as a group. There are even indications that labor holds itself responsible for the education of employers after a fashion that would have been inconceivable a decade or two ago.

In considering the kinds of questions appropriate for labor-management discussion and research, the adjustment of grievances should be put to one side. Theoretically, in a well-run enterprise there are no grievances. They are a decidedly negative factor. When they arise they should be handled expeditiously, according to an agreed procedure. If the idea of a common attack on production problems gets enmeshed in grievance machinery it might as well be abandoned. The further apart the two functions are kept the better. The techniques suited to battling over grievances are seldom those useful in solving production problems.

A secondary objective of labor-management cooperation is to give employees at least as much information about the business as the firm makes available to its shareholders. The major purpose is to have organized labor take part in analyzing the problems of industry, in studying the problems of management, in adapting the policies and relationships of the enterprise to the conditions which provide its economic opportunity for existence and ultimately control its destiny. The knowledge needed in dealing with such problems may call for formal study under the guidance of experts, as well as the knowledge gained through daily experience on the job. Labor-management discussion and research is usually a process which combines and utilizes both types of knowledge, sifting the facts, stating them clearly, and analyzing their implications. This sort of fact organizing and diagnosis leads to definition of objectives and then to ways and means.

Several bits of testimony may clarify the process and its possibilities. The manager of an exceptionally well-managed plant manufacturing large, complicated machines writes:

> I found that by taking time off to discuss production methods with the men in the shop I was able to devise, through their suggestions and assistance, methods which saved millions of dollars in a few years' time. I discovered that the men in the shops,

although having much knowledge which could be applied with benefit, hesitated to advance any suggestions unless approached in an informal way and questioned.

And from Charlton Ogburn, well known attorney for labor organizations:

Several years ago I acted as impartial arbitrator between the Georgia Power Company and its transportation employees in the City of Atlanta. In addition to wages and hours I had many questions involving conditions of work to settle by an arbitration award. One question involved a change of schedule of street cars, especially to decrease the number of swing runs. The Company maintained that the changes demanded by the union were absolutely impossible. The union's position was that by re-routing of cars, etc., these changes could easily be made. I asked the Company if it would consent to let a committee of the union have access to its schedules, spend several days in going over them, and then bring forward the revised schedules as the union stated the schedules should be. The Company seemed to hesitate, said it was futile but, nevertheless, on my insistence, agreed. I adjourned the hearing for a week. At the end of the week the union brought in its new schedules. The Company seemed greatly surprised that they did, in fact, accomplish the demands of the union and decreased the swing runs, made many other improvements and instead of costing the Company anything to make these changes an actual saving resulted.

Even more convincing is the testimony of Wallace Clark, a leading industrial engineer based on practice in twelve European countries and service to four governments, including our own:

Differences of industry, business conditions, geography, family or national temperament, psychology, language, politics or government, present no real obstacle when there is simple agreement on what is to be done. On the contrary, a planning technique which is scientific, automatically and impersonally removes all seeming obstacles, and clears the way to results which had been considered impossible.

There has been an unusual opportunity to contrast industry which is autocratic with that which is not. In the former, agreement is more quickly reached and action is taken with greater singleness of purpose. But democratic control draws deeper drafts of technical knowledge, skill, administrative and creative abilities of all who are concerned.

This experience has deepened the conviction that scientific planning, which is democratic in purpose, methods and control can evoke and direct dynamic forces which are invincible and can realize, in the most practical, workmanlike manner, the greatest measure of prosperity and security.[4]

It is encouraging to note that these same democratic techniques are being applied with marked success in areas quite distinct from industry. The operations of the Farm Security Administration, for example, are continually influenced by a stream of suggestions and recommendations flowing upwards from FSA borrowers, county supervisors, and voluntary local committees. Some of the recommendations from borrowers have resulted in changes in operations on a national scale. Thus the form for the farm and home plan, which is the foundation for standard rehabilitation loans, has been revised several times to meet the suggestions of borrowers and county supervisors. In a number of instances a single field employee has profoundly influenced the agency's entire program.

While fully recognizing the value of collegiate and other specialized forms of training for expert service, even in the scientific field it is admitted that the highest grade of work in many lines can be conducted by those with aptitude and devotion but without the slightest trace of orthodox technical education. As one savant quaintly puts it, "You do not have to know French to use plaster of Paris." In the Carnegie Nutrition Laboratory in Cambridge, Massachusetts, some years ago the distinguished Director found satisfaction in the fact that included among the small staff engaged in attenuated scientific researches were a number whose only technical training had been obtained right in that laboratory doing the day's work. Among them was a man who had formerly been an express driver and one woman—formerly a nursemaid—who was now "as competent in gas analyses as any one in the world." The Colorado Museum of Natural History in Denver some years back, needing a man to tend boilers, employed one whose only training had been in heavy toil in an iron works. After two years on the boilers he was given an opportunity to work on the exhibits of extinct plants and animals with the result that today he is among our most experienced and respected paleontologists.

The La Guardia administration in New York City is responsible for the appointment of a liberal Board of Higher Education, and the Board in turn is liberalizing the administration of the city colleges, which annually enroll more than 30,000 students.

The Board has adopted for the College of the City of New York a new set of regulations under which the members of the faculty elect their own heads of departments and matters of policy are settled in conference by the interested staff members, instead of being handed down from the top. This democratic change, it is reported, has greatly impressed the student body, and out of it is coming not only increased administrative efficiency but, even more valuable, a harmonious relationship between students and faculty on a traditionally stormy campus. The results are apparent throughout these city institutions, in practical matters, as well as in attitudes and spirit. A chronic traffic jam at the elevators in one of the skyscraper buildings resulted in a condition of constant lateness in getting to classes. As part of their course in business management, and under the direction of their professor, a group of selected students tackled the problem and worked out and put into operation a plan which increased the effectiveness of the service by 50 per cent. The improvement was so well received by the student body that it became a permanent feature of the college administration, students forming their own lines in the absence of a traffic director and entering the elevators without confusion.

The methods here discussed, bringing about maximum collaboration between labor and management to increase production, represent no departure from tested American theory and practice. The object is not to determine what part of the rewards of industry and commerce should belong to management, ownership, and labor; to establish a scheme which gives employees a predetermined monetary share in profits; to have labor assume management's indispensable authority and responsibility; to duplicate personnel management by having employee groups take part in disciplinary action; nor to mediate grievances and settle strikes. The objective is none of these things. The goal is to establish mechanisms which will make organized labor an active participant in determining production procedures and administrative policies designed to increase the output and distribution of goods and services.

Labor's traditional attitude has been a serious obstacle to the collaboration here discussed, for labor wants security of tenure for the worker's job and instinctively opposes enlarged production in fear of technological unemployment. But management's attitude is an equally stubborn obstacle, for management insists that it has the sole responsibility for production and hence cannot risk any dilution of its authority. Ultimately both types of opposition can and must be resolved. The dearth of experience and techniques required for so fundamental a change in attitude and procedure is painfully apparent.[5] However, recognition of the opportunity is half the battle. Granted that the suggested change will be of long-run social benefit, it seems safe to assume that the means requisite to its accomplishment will be found.

If we look forward to an era when American industry is again as virile as its past, and at the same time as productive as modern science and invention can make it, then this new status for labor becomes an imperative demand. The capacity of the democracies so to organize their economic life is challenged by the authoritarian countries in which individual rights and the rights of labor are ruthlessly sacrificed. Implicit in the world situation today is the necessity to increase the capacity of this country to produce and to consume, not by rigid authoritarianism but by giving free play to the democratic principle. And if over-centralization is the hallmark of the totalitarian state, then freedom and opportunity are the proofs of democracy. A potent force on the side of the American scheme of things is the effort to give every worker a responsible part in the enterprise to which he contributes his skill and his labor and through which he strives to maintain and to improve his standard of living.[6] A potent influence in bringing about the scheme of things here advocated will be adult education facilities of a type discussed in the next chapter.

CHAPTER 18

ADULT EDUCATION FOR MANAGEMENT AND MEN

More than a century ago, in March, 1834, the trade-unions of the country convened in New York to protest the existing "monopoly of education" by the "privileged classes," and to urge an "equal and universal system of education." Free public education was not one of the original doctrines of the American people, and agitation by the trade-unions was largely responsible for its development. In a rapidly expanding economy labor saw in education the opportunity for the individual to acquire the productive skill and cultural background which would further his economic and social betterment. Plenty of jobs and the flexibility of the social structure made education seem the one thing needed to fulfill the ambitions of the worker.

American industrial life developed and productive processes became more complicated, formal education and training were increasingly important, and schooling was accepted as a public responsibility. Trade and vocational schools were gradually established to supplement grade and high schools, while engineering colleges and business schools appeared and began to turn out specialized candidates for "white collar" jobs. Within a century after that protest meeting in New York, a vast educational system endowed with billions of dollars, public and private, had grown up to train the youth of a rapidly expanding industrial civilization.

How well this complicated and expensive educational machinery does its job is a question widely discussed today. American schools and schooling are in a cross fire of criticism. Subject to thousands of uncoordinated local controls, ponderous and inflexible, its funds and jobs always alluring to political bosses, American education is charged with being uncertain in aim, fumbling in method, smothered in outworn academic trappings, remote from the lives and interests of the students who attend the schools and the taxpayers who support them. This dissatisfaction is expressed in the many current experiments with new curricula, new tools and methods of instruction; and in elaborate studies of the educational system and its product, most notable among them being the monumental Regents' Inquiry Into the Character and Cost of Public Education in New York State, characterized as "the most important educational document of the decade."[1]

Along with this yeasty ferment in the going educational system, is a growing conviction that education has been too much limited to school and college classrooms, and to immature years. There is emerging a broader concept of education as a lifelong adventure, and an increasing emphasis on educational opportunity for adults. Adult education—vocational, cultural, recreational—is not a new thing in this country, though the movement has reached no such stature as it has attained in other countries, particularly in Denmark and Sweden, where today it is the cornerstone of economic and political life.[2]

The earliest adult education efforts in this country go back to colonial days when, before the beginnings of public education, schoolmasters often conducted evening schools for the men of the community. As in the day schools for children, a fee was paid for instruction, and the subjects offered accorded with the demands of the pupils. All classes of society attended these evening schools, but they were particularly popular with young and ambitious clerks and mechanics. An advertisement printed in the *New York Gazette* in 1755 gives quite a picture of the evening schools of two hundred years ago:[3]

NOTICE is hereby GIVEN that
JOHN SEARSON
Who teaches School at the House of Mrs. Coon opposite to the Post Office, proposes (God Willing) to open an Evening School, on Thursday the 25th of this Instant September; where may be learned Writing, Arithmetic Vulgar and Decimal, Merchants Ac-

counts, Mensuration, Geometry, Trigonometry, Surveying, Dialling, and Navigation in a short, plain and methodical Manner, and at very reasonable Rates. Said Searson having a large and commodious Room, together with his own dilligent Attendance, the Scholars will have it in their Power to make a good Progress in a short Time.

With the establishment of public schools, many communities continued or adopted the custom of evening schools for adults employed during the day. Night schools, as they came to be called, are today an important part of the public school systems of many states and cities. They have, in many communities, developed special classes and courses for foreign-born men and women who want to learn to speak, read and write English, and to acquire the elementary knowledge of American history and civics required for citizenship. Classes for illiterates, native and foreign born; courses leading to eighth grade and high school diplomas for those forced to leave school at an early age; vocational and trade training; classes in music, art and drama; in social and aesthetic dancing—a detailed list of the offerings of the night schools for adults today would fill many pages. University extension courses are an adaptation of the old colonial evening school on a higher educational level. Hundreds of thousands of eager students make use of such opportunities during each week of the school year.

In addition to formal classes and courses, there are scores of less rigidly organized adult education projects in this country. Since the early days of the lyceums and the Chautauquas, such undertakings have appeared in countless forms and under many auspices. Forums, discussion groups, reading clubs, lecture courses, correspondence courses—the list could be endlessly extended, and divided into efforts which are purely recreational and cultural, and those designed to increase the student's vocational equipment and hence add to his earning capacity.[4]

But admirable as is all this opportunity for self-improvement and the creative use of leisure, it has no direct bearing on the subject of this book. For, like the education offered children and young people today, adult education in general seldom comes to grips with the labor-management problem of production.

Institutions of higher learning have always accepted a responsibility toward the learned professions. Indeed, college enrollments of a few generations ago were largely made up of young men looking forward to careers in the ministry, in education, or in law. Educational institutions have in the last two or three decades taken an increasing interest in training for leadership in business and industry as well as in professions. Today, well-endowed schools of business administration stand cheek by jowl with schools of law and education on many university and college campuses.

But while the training of management leaders has progressed to a place in the educational system, the training of labor leaders is pretty much left to chance. So far as anyone takes any responsibility for it, it is left to the labor movement itself. Many present-day leaders in business and industry began their lifework with formal training for their careers. The labor leaders of this generation, on the other hand, were generally forced to leave school not only without preparation for leadership, but when they were too young to have acquired habits of reading and study. After being elected to office by his union, the labor leader tries to pick up whatever knowledge and skill he can to fit himself for his new responsibilities. He often feels the handicap of his limited schooling, and yet the contradiction between what he was taught in school and the realities of his industrial experience is apt to make him suspicious of educators. According to Meiklejohn college graduates frequently entertain like sentiments.

Training courses developed by large corporations and business houses for their employees have been primarily vocational. Plant schools, training institutes, and correspondence courses, often conducted with the cooperation of university extension divisions or the vocational schools of the community, have sought to enhance the worker's skill but have not been concerned with his background or with his relationship to larger social-economic problems. By increasing the employee's skill, his productivity and hence his value to the employer is increased. "Training on the job" has become a popular management activity but its purposes have been strictly limited to improving the trainee as a worker.

Out of the needs of the labor movement, there has therefore developed a special type of adult education, known as workers' education. Like other kinds of after-school opportunity, workers' education in this country has lagged behind the movement in other industrial nations. But in the last decade, workers' education has moved forward rapidly in the United States, not only in the number of participants, but in philosophy and method, in preparation of appropriate study materials, and in widespread recognition of its importance by educators and by the public.

Workers' education grew out of the failure of educators to afford wage earners, in school or as adults, opportunity to study their own problems from the labor viewpoint. It has developed a scheme of thought and teaching which is distinct from other forms of education. To this new agency, thousands of wage earners now turn for an understanding of the background and the current issues of industrial enterprise, and for the training of their leaders.

In 1918, the American Federation of Labor appointed a committee to study and report on workers' education. Educational programs were undertaken by central labor unions in several industrial cities, and in 1921 the Workers' Education Bureau of America was established as a clearing house of information and a guidance center for the growing movement. Two years later, the A. F. of L. made the bureau its official educational agency.

During the Twenties a number of resident schools for workers were established. One of the best known of these was the summer school for women workers in industry, first established on the Bryn Mawr campus, now located in a building of its own at Vineyard Shore, New York. The University of Wisconsin conducted a similar summer school, enrolling both men and women. Today five workers' schools, i.e., Bryn Mawr; Berkeley, California; Madison, Wisconsin; Asheville, North Carolina; Chicago, Illinois, are associated together as The Affiliated Schools for Workers.

Workers' classes, forums, week-end institutes, and resident schools emphasize the teaching of labor economics, social history, and labor problems. Most of these undertakings maintain a precarious existence, since they are financed only by the unions and by contributions from liberal friends of the labor movement. With few exceptions public funds were not available for workers' education until federal money was appropriated for work relief, including projects creating jobs for unemployed teachers.

The growth of union organization since 1934 has greatly increased the interest of the labor movement in education. While many older union leaders look on education as an unnecessary "frill," the enlargement of the labor movement, and with it, the sudden promotion of thousands of workers to responsible positions, has created a mounting demand for training in union leadership.

Foremost in meeting this need has been the Workers' Education Division of the Works Progress Administration, which has assigned unemployed teachers to help build union programs, and has worked out much up-to-date, inexpensive study material. Many of the new CIO unions have made workers' education one of their official activities, while older unions like the Amalgamated Clothing Workers have greatly expanded their efforts in this field.

New emphasis is being placed upon training officers in meeting the day-to-day problems of union administration. The Steel Workers Organizing Committee, the United Rubber Workers, the Textile Workers Union, and the United Auto Workers are among the larger unions which have organized systematic courses in grievance adjustment procedures, management relations, and "tool" courses in public speaking, union bookkeeping, labor journalism, and parliamentary law. Instruction is given at central labor schools, through regional training conferences, and at week-end institutes, as well as at resident summer short courses and summer camps. In 1939 more than a thousand officers from eight international unions were receiving intensive training in union administrative techniques at a summer camp in Pennsylvania conducted by the CIO.

The formal training of the present generation of management leaders, insofar as it was concerned with labor at all, dealt almost exclusively with the worker in terms of his efficiency as a unit of production. According to the Wickenden Report, sponsored by the Society for the Promotion of Engineering Education, in 1929 only 13 per cent of the curricula of schools of engineering was concerned with nontechnical subjects. Most engineering students, unlike most candidates for law, medicine, the ministry, and education, go direct from high school to a technical school. There they are highly trained in the arts of production, but the products of engineering education are turned out with at best a meager introduction to the problems of distribution, consumption, and of industrial relations.

Another great training field for management, the schools of commerce and business administration, has largely adjusted its teaching to the attitudes of the business world for which its students are prepared. On the whole, the views current in such schools accord with those of the typical business leader, and are antagonistic to organized labor. Courses in personnel management and industrial relations have usually dwelt on incentive and bonus systems, welfare plans, and labor turnover—all from the point of view of "efficiency." Little attention has been given to union-management relations, or to the worker's standard of living, his job security, or the problem of old age. Courses in money and banking, corporation structure and finance, accounting, advertising, and taxation have not encouraged critical examination of existing practices except from the standpoint of their effectiveness as profit-making or money-saving devices. Certainly few management leaders have been fitted by their formal education to develop broad social vision or sympathetic understanding of labor problems and practices.

During the five years between 1934 and 1939, the new labor legislation and the increasingly important role of organized labor in industrial affairs have stimulated a fresh interest in labor viewpoints among management leaders. While this concern is often apprehensive rather than sympathetic, it has led to analysis of long-established practices and prejudices.

Management officials are extending their knowledge of labor questions by attending short courses and conferences for business executives which have been organized by Princeton, Massachusetts Institute of Technology, Pennsylvania State College, the University of Michigan, and other institutions. Economists and specialists in industrial research, whose study has given them insight into both labor and management attitudes, have helped formulate rounded and objective programs for these adult education projects. At their instigation, prominent labor leaders have been invited to a number of campuses to address audiences of management leaders, and to contribute to round-table discussions of union-management relations.

Similarly, labor problems have gained a prominent place on the programs of annual conferences of business associations, and union leaders have been asked to speak at sessions of such bodies as the Society for the Advancement of Management, the Personnel Research Federation, the American Management Association, and the National Industrial Conference Board.

Since 1929 labor problems and industrial relations have had a more important place in the curricula of business schools. Labor leaders have been called in to lecture to classes and sometimes have stayed over for informal "bull sessions" in the evening, covering a wide range of subjects bearing on labor organization.

In industry itself, new problems arising from collective bargaining are being discussed in special courses and conferences for lower supervisory employees. While foreman training is not an innovation, current emphasis upon the foreman's responsibility in establishing harmonious relations with unionized employees is a new and significant phase of management training.

On the other hand, unions are inviting representatives of management to meet with them and talk over new ideas in the field of economics and industrial relations. In the spring of 1939, thirty steel executives met in Pittsburgh as guests of the Steel Workers Organizing Committee, to hear and discuss an address by a nationally known economist. A similar educational experiment by the Steel Workers Organizing Committee is the monthly meeting at McKees Rocks, near Pittsburgh, where local union officers from seventeen steel plants play host to their foremen and supervisors, and join with them in examining the causes of friction in their collective bargaining relations. The frank exchange of ideas by union and management spokesmen at these conferences has generated a better spirit and a clearer understanding of the industry's problems and practices as seen by employers and workers.

Across the continent a similar plan is operated in reverse. There the California plant of the Paraffine Companies, Incorporated, sponsors a course for union leaders. The course is conducted by the California State Department of Education and the management on company property, with two University of California Instructors as teachers, the officers of the eighteen CIO and A.F. of L. unions represented in the plant, as students. The program deals with collective bargaining problems, developed from the labor point of view. Unlike the union-initiated meetings at McKees Rocks, management representatives are excluded from the class.

Although each situation must be separately considered, under most circumstances there are many advantages in inviting management representatives at least to some sessions of workers' educational projects, and *vice versa*. Joint courses might even be tried. Too often employers and employees come to close quarters only in the tense and emotional atmosphere of a controversy or a strike. The exchange of ideas in a friendly setting provides opportunity for patterns of group thinking and cooperative action to evolve.

So long as the right to organize was blocked, and unions struggled for status in a hostile environment, the intellectual insolation of business and labor from one another was inevitable. Workers' education has developed in an atmosphere of conflict, and its teaching for years reflected the grimness of labor's fight. Partisan to the labor cause, cut off from other educational agencies, workers' education has been in the eyes of most educators "propaganda" rather than education. Proponents of workers' education in turn pointed to the unreality of the "classical" economics taught by the schools, and the close parallel with the conservative concepts prevailing in business circles. As new viewpoints begin to bridge the gap between the thinking of business and of labor groups, and as universities widen their horizons by objective research in economics and labor problems, higher educational institutions may be expected to adapt themselves to the training needs of both management and men. Then the unions need not try to carry the full responsibility for training their leaders.

There is also a place in the public schools, particularly on the secondary level, for courses laying the groundwork for union leadership. Nor would such consideration of the labor point of view on the productive process and industrial relations come amiss in the education of future business leaders and professional workers. And if labor were convinced it could trust the fairness and objectivity of the public school system, there would be many advantages in having workers' education a part of the adult education program now going forward in the schools of many communities.

There is a precedent for publicly financed workers' education in the program of the Works Progress Administration. It is obvious, however, that the limitations of a relief set-up cannot adequately meet the need for a well-planned, continuing program with specially equipped teachers. Workers' education, financed by state funds and carried on by the universities of California and Wisconsin, and by Rutgers University more clearly mark out the direction of effective labor leadership training under public auspices.

Training in specific union organizational and administrative techniques is properly the function of the unions themselves. But in the broader study of economic and social questions, labor legislation and history, the colleges and universities—public and private—should have a part to play. To teach mature and skeptical adult workers, however, requires methods and materials differing from those effective in teaching youth. In successful workers' education, abstractions and theory as such are to be avoided. The emphasis must rather be placed on concrete facts and practical situations, from the discussion of which, with wise guidance, general principles emerge. Tact, imagination, and flexibility are required of the teacher of adult workers, and experience demonstrates that by no means all successful college and university instructors succeed with worker-students.

In several industrial centers, university extension evening

classes for workers are being conducted during the college year dealing with industrial relations problems. These might well be extended and supplemented with summer short courses for industrial workers, similar to the conferences and institutes now provided on many college campuses for business executives, farmers, and professional groups. Under such a plan, wage earners could have an intensive one- or two-week course during their paid vacation period without loss of income or risk of losing their jobs. Not only the union and the individual worker but also the college stands to gain from such projects. Interested faculty members would have opportunity to study social and economic problems from life rather than from books; and their thinking and "book learning" would be challenged by the realism of those who spend their lives as wage earners. Such an experience in workers' education would enrich their regular academic work.

Beyond the problem of bringing labor viewpoints into the schools and colleges, and of workers' education projects, is the problem of teacher training. If teachers are to understand the forces at work in an industrial economy, and contribute to enlightened thinking in their classrooms, their professional education must give them not only acquaintance with approved methods of teaching, but insight into the problems and issues of the world beyond the shelter of academic walls. With few exceptions, this will be possible only as teachers' colleges become more flexible and more realistic in what and how they teach their students.

There is of course no cure-all for the difficulties of industrial relations. But it is beyond question that if such education as we have discussed in this chapter were general throughout the ranks of management and labor, it would raise the objectives and the activities of employer associations and of labor unions to a higher plane. Certainly the quiet, undramatic forces of education are the most effective weapons for destroying the power of bureaucrats and racketeers on both sides.

Already recognition of labor organizations by employers, and joint participation of both groups in the handling of common problems, are turning warring industrial factions toward socially constructive activity. One result of this is

ADULT EDUCATION

that labor leaders are taking a more active part in public affairs. The value of such recruits in the battle for good government was well described recently by Newbold Morris, president of the Council of the City of New York:

> No group of civic associations has ever been successful in arousing more than a spontaneous effort to eliminate graft and waste from City government. There have been occasional victories, but good government must have a stronger foundation for sustaining influences. I earnestly hope that you (the Committee of Seventy, Philadelphia) will turn to the great masses of citizens for support. Go to organized labor and ask the leaders of organized labor to make your cause theirs, for no decent labor movement can grow where municipal corruption exists. In New York City we have found that the two great movements, the labor movement and municipal reform, go hand in hand.[5]

Mr. Morris was discussing city government. His words apply with equal force to state and national affairs.

In earlier chapters of this book we have pointed out, that many of the major problems besetting our national life today are only solvable through the joint efforts of management and organized labor. Persistent large-scale unemployment, technological change, insecurity of earnings, the competition of sub-standard employers—these are among the grave matters that press for solution. Whether these, and equal maladjustments can be resolved within the framework of American democracy depends in large part upon the wisdom and skill which leaders of the employers and of the unions bring to bear on their responsibilities. Here is the urgent need, the vast opportunity of adult education for both management and men.

CHAPTER 19

A FREE SOCIETY AND A BETTER LIFE

It is the fashion to be pessimistic about the future of American democracy. Discount as heavily as we please the propagandistic pessimism of "Big Business," and the imitative pessimism of little business, we yet must recognize that hosts of fair-minded men and women look without much hope toward the future of our economic and political system. Progress, we are told, is an illusion, bred of a century and a half in which the western countries, mercilessly exploiting their own natural resources, could thrust the liabilities of technical advance upon the masses of Asia and Africa, bound hand and foot by their traditional economic methods. The natural resources have in large measure been wasted, and the countries that counted as backward a century ago have made great strides in industrialism, presenting a redoubtable competition to the United States and Western Europe. We are told that the epoch of imperialistic trade is closing, and that the economic expansion which followed that trade is approaching its end. It appears to follow, then, that the economic depression persisting with us since 1929 has come to stay, unless we go over to a scheme of economic organization radically different from the traditional scheme of free enterprise, or as it is usually named, the profit system.

Democracy, as we have known it in the modern world, has been a concomitant of the extension of economic opportunity. The early American colonists had no notion that they were setting up a system under which all persons would have equal political rights. Every colony had its upper and middle class, its servants bound and free. Opportunity, consisting through the first three hundred years of American history of free land, broke up the remnants of the feudal

A FREE SOCIETY AND A BETTER LIFE 235

order and established political equality. Trade-unionism, facilitated in its strivings by the forces of economic expansion, endowed a large section of the landless with the economic security and self-respect that are essential prerequisites of a realistic democracy. In Western Europe the labor movement, through the era of economic expansion, succeeded in winning for the worker political enfranchisement and, what is far more important, political competence. Even without the opportunity represented by vast tracts of free land, war-free nations like Switzerland and the Scandinavian countries succeeded in establishing a political system quite as democratic as that of the United States. England and France also earned the title of democracy, in spite of class control in many important areas, including foreign and imperial affairs, peace and war. But to repeat, all these achievements of democracy rested upon the economic expansion of the western world, upon that economic expansion which we are now assured has come to its final conclusion.

What truth is there in the doctrine that economic expansion is a phenomenon of the past, and that for the future we must take in our economic sails? The prime mover in economics is today, as it ever has been and ever will be, economic needs backed by purchasing power. It makes no difference, from the economic point of view, whether the needs that invite us to produce are domestic, colonial or international. It is their volume that counts. So it is the volume of available purchasing power, wherever located, that counts. And in spite of latter-day skepticism, one may still affirm that by and large purchasing power arises out of productive power.

The western world never had so great a volume of conscious unsatisfied needs as today. It never commanded so vast a volume of unused productive power. The prime movers of a vast economic expansion are at hand, but we have not known how to gear them in.

Our industrial population needs more milk, meat, fruit, fresh vegetables than it gets. Our farmers need more clothing, better housing, more cars, more electric power, than they get. Here are obvious reciprocal markets, but they fail to mesh. Wherever one looks in our economic system one becomes conscious of needs reciprocally related, of productive powers reciprocally related, and the failure of meshing.

That is one aspect of the present crisis. Another is the presence in every industrial country of branches of trade and industry that are excessively developed in relation to any prospective need, and of other branches that are dying. The world is geared to produce more sugar than it can eat, more cotton than it will wear. In every highly developed country the heavy industries are overdeveloped relatively to the work they have to do in replacing equipment and in providing for a conservative expansion of plants. The silk worm is threatened with the fate of the indigo plant, as invention extends the scope of industrial textiles.

A condition like this, a vast volume of needs unsupplied—pressing needs, for decent housing and clothing and adequate food; a vast volume of unemployed or partially employed labor power and mechanical power together with the patent evidence of hopeless misadjustment, inevitably causes old men to see visions and young men to dream dreams. Were this not so we should be in a bad way. We should prove ourselves inertly despairing, like Bengalese under flood or drought. Our visions and dreams are at least active responses to a situation we have no right to respond to passively. That the Technocrats, Upton Sinclair, the Townsendites, the spend-ourselves-rich crowd, the inflationists, the deflationists, the budget balancers, Dr. Ezekiel and many other political inventors have won wide followings is an encouraging symptom of the real state of the national mind. The mass of Americans do not follow the press and its financial backers in the puerile formula, "Beat Roosevelt and all will be well." The plain man knows that the job is bigger than that.

We must regularize employment: to this all but the Neanderthal reactionaries will agree in principle. Ten or twelve million unemployed after nine years of effort to cope with the problem is a frightful indictment of our system. Grant that some millions of them would have been unemployed even if these had been boom years: this only shows that the evil is deeper than depression.

We must abate the evil, or confess our inability to prevent its growing to disastrous proportions in a coming crisis: pro-

A FREE SOCIETY AND A BETTER LIFE

portions disastrous first of all to the victims, starving and freezing, but next to our entire economic and social system. In what we once judged to be the most orderly nation in the world we have seen the unemployed mobilized to establish the dictatorship of National Socialism, which holds in the hollow of its hand every right whether of labor or of property and proudly boasts that it has completely extirpated the democratic idea and all the liberties of speech, of conscience, of domicile and movement that go with it. We are not reputed a specially orderly people. We cannot carry the risk of chronic and increasing unemployment.

The Soviet and the Nazi governments have eliminated unemployment through the institutions of economic planning, and through absolute control of labor and property. So far, good. But if one examines the cases more closely they do not look so good. By thrusting millions of men into the armies and other millions into armament factories and the building of military roads and fortifications those governments have relieved the labor market of the unemployed. But their planning has no place for a decent standard of living: on the contrary, the worker is supplied with cannon instead of butter, propaganda instead of meat. And if the underfed worker's knees tremble on the job, to the detriment of his performance, an hour or two must be added to his working day. He does not remonstrate, because the government has powerful means for quelling even the mildest protest.

That is not our road to the future.

But if Germany and Russia can plan their economy for war, is it possible for us to plan our economy for peace? For a time we listened to the seductive plans of the Technocrats. Place the engineer in charge of our economic system. Let him calculate the consumption needs of the people, and satisfy them by the most efficient means known to the engineering profession. An average of four hours' work—sometimes it was put much lower—would supply the needs of all the population far more abundantly than they are now supplied. To hosts of people the project at first seemed sound in principle. There are undoubtedly tremendous wastes in our system: badly located, inefficient plants operated along with plants properly located and efficiently equipped, and perhaps tied together with a financial net extracting out of the consumer enough to cover highest costs. No one with eyes can have failed to note instances of production, not controlled by the engineer who understands production, but miscontrolled by the financier who does not understand it.

There are abundant expert criticisms of the Technocratic scheme, but this was not what killed interest in it. On second thought the average American could not see himself making a good life out of suckling his sustenance from automatic machinery under distant control. He could not see the promise of democratic personal independence under engineers with sufficiently autocratic power to operate so grandiose a system efficiently.

And the same condemnation has been extended to most of the later schemes of national industrial planning. The average man knows that to plan the operations of even a comparatively simple enterprise like a modern hotel and keep it running smoothly takes all the attention of a first-rate man, who must not be interfered with by financial or administrative higher ups. There are indeed great corporations that operate a miscellany of diverse enterprises, but one hears enough gossip from the inside of the evils of bureaucracy, the senseless interference from the New York office, to doubt that "general planning" is much more than a paper function, the real sources of the strength of such a corporation lying elsewhere, probably in Wall Street.

And if we are told that Germany manages to plan its industry effectively, dictating to each factory what quantities and what qualities it shall produce, what raw material it shall buy, what loans it shall have, what it must pay labor and what prices it must fix on its product, the answer is promptly forthcoming: German industry can not compete on any international market except by aid of subsidies or by political pressure.

This is not our road.

Suppose we consider the opposite extreme, to win order out of the planlessness of the existing situation by a method akin to insurance. This proposal has been brilliantly elucidated by Mordecai Ezekiel.

As matters stand today, when a factory fails to secure

A FREE SOCIETY AND A BETTER LIFE 239

orders it lays off men. The drying up of the pay roll immediately hits the local merchant who must curtail his orders for goods, to the distress of other producers; and thus the evil spreads concentrically, a single item in the mechanism of depression. Let the government agree to take the products as the factory turns them out, in case the market will not take them. The government will take the products, at a remunerative, but not highly lucrative price, and trust to its ability to unload them later. Pay rolls would maintain their level, local trade would continue as usual, and since the system would be in force generally, how could a depression get under way?

Dr. Ezekiel will regard this brief statement as a thumbnail caricature of his really profound analysis. If, however, his plan could be put adequately in a few lines he would not have written a long book. But here only a few lines are available. Are taxpayers prepared to take steel billets at a price the Iron and Steel Institute would consider remunerative? Will the iron and steel men let us sell our holdings when the market again booms and they have a chance at a killing, or will they force a gentlemen's agreement upon the government restricting public sales to Patagonia or Guam? It is universal experience that when government does business with business, government gets stung and business gets sore, forgetting promptly that government saved its skin. It is hard to find a businessman saved from bankruptcy by PWA orders who is not now roaring about a balanced budget.

This is obviously the simplest case, a raw material which may be stored indefinitely at no other cost than interest on the capital required to hold it. How large a proportion of our production falls into this class? Possibly ten per cent, although this figure is probably an exaggeration. All other commodities are subject to deterioration or fluctuations in style. Stabilization of even ten per cent of our production would help, but by itself would hardly do the job. To work the plan effectively the government would need to accept the losses from deterioration and obsolescence over a wide range of production. The government might be in for heavy losses in spite of the insurance feature provided.

We might more safely follow a plan proposed by the late

Malcolm Rorty, to subsidize the marketing of industrial and agricultural products at home as we now subsidize the low cost housing industry and the export of cotton. There is some price at which it is possible to sell our normal production of automobiles, refrigerators, Diesel locomotives, clothing, shoes, hats. Perhaps this price falls twenty per cent under cost of production. Let the government stand ready to make up the difference. The government would take a loss once for all, but the national economy would escape the losses of interest on capital tied up in stored goods and of deterioration and obsolescence. Even so, would not the cost be colossal, in a depression profound enough to reduce national income from eighty to forty-five billions?

Mr. Rorty's answer was that no depression could have gone so deep if his plan had been operating. The subsidized industries would be doing business as usual, keeping up their pay rolls as usual. Goods would move in the wholesale and retail trades as usual; if at the lower prices contemplated in the subsidy grant, they would move more rapidly than usual. Gradually the subsidy would eliminate itself under rising prices.

Is that our road? Note that it would operate to freeze industry just where it stands. It would oversubsidize the more efficient plant in order to keep the less efficient alive. It would hold up the sinking industries and perpetuate the evil of overexpansion, unless the government, like that of Germany, entered into the accounts of each individual concern and considered its particular need; and adopted a plan for gradually curtailing the overgrown branches and pruning away the dying ones. But that would be virtually government operation—government operation not for profits but for losses.

It is not our road.

How about spending ourselves out of depression? This idea, so revolting to tradition-minded economists and often to businessmen who have been saved from bankruptcy by it has been entertained by multitudes of lay thinkers for hundreds of years. In the seventeenth century it found delightful expression in Mandeville's Fable of the Bees; in recent years it attained respectability through the powerful

A FREE SOCIETY AND A BETTER LIFE 241

arguments of John Maynard Keynes and his school. It is now by way of becoming orthodox economics.

As we have already noted, the prime movers in economic life are conscious, unsatisfied needs, and available purchasing power. There are no exact figures for needs; it is sufficient to know that they exceed all probable production. Nor are there wholly dependable figures for purchasing power. It consists of the national income minus hoarding and net credit shrinkage, or plus net credit expansion. We assume that the figure for normal times is seventy-five billions.

What is characteristic of all economic crises is a drastic shrinkage of purchasing power. A violent fall in farm prices, whether resulting from overproduction or the closing of important foreign markets, cuts off farm purchases and eats its way into industrial pay rolls, with resultant spreading of the malignant influence. The sudden adoption of a bona fide disarmament program by all the nations would flatten out the armament industry and set in motion powerful forces of depression in every country. Whatever upsets the calculations of any great body of producers may serve as the germ of a budding depression. If the disturbance is widespread, it shakes "confidence"; nobody buys anything he can do without and the volume of hoarding increases and the volume of credit shrinks. There is theoretically a bottom level below which the economy cannot sink, because some needs are so imperative that no impulse toward hoarding can altogether check the movement of goods. But we do not know where that bottom level is to be established.

Advocates of the principle of spending urge that if the volume of purchasing power falls below the normal, the government can restore the equilibrium by a policy of spending enough beyond its normal income to take up the slack. If the normal income has fallen away ten billions the government should increase its expenditures, but not by ten billions, since the spending of one billion means pensions or pay rolls or purchases of materials, to be spent with varying promptness for other goods and services, and so on. The billion spent by government thus must be multiplied by some figure, say three or four, in calculating its effect upon the annual volume of purchasing power.

By a spending policy the government can theoretically raise the purchasing power of a country to its normal level, no matter how deep the depression, if the government is prepared to spend enough. Where will it get the money? It would be of no use to try to get the money through taxes of wide incidence. Every billion taken out of the pockets of those who are forced to spend all their income means a corresponding reduction in the volume of free purchasing power. In spending the billion the government would be merely throwing back into the pool, after more or less delay, the purchasing power it had syphoned out.

The same cannot be said of taxes laid exclusively on capital or on income so large that they lead to hoarding in slack times. Here the process may have the effect of transforming inactive into active purchasing power. But there may be, and usually would be, offsetting forces set in motion. The large incomes and capitals commonly serve as nuclei of the credit structure, and an attack on these nuclei may result in a shrinkage of credit purchasing power that may equal or exceed the purchasing power set afloat by government spending.

Hence the inevitable resort to credit by any government that wishes to abate a depression by a spending policy. So long as the credit of a government remains good, a billion raised by bonds operates exactly like a billion raised from inactive hoards, unless the flotation of bonds dries up the sources of private credit, or starts a credit-destroying panic among moneyed men suckled on the dogma of a balanced budget.

In the first instance the effect of government credit spending appears to depend on quantity alone. Whether the money is spent for pensions and relief or for useful buildings, bridges and roads, makes little difference, except that the "unproductive" grants will be more promptly respent, and respent more frequently in the course of a year, than the money expended for the steel, cement, etc., that make up a large proportion of the productive expenditures. In the long run, however, the credit of the government is strengthened by an imposing array of permanent improvements; weakened by an apparently endless series of unproductive expenditures.

A FREE SOCIETY AND A BETTER LIFE 243

Still more important, the policy of spending for permanent improvements places the stimulus where it is likely to do the most good. In time of depression the industries that are first to succumb, that sink deepest and are the last to recover, are the heavy industries. Broadcast spending does not easily reach them. Expenditures for public improvements reach them directly. Rightly or wrongly, the heavy industries are regarded as a barometer of business conditions. If the spending policy reanimates them the effect on morale, on "confidence," may count for more than its cost.

This is not to argue that the so-called "unproductive expenditures" should be restricted in time of depression. Nothing is more dangerous to a free society than a hard-boiled attitude toward human misery on the part of government. But the problem of relief to the old and the disabled is not merely a depression problem. To be sure, widespread unemployment demands government action, and involves heavy expenditures that may or may not be productive.

The point here is that the mere granting of relief, the distribution of "doles," will never yield a sufficient increment in purchasing power to make up for the general decline under depression. A million men employed contribute their wages to the volume of purchasing power. The profits from their employment represent another contribution. No country has ever attempted to grant doles that were more than a fraction of normal earnings. There are no profits arising in connection with doles to add to purchasing power. A system of doles will abate human distress, and will release purchasing power. It can never be adequate to the task of checking depression.

If we face realities we will recognize that any system based on private initiative will have a price structure based partly on consumer demand, partly on investment demand, the latter realizing itself in the building of factories and warehouses, the production of machinery and the various raw materials required for capital goods production. Depression, with its concomitant distrust of the future, strikes the investment demand first of all: hence the distress of the heavy industries. If a country means seriously to check the development of a depression it will be prepared to launch a volume of public investments sufficient to balance the falling off in private investments. It will not permit an antiquated system of government bookkeeping to confuse its investment policy with its spending policy, and stir up panic over the "unbalanced budget" in the souls of businessmen who would be retired for incompetence if they entertained a similar confusion in their own spending and investment policies.

With regret it is to be observed that this analysis discloses no panacea for the ills of our economic system. It cannot even indulge the Job's comfort of finding that these ills are so many and so serious that the system must very soon collapse and make way for another nearer the heart's desire. On the contrary, it is compelled to accept the view that there is still great vitality in the present economic system. There is enough vitality at any rate to justify serious efforts toward abating its ills. We say "abating" advisedly, for we can conceive of no way by which all uncertainty, all miscalculation, all layoffs, all injustices can be removed. Similarly, although our democracy can be improved, although it can be made more and more dangerous for elected representatives to forget about their constituents' interests in their desperate personal political squabbles, this country cannot look forward at an early time to a Congress and to state legislatures wholly made up of intelligent and public-spirited men and women. A dictatorship might conceivably be one-hundred per cent efficient; a democracy cannot be. Just so an undertaker's—or "mortician's"—establishment may be one-hundred per cent efficient, but a university cannot be. Democracies and universities thrive by the play of living forces, a play that involves clash as well as cooperation, waste as well as achievement. To aid our readers in their consideration of the existing economic order and the various suggestions responsibly made for its revamping there will be found on the opposite page a graphic representation of our total national economic income with indications as to possible developments of its constituent elements in succeeding decades.

A system of free enterprise and political democracy is not tantamount to a system without order. It admits of controls. It admits of centralized planning, of a sort, but of a sort

A FREE SOCIETY AND A BETTER LIFE 245

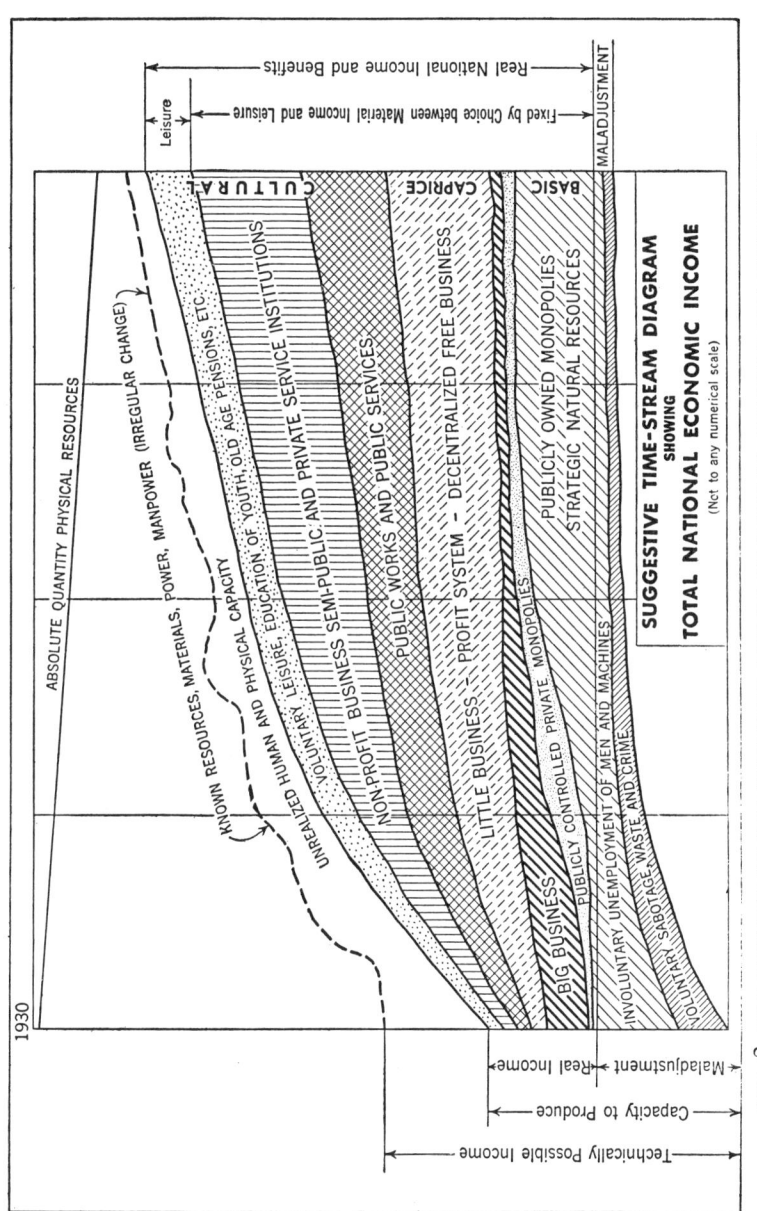

FIG. 3. THE DIVISION IN OUR NATIONAL ECONOMIC INCOME—GRAPHICALLY REPRESENTED.

that does not weaken liberty and initiative, the forces upon which we must count for the making of a better world. We need in Washington and in each of the state capitals permanent economic commissions able whenever the need arises to present a picture of our whole economic life, to show what branches are overdeveloped, what branches could profitably be developed farther. We need a financial system so completely subject to the public interest that investment funds will flow naturally to the enterprises, little as well as big, that can advantageously be expanded, instead of being subject as now to diversion mainly in favor of concerns that may have nothing to recommend them but their colossal size and their highly advertised position.

To maintain a continuous survey available to the public of all national operations is, to be sure, only a first step toward an intelligent economic policy; to assure the free and impartial flow of investment funds is not more than a second step. If we are to meet responsibly the problems that must inevitably present themselves in a complicated, delicately balanced system of free labor and free enterprise we have to give reality to the vague professions of responsibility and public spirit often so glibly circulated by leaders of both labor and capital. Down to the beginning of the present depression it was not remarkable that almost all Americans regarded the feathering of their own nests as practically the whole duty of man. The captain of industry looked to his balance sheet: if laying off half his workers would immediately improve his position his duty appeared to be clear. The labor union looked to wages and hours: if a single craft could hold up a great industry until its particular demands were met, this appeared to be the thing to do. The depression has taught us that wholesale layoffs, strikes that disorganize industry, are not localized matters. The inevitable drying up of pay rolls transmits baleful influences in ever-widening circles.

In this country, we need to hold both employer and employee to a sense of the responsibility for continuing production; where the forces of a gathering depression are too powerful for private good will and cooperation, we need the intervention of government, whether through the method

A FREE SOCIETY AND A BETTER LIFE

of subsidy or through the launching of public works to take up the slack in purchasing power.

Cooperation of government, employee and employer to carry responsibility for the uninterrupted flow of production and income implies, as we have tried to show in this book, far-reaching changes in attitudes and organization. It will be necessary to get rid of the obsolete conception of government as essentially honorific and coercive and recognize in it an instrument of increasing value to the economic system in normal times and a powerful resort in time of threatened crisis. There is need for a new type of organization of employers, with a leadership not stupefied by class dogma, not limited in its objectives to class interests, but prepared to assume the responsibilities of economic statesmanship. Similarly we need labor organizations that will not merely advance the immediate interests of particular groups of labor, but will regard the interests of the industry as a whole, including the workers, and of the economic system. And this means that whatever efforts are made to conserve the values of the traditional craft unions, the ultimate control of labor policy must rest with an organization wide enough to take a whole industry within its purview. We shall never be free from struggles between employers and workers, industry and industry, so long as we remain free men. But our economic system cannot stand the stoppage of a whole industry, the tying up of extensive pay rolls just because a craft representing a small fraction of the total personnel has a particularistic quarrel with the employer, or perhaps with another craft.

Instead of the one thing needful to set up a Utopia, this analysis indicates that many things are needful, things difficult of realization, which realized would give us not a Utopia, but a world that would still remain one of struggle, of risks and misadjustments and disappointments. For all that it will be a more livable world, a freer world.

We have not been dealing in this book with invented tendencies, but with tendencies actually operating and gaining force. A generation ago only a skeleton file of so-called radicals could see the necessity of a creative role of government in the economic system. Today only a reactionary fragment gradually dwindling under the scythe of the grim reaper questions the necessity of government aid to low rent housing, of government intervention in the flow of purchasing power. As younger and better-trained men rise into positions of industrial leadership there is multiplying evidence of the infiltration of social-mindedness into the stubborn tissue of business self-interest. We see great labor unions taking seriously the idea of responsibility for continued production. We see important progress making toward more extended and better administered social security. We see the farmer, always before an economic exile, brought into the scope of national economic policy, and in time we shall form rational ideas as to what to do with him.

It would be premature to say that we have already made such progress that our liberal democratic constitution is safe. A constitution rests ultimately not upon courts or army or legislative bodies but upon the people. Our liberal democratic constitution will survive and develop increasing security as we maintain and increase the proportion of our citizenry that feels free from dictation and reasonably secure in its living. The exploited casual laborers of California and the feudalistic bosses that exploit them are no part of the foundation of a liberal democratic constitution. Neither are the unhappy serfs of the unorganized mills and factories. We who have seen great and powerful unions in the clothing trades rise up out of the morasses of the sweatshop will not believe that these abuses are ineradicable.

Through science and technology the American environment has grown progressively richer. Yet we are only on the threshold of man's power over nature. If all we wished for were an unexampled progress in wealth, we could have it on terms that appear simple. Let men be free: crush every medieval impulse toward discrimination between man and man, toward the rejection of the good gifts offered by variety of ethnic and cultural origins. But we want more than wealth. We want a good life, health, security, happiness for the great masses, and the personal independence and dignity upon which alone a democratic constitution can rest securely. If we must choose between increasing material prosperity and the democratic life, we will choose the latter.

A FREE SOCIETY AND A BETTER LIFE

But this is not a real choice. The solidly founded liberal democratic society is the only seedbed in which ideas and inventions are sure to thrive. A dictatorship may temporarily be more efficient, but only under freedom can there be immunity from dry rot and a resistless forward movement of the creative forces inherent in human life.

A DIALOGUE BETWEEN THE AUTHORS

COOKE: Now that our manuscript is almost completed without, our having uncovered any irreconcilable differences of opinion, I recall that when we first discussed the outline of this book while lunching at the Commodore Hotel in New York City, we each reserved the right to develop in a final dialogue such differences as might have cropped up. This chapter was to have been a sort of verbal rough and tumble with no holds barred.

MURRAY: We expected to quarrel more than we actually did.

COOKE: Yes; but as long as we have been able to express in the book itself what is essential in our different approaches, why not use this epilogue to emphasize further our common ground? There is enough of that to keep right-minded folk busy for some time. So I ask, "Where do you think we should go from here? What are the next steps?"

MURRAY: Before we go much farther on our travels along the road of collective bargaining, we'd better send someone back to pick up the rest of our party who missed the train.

COOKE: And who are they?

MURRAY: What I mean is this: the labor movement in the United States embraces, at the most, 8,000,000 wage earners who have reached various stages of development in organized relations with management. But three times as many more workers have been either forgotten or ignored by unionism or restrained by reactionary and lawless employers. Our next step, therefore, is to lend a hand to these people and to help them join the parade. If we go on without them, we are going to find ourselves at some time dragged down by their lower standards and at another advancing at their expense. We have experienced both already. The real split in labor is between the organized and the unorganized. We must bring up the rear, for if "every kingdom divided against itself is brought to desolation, and every city or house divided against itself shall not stand," the same is true for the labor movement. And after our mass is thus increased, we shall be better able to advance, more or less as a unit.

COOKE: The Scotsman in you surely knows how to quote his Bible. But what steps would you take?

MURRAY: The next step is the recognition of the interest that labor has in the conduct of business. Today the ownership of industry is sharply separated from the control. The stockholder usually has no voice whatsoever in the administration of his company. Only an exceedingly small percentage of them can or do attend stockholders' meetings. Proxies are gathered by the management at corporate expense. No one but a fabulously wealthy and influential stockholder like John D. Rockefeller, Jr., could successfully assert his rights as part owner against a hostile directorship. Management has usurped the prerogatives of ownership and is in fact responsible to no one but its patrons, finance capital. When management resists labor organization, it is fighting to preserve this usurpation at the expense of the ownership. When the Youngstown Sheet and Tube Company provoked a strike at its plants, the chairman of the board of the directors got into an epistolary battle with his own stockholders, many of whom opposed his policies. One of these, a former associate justice of the United States Supreme Court, wrote in answer to a circular giving the "company's" position: "Really, my dear Mr. Dalton (H. G. Dalton, chairman of the board of directors, Youngstown Sheet and Tube Company), the difference which has resulted in this shocking strike now in progress as stated in this circular seems to narrow down to a question of personal pride or aversion on the part of the parties concerned to sit down at a table and talk the subject out as equals—as will certainly be necessary before settlement is reached." This stockholder, the Hon. John H. Clarke, former associate justice of the U. S. Supreme Court, had no more weight in determining the policies of the company than the 20,000 employees who demanded union recognition. Here management had set itself apart and above the interests or desires of ownership and employees, to neither of whom did it in any way consider itself responsible.

The next step, therefore, is to raise ownership and labor to a common level with management, and when this is done, we can take the next great voluntary move forward in the solution of the problems of unemployment and job security. If this effort fails, then government regulation, either benevolent or fascistic, is the only road remaining.

COOKE: That's fine, Mr. Murray. Now—"answer me another!" I am completely convinced that right here in the United States will be enacted the next important acts in the drama of man's development of a well-balanced civilization. Anything which tends to confirm this possibility greatly excites me. While writing this book with you it has been gradually dawning on me that only recently something wonderful in the history of labor and society has been developing.

MURRAY: You're optimistic. I hope you're right. But what is it?

COOKE: Two things have become clear and another has happened which three taken together spell, as I see it, a fundamental change in the situation. First, unemployment in all developed countries is now looked upon as a chronic condition. The civilized world may never again have a scarcity of labor quite in the sense heretofore known. Second, with machine power and machine skill largely supplanting hand labor and craft skill the old craft idea on which labor has been basing its hopes since the beginning of the industrial revolution loses much of its potency. Third, the passage of the Wagner Act opens the door wide to a new twentieth-century opportunity for labor. If these three propositions have the significance which I attribute to them this book could not have been written ten years ago, or even as late as last year. Have we, in your opinion, arrived at such a point in the evolution of industry and labor as to promise for the future a life for the workers, and a productivity for industry, far above anything we have known in the past?

MURRAY: Yes, I think we have. These last depression years have been the crisis. The world has had to choose a course of action. The complacent individualistic excesses of the 1920's were out of the question as long as the effects

A DIALOGUE BETWEEN THE AUTHORS

could be remembered. South America turned to revolution; England to Tory government and Germany to National Socialism. France elected a Popular Front which disintegrated more rapidly than it was formed. In the United States we tried to widen the application of democracy, at the same time placing restriction on its abuse. Here the emphasis was on protecting a labor organization's right to exist and function, and thus directly take a part in controlling its destinies. Its success in this has been fully discussed in this book. It has been so successful that it will survive any change in the conditions which made its rapid growth possible. We are now in a wave of reaction. Many states have already drastically revised or repealed their "Little Wagner Acts." Yet labor continues to advance, with its three most notable victories in Wisconsin, Michigan, and Pennsylvania in spite of their having been the first states to abandon the New Deal.

COOKE: You think then that we have progressed.

MURRAY: Yes, we have arrived at such a point where the promise is hopeful for the future you envision.

Now, Mr. Cooke, I would like to get your reaction to a problem that constantly bothers me.

COOKE: I can't guarantee an answer, but I'll try.

MURRAY: The standard economists tell us that technological unemployment is a myth or at worst a temporary inconvenience, resulting in more jobs later through cheaper products. But the workers who lose their jobs, the communities which become ghost towns—Martins Ferry, Ohio; Mingo Junction, Ohio; New Castle, Pennsylvania; Creighton, Pennsylvania; for example—have been somewhat neglected by this school of thought. When an entire plant is shut down, as has frequently been the case following the introduction of the almost automatically operated continuous strip mills in steel, the average age of the displaced employees is high, usually above the hiring limits in the industry. These men have, for the most part, given long service in a process which is now obsolete. Even if new jobs were available, the companies refuse to transfer most of them on the ground that they are too old to learn a new occupation. I understand that the telephone industry is attempting to alleviate the suffering caused by this

254 ORGANIZED LABOR AND PRODUCTION

problem by introducing dial systems only to the extent that their switchboard girls naturally retire from service. Without affecting the advance of industrial techniques, do you think that the welfare of labor also ought to be a major consideration when new machinery is contemplated? If so, in view of the vast importance of the problem, how would you go about attempting to solve it?

COOKE: Now you have posed the most important, perhaps the most difficult, problem of all. Considering it as a deep-seated disease, the faulty manner in which we have integrated the new technology into our society can, I believe, be remedied by combining patience with vision and positive remedial action, but not by the application of any quick-acting liniments or poultices.

MURRAY: What are some of the better remedies?

COOKE: First let me paint the picture a little more clearly. The economists—with the exception of a few among the older of them, and most of the younger generation now coming to the front—have been more scholarly than realistic. Economics began as an interpretation of the economic experience of the day. It was good interpretation, and led to generalizations, called principles. An initial error was the assumption that these principles were enduring natural laws instead of inferences based on practices of the day which were sure to change. The second error of the economists was to continue teaching these principles as natural laws, without adequate modification of them, while the structure, institutions and practices of economic activity were changing profoundly. The result is survival of an "economic science" that does not fit.

MURRAY: You're right about that, Cooke.

COOKE: A hundred, seventy-five, fifty years ago our economy was in process of expansion through discovery and settlement of new areas, and the exploitation of new resources—a vast store of new capital. This exploitation made new jobs so fast—jobs of a kind that did not require highly developed skills—that workers displaced by technical advance were promptly reabsorbed. And it is a historic fact that the new jobs—the expansion—created such purchasing power, and technical improvements in a competitive system so lowered prices, that the industries in which the technical improvements were made called for an increasing number of workers. Generally, although displaced workers suffered temporary inconvenience or even distress, within a short time they had new and frequently, better jobs in the expanding economy.

But these things have changed. Improved technology has been introduced into economic society at an accelerating rate; at the same time the expansion of the economy has been slowing down. New areas are not being discovered and settled; new resources are not being appropriated and exploited, thereby creating new jobs. And in the older industries concentrations of control of capital, and of effective control of managements, if not literally of ownership, have made possible the destruction of vital parts of the competitive economy through various kinds and degrees of price maintenance, thereby diminishing expansion and new jobs. Many displaced workers today suffer not merely temporary inconvenience and distress, but are pushed into a rapidly developing class of irregularly employed or of a permanently unemployed proletariat.

The situation is ominous and the problem gigantic. It means an attack for solution along many fronts.

MURRAY: Well, I ask again, what are you going to do about it?
COOKE: Perhaps, to begin with there should be a regulated, better-measured introduction of the new technology such as you have stated is exemplified by the American Telephone and Telegraph Company. In another case I know about there has been a deliberate retarding of progress pending the development of increased demands for existing products and for new products. It may be said that the company has been deliberately "soldiering" in the interests of its employees. Fortunately, this company is in a financial position to do this and is looking ahead at least a generation rather than being concerned with immediate savings. Such procedures are praiseworthy and should be followed more generally. However, they are not generally applicable and are possible only where an industry is controlled by an essential monopoly; otherwise some competitor will try to get the jump on the others by going the limit with new devices and thereby force the others to

come along. Also a monopoly may not act so wisely as in your illustration. One trouble in the steel industry is that a great dominant corporation has for years withheld discarding early equipment as depreciated and obsolescent, and is now proceeding to correct that situation all in one move.

Therefore there must be regulation of the introduction of new technology, not by the sum of the decisions of separate enterprises, but in a broad way under supervision of the public, which means of its government. It means some degree of regulation, not only of the introduction of new devices, but also of capital formation, investment, and additions of plant and equipment to industries. It means especially renewal of expansion of the economy through restoration of price flexibility throughout the economy. If this cannot be accomplished directly by legislation governing monopolies—and it is doubtful whether it can—then we must resort to wider applications of the yardstick principle of control of the price structure of each faulty industry by competing public or non-profit cooperative enterprises. Some other people in countries that remain most democratic, such as the Scandinavian, are working it out this way. They are small countries and are managing it much more easily than we could, but we have the problem and they have shown us the most effective way thus far.

MURRAY: It is clear that we must work for improvement on a wide front. You evidently agree with me in that.

COOKE: But to one statement of yours, Murray, I must take violent exception. You say, "even if new jobs were available, the companies refuse to transfer most of them on the grounds that they are too old to learn a new occupation." To me any such claim by the companies is pure bunk and in a plant operated under Scientific Management such an alibi would not be at all valid. No man before pensioning age should be regarded as too old to learn a new occupation provided he is afforded proper instruction, if the work is properly planned and if he is not assigned to something which is beyond his mental and physical capacity. This is not theory but the very definite practice of every Scientific Management plant.

A DIALOGUE BETWEEN THE AUTHORS

MURRAY: Labor, in other words, must come first.
COOKE: Yes, the welfare of labor, which is the bulk of a nation's citizenship, is the primary consideration. Its welfare must be maintained at all costs. The least cost is through greater productivity which calls for jobs for all. Industry should include in its plans for change the human as well as the mechanistic factors involved, and this means that the individual employer should lay as definite plans for the full utilization of his working force as is at all feasible. But it must now be recognized that greater productivity is a problem of expansion of the economy through wise and measured collective control, now that expansion through discovery and exploitation of new geographical frontiers has come to an end.

It is my experience in negotiations growing out of collective bargaining that the union representatives frequently require expert assistance. Do you see any disadvantage in using a company's funds in paying for such services if it is fully understood all around and the union is untrammeled in choosing the experts?

MURRAY: In the light of union experiences to date it is pretty difficult to visualize any company willing to provide funds for the employment of expert assistance by a union, which in turn would use same in the collective bargaining process. As I see the situation, there must be much more complete and full acceptance of unions as an integral part of the productive process by employers before any such arrangements can be either practical or possible. Given the now generally prevailing lack of confidence among our members in the good faith and sincerity of most employers in dealing with unions, union members would be inclined to question the accuracy of any data and the impartiality of any expert whose services were made possible by funds provided by an employer. This general distrust of employers' motives may be better understood if it is kept in mind that the National Association of Manufacturers, which professes to be the "voice of American industry," has only about three thousand members, and its development of policy comes from but a small number of the largest corporations in the United States. This has been very clearly shown by the Senate Subcommittee on Civil Liberties report on labor policies of employer associations, part 3, p. 222:

> "The National Association of Manufacturers is largely financed by a small group of powerful corporations, representing in 1937 less than 10% of its membership of 3,000 companies. A much smaller clique of large corporations, not more than 60 in number, have supplied it with active leadership. Through the National Association of Manufacturers and its affiliated national network of employers' associations in the National Industrial Council this small group of powerful interests have organized the strategy for a national program of employer opposition to labor unions and to governmental action to improve conditions of labor."

And when one remembers the stooge American Workman's Protective Association sponsored by the NAM, and that the same NAM officers who perpetrated this deception are still on the staff of the NAM the lack of confidence of labor becomes understood.

No, if union representatives require assistance they will provide it themselves. Indeed, union officials in some fields are recognized as the foremost experts in the industry. Gen. Hugh Johnson, some months ago, ran a column in his newspaper syndicate praising John L. Lewis as the best informed mind either as operator or worker in the coal industry. Then too, most unions have established their own research departments.

I am often asked how we can expect labor to plunge wholeheartedly into high productivity so long as there are many unemployed—so long as we have these periods of depression and the loss of jobs and savings. We all know that many jobs now done with a steam shovel would give more people some semblance of a living if done with hand shovels. But to do it would lower the standard of living—the standard of living, of course, varies directly with productivity. What is the answer?

COOKE: Of course you know the answer. There is some sense in thinking an average lower standard of living, with everybody living and self-respecting, to be somewhat better than an average higher standard with ten to fifteen million unemployed and on public charity. There was something noble about the self-sufficient community of the great-grandparents of living Americans, even though they wore homespun and didn't have telephones, autos and movies. A higher standard doesn't mean merely a higher average; it means a higher average of well-distributed incomes. This is not an average got by adding $25,000 to $1,000 and getting $13,000; but an average got by adding five at $2,000, four at $2,500 and one at $6,000, which likewise is $13,000.

Our problem is one of securing as high a standard of living as possible, and the only way is by high productivity. At the same time we must secure the high standard under conditions of equitable—not equal, but equitable—income, with everybody sharing according to his ability to contribute.

This means organizing our economic process so that every bit of work done on individual initiative, and the supplementary work done on public initiative, meets a genuine need; does not represent speculative over-investment or speculative over-production with existing investment. Balance is what is needed. Given balance, the economy will expand automatically from innumerable individual efforts. Keep everybody busy and reduce, if not absolutely eliminate, unemployment. This does not mean a static society. It means, rather, a growing society, a society progressing, but kept in balance.

We must remember that while human wants are limitless as a whole, many are limited at any particular time. What people desire—the proportions—change gradually. Production should be such as to meet balanced demand; and investment in facilities should be such as to provide balanced production facilities.

Now that we are trying to be quite frank with each other may I say that nine out of ten businessmen I meet, the moment labor unions are mentioned, immediately refer to what they call their "excesses." You must have a stock answer for remarks of this kind. What is it?

MURRAY: Employers generally get the kind of labor relations they ask for. If the union indulges in "excesses," then the employer as a rule has no one but himself to blame for it. For instance, if he engages the services of labor espionage agencies such as Railway Audit, Pinkerton's, or others, if he stocks up his plant with tear gas, hand grenades, sub-machine guns, blackjacks, rifles, and other implements of war, if he hires high-priced Wall Street lawyers to harass the union before the Labor Board and in the courts, if he distributes to his foremen anti-union literature and lets it be known to them that any harm they can do to the union would be forgiven by him, if he contributes to anti-labor organizations such as the notorious Johnstown Citizens' Committee, if he quibbles over words, if he refuses to consent to an election or to sign a contract when he knows the union has a majority, if after a contract has been forced from him he delays and hampers the settlement of grievances, if he continues to discriminate against union members, then labor will answer in kind and nine out of ten businessmen, viewing it from afar, will say, "Ah, another 'excess.'"

Take the Steel Workers' Organizing Committee. During the early days the SWOC encountered considerable opposition, but among those companies which negotiated signed contracts with the SWOC and which sincerely and wholeheartedly entered into these agreements, no one has been able to say that the SWOC has gone to "excess." Indeed, the steel workers' union is constantly referred to as a model of respectability and intelligent relations. The Jones and Laughlin Steel Corporation had fought the union in 1936 and the early part of 1937. As a result the union was forced to strike in order to gain recognition, but after the strike a new era opened. The company abandoned its anti-union policy and embarked upon a sincere experiment in labor relations. As a result the Jones and Laughlin Steel Corporation is enjoying a period of harmonious labor relations. There are no "excesses" at the plants of this company. Indeed labor relations here have become a model for the entire industry. A booklet has been published describing them.

The point is that when companies oppose unions, the unions elect as their leaders belligerent and willful men. No other type could survive. If, on the other hand, the company does not oppose the union with unlawful methods, the union is likely to choose for its leadership men noted not for their fighting qualities but for their ability as negotiators. This largely accounts for the businessmen's reaction you refer to.

COOKE: It seems to be a choice between facts and fights but of the two, facts usually pay better.

MURRAY: I have seen so many vexing problems solved simply by getting the facts and then weighing them dispassionately that the Scientific Management approach as practiced by you and your colleagues makes a strong appeal. And yet under the guise of "scientific management" a good many practices have been put into effect which were less scientific than extortionate. That is, instead of finding a better way of doing things the new management methods discovered how to get more out of labor without a proportionate return. As a result wage earners generally hate and fear the efficiency expert. What do you suggest be done about it?

COOKE: I am glad you asked that. It is a very pertinent question. However, the terms "Scientific Management" and "efficiency system" should not be used as synonyms. The objection of the wage earners is not an objection to Scientific Management, but to something which masquerades thinly disguised as Scientific Management, or "something just as good." The management engineer who tries conscientiously to follow the true Scientific Management techniques and principles shudders when the term "efficiency engineer" is applied to him, because of the unsavory record of the latter term, which has been used to cover a multitude of sins. The profession of management engineering, like the professions of law and medicine before they had developed scientific standards, has had its deep fringe of quacks and shysters. Occasionally they have used the term "Scientific Management," but more generally the term "efficiency engineer" as having a better sales appeal; being less high-brow, and more related to something the typical businessman understands—efficiency.

The engineer who represents genuine Scientific Management painstakingly attempts to discover and evaluate all the facts bearing on a managerial situation, including those pertaining to labor's interests, and then seeks to devise a system of management which fits the particular situation. No two of these systems are ever alike in detail because no two managerial situations are ever alike in detail. The efficiency engineer, on the other hand, rushes through some preconceived or hastily devised system, with his weather eye always on the interest of the employer who pays his fee, gets the job done quickly, collects his fee, and rushes on to the next job. The former is creative of something enduring because it fits the situation in respect of every element; the latter is highly commercial.

MURRAY: The name doesn't interest me. It is what some of these so-called experts do to labor.

COOKE: The conditions you refer to frequently occur where incentives are fixed by foremen or others without adequate time studies or where the time studies are improperly made and without due regard to operating methods. Wage earners should see to it that practices which involve wage payments and other operating set-ups are developed in such a way as to include in the research all factors which are rightly involved. This is true Scientific Management. This necessitates: (1) a production control that will distribute the work equitably and eliminate lost time; (2) development of standard methods along with the introduction of production control; (3) studies of fatigue where this is involved; (4) training of the operatives to work in the easiest way; (5) increase in pay where increased effort or skill is required—all carried on with the full knowledge of the workers affected.

As in so many other situations, education is a large part of the answer, particularly of executives and all others in financial control of industry, as well as of the men at the head of organized labor and all their subordinates pretty well down the line. Education of the workmen, I think, will be relatively easy. The pity of it is that most of the people in control of industry are too lazy to take the trouble to understand Scientific Management and too ignorant to distinguish between it and the superficial makeshifts of the "efficiency engineers," who seem to offer an easy way with little or no responsibility placed upon management. No management engineer worth his salt ever suggests that the

A DIALOGUE BETWEEN THE AUTHORS

introduction and gradual development of Scientific Management is either a short-time proposition or easy of accomplishment. The ends to be accomplished are too important and far-reaching to make it an easy job. Taylor advised employers, "Don't start unless you are ready to stay with the development for at least five years!" One of the best management engineers I know does not begin time studies during the first five years.

MURRAY: It's a serious confusion that you point out.

COOKE: Every party at interest must bear a share of responsibility for this confusion between Scientific Management and the numerous varieties of "just-as-good" substitutes. The Scientific Management engineer, because he has been too technical, too summary and one-sided in his explanations; employers, because they have thought too much in terms of lower costs and too little in terms of human relations; labor, because it has failed to make serious and sustained effort to learn the distinction between true Scientific Management and "efficiency."

MURRAY: What should be done about it?

COOKE: What should be done about it! The obvious, simple, direct, step is for organized labor, progressive employers, and professionally-minded engineers to get together to put management engineering by whatever name you call it on the dissecting table, and as a result of such laboratory work put on record so that everybody can understand, the anatomy, physiology and pathology of management engineering. You should have in mind that there is already a rich literature of Scientific Management easily available. A reading of the Bulletin of the Taylor Society affords quite an education as to the best in management.[1] Quite a few labor leaders have contributed to it.

MURRAY: I hope you can get them all to read it.

COOKE: Now, let me ask one, Murray. It's this: assuming a time when labor's fight for organization has been pretty generally won, what in your opinion will take the place of the "scrap" in keeping up rank and file interest in the labor movement?

MURRAY: As I pointed out in answer to your first question, labor's fight for organization is not pretty generally won; but applying this thought to those industries where substantial recognition is being achieved I would say that the thing labor has been fighting for from earliest days will take the place of the "scrap" in keeping up rank and file interest in the labor movement. The need for battle to stimulate support is one of the popular fallacies of unionism. The Amalgamated Clothing Workers, for example, have not had a major strike in years; yet member enthusiasm is as great as ever. It is just as easy, and far more desirable, to arouse fervor for the fundamental work and accomplishments of unionism as it is to hold a picket line. In fact, one of the results of a walkout is a heightened interest in carrying on the real job of collective bargaining.

The rank and file is more concerned about pay and job security than about "scraps." A liberal seniority clause is more exciting than a soup kitchen. The point is that there are "scraps" only because they are necessary to bring about certain gains. And as they become no longer necessary the energy they consume will be diverted to more useful channels.

No artificial device is needed to keep up interest in the labor movement. The desire to enjoy a democratic, reasonably secure and comfortable economic life will always be the main source of rank and file interest in the labor movement. Now let me ask you a question.

COOKE: Go ahead.

MURRAY: American industry today is split into two camps: those which have accepted collective bargaining and those which still actively resist it. Because a single anti-union company may imperil the constructive unionism in conjunction with advanced employers, such as we discuss in this book, do you not think it is the responsibility of all of us to bring the old-line reactionaries into line?

COOKE: The law of the land being what it is, there can be only one answer to your question. The means by which more general collective bargaining is to be brought about is the problem. We *should* be able to rely on social pressure to influence a wider observance of the law, but something tells me that little help can be expected from this direction. Our principal purpose in writing this book was to demonstrate to the open-minded that collective bargaining works—that the net gains are worth all the effort needed to put the system into effective operation. The experiences and testimony of labor leaders and employers who have satisfactorily tested out the system should be influential. To get these arguments before the American public perhaps an association would be useful. Its board might be constituted on a 50-50 basis of employers and employees with a sprinkling of economists, engineers and other specialists. The meetings would afford a forum in which model contracts and progressive techniques could be publicized and difficulties discussed. There would be many ways in which such an organization could not only increase the total volume of collective bargaining but qualitatively improve it as well.

With your familiarity with labor's past struggles I need not tell you that our principal dependence for the extension of collective bargaining must be placed on labor's own activities, on its insistence on collective bargaining and its efforts to make its practice serve broad social purposes.

Do you allow yourself to speculate on probable trends in case we are unsuccessful in having collective bargaining generally adopted somewhat after the plan recommended in this book?

MURRAY: I don't like to speculate on the probable trends in case we are unsuccessful in putting over collective bargaining somewhat after the plan recommended in this book. It is too dismal an outlook. We are just leaving a period in which collective bargaining was scarcely ever really accepted. Employers dealt with unions only because they had to. If we go back to such conditions now in view of the present world-wide attacks upon democracy the outcome may well be a weakening of democratic processes here and a possible setting of the scene for a dictatorship. If American political democracy is to survive, we must succeed. We must have democracy in industry.

NOTES AND REFERENCES

Chapter 1

[1] "History of Scientific Management in America," *Mechanical Engineering*, September, 1939, p. 674.

Chapter 3

[1] John A. Hobson, *The Evolution of Modern Capitalism* (New York: Scribner's, 1904), p. 57.
[2] *Ibid.*, pp. 61-67.
[3] Herbert Heaton, "Industrial Revolution," *Encyclopaedia of the Social Sciences*, Vol. 8, p. 8.
[4] Thorstein Veblen, *Imperial Germany and the Industrial Revolution* (New York: B. W. Huebsch, 1915), pp. 124-28.
[5] Heaton, *op. cit.*, Vol. 8, p. 9.
[6] J. L. and Barbara Hammond, *The Town Labourer, 1760-1832* (New York: Longmans, Green, 1920), pp. 19-20.
[7] *Ibid.*, Chapter VIII, "The Employment of Children," pp. 143-93.
[8] G. D. H. Cole, *Short History of the British Working Class Movement, 1789-1937* (London: Allen and Unwin, 1937), p. 51 ff.
[9] Carroll R. Daugherty, *Labor Problems in American Industry* (Boston: Houghton Mifflin, 1933), pp. 52-53.
[10] A. A. Berle, Jr. and Gardiner C. Means, "Corporation," *Encyclopaedia of the Social Sciences*, Vol. 4, p. 422.

Selected References (excluding those mentioned above):
Walton H. Hamilton, *Current Economic Problems* (University of Chicago Press, 1925), 3rd ed., 960 pp.
Harry Elmer Barnes, *An Economic History of the Western World* (New York: Harcourt, Brace and Co., 1937), 790 pp.
Sidney and Beatrice Webb, *The History of Trade Unionism* (New York: Longmans, Green, 1920), 784 pp.

Chapter 5

[1-4] These items are discussed in detail in the Decision and Order of the National Labor Relations Board in the Matter of Republic Steel Corporation and Steel Workers Organizing Committee, Case No. C-184; and in the Reports and Transcripts, Parts 23-34, of the LaFollette Senate Civil Liberties Committee (S. Res. 266, 74th Congress).
[5] Report of the President's Commission on Industrial Relations in Great Britain, Released September 2, 1938. Government Printing Office.
[6] V. Henry Rothschild, 2nd, "Government Regulation of Trade Unions in

NOTES AND REFERENCES

Great Britain," *Columbia Law Review*, Vol. XXXVIII, Nos. 1, 8, January and December, 1938.

[7] William M. Leiserson: presented to Hon. Elbert D. Thomas, chairman, Committee on Education, Labor, U. S. Senate, on May 9, 1939.

[8] Fansteel Metallurgical Corporations vs. N.L.R.B., 35 U.S. 240; 59 S. Ct. 490.

[9] Henry M. Hart, Jr. and Edward F. Prichard, Jr., "The Fansteel Case—Employee Misconduct and the Remedial Powers of the National Labor Relations Board," *Harvard Law Review*, Vol. 52, p. 1275. June, 1939.

[10] Financial report of the United Mine Workers of America, New York *Times*, January 26, 1938, p. 1.

[11] Frederick H. Harbison, "The Seniority Principle in Union-Management Relations," Industrial Relations Section, Princeton University.

Chapter 6

[1] Commercial and Industrial Organization of the United States. Domestic Commerce Series No. 5. Bureau of Foreign and Domestic Commerce. U. S. Department of Commerce. Government Printing Office.

Chapter 7

[1] Mary P. Follett: "The Illusion of Final Authority," *Taylor Society Bulletin*.

[2] *Ibid*.

[3] John H. Williams, *The Flexible Budget* (New York: McGraw-Hill Book Company, 1934).

[4] Robert B. Wolf, "Non-financial Incentives," a paper before the A. S. M. E., *Transactions*, Vol. 40 (1918), pp. 925-946.

[5] Otis Ferguson in the *New Republic*.

Chapter 8

[1] Committee on the Elimination of Waste in Industry of the Federated American Engineering Societies, *Waste in Industry* (New York: McGraw-Hill Book Company, 1921).

[2] B. Seebohn Rowntree, chairman of the Board of the Rowntree Chocolate Company, Ltd., York, England: "Capital & Labor Co-operate," Department of Christian Social Service, New York City.

Chapter 9

[1] Geoffrey C. Brown, "The Bedaux System," *American Federationist*, September, 1935.

[2] Sanford E. Thompson, "Smoothing the Wrinkles out of Management."

[3] Frederick W. Taylor, *The Principles of Scientific Management* (New York: Harper Brothers, 1911).

Chapter 10

[1] See the brief prepared for the Attorney-General of Pennsylvania and entered in the case of defense of the State's 44-Hour Law, March-April, 1938.

268 ORGANIZED LABOR AND PRODUCTION

[2] *Ibid.* Also in case of Bunting vs. State of Oregon see elaborate statement of the health argument in "The Case for the Shorter Day."
[3] Alan G. B. Fisher, *Some Problems of Wages and Their Regulation in Gt. Britain Since 1918* (London: P. S. King & Son, 1926), pp. 42-3.
[4] *Ibid. supra.*
[5] William G. Smith, Secretary-Treasurer, American Federation of Hosiery Workers. Pennsylvania Brief, pp. 64-5.
[6] Sidney and Beatrice Webb, *Industrial Democracy* (Longmans, Green, 1920), pp. 717-18.
[7] *Ibid.*
[8] See press releases of the Wages and Hours Administration.
[9] Harlow S. Person, "Work Week or the Work Life," *Bulletin of the Taylor Society*, Vol. XIII, No. 6, pp. 230-32, with discussion, December, 1928.

Chapter 11

[1] E. T. Coil, "Democracies Must Also Plan," *Plan Age*, May, 1939.
[2] It is an interesting historical fact that Taylor himself did not coin the term, "Scientific Management"; it was coined by a committee of engineers at the request of an attorney who wanted a striking, concrete, descriptive term to use in a case he was conducting. This attorney was Louis D. Brandeis, of Boston, Mass., who later became one of the great associate justices of the United States Supreme Court.
[3] "History of Scientific Management in America," in *Mechanical Engineering*, September, 1939.
[4] *Ibid.*
[5] Harlow S. Person, "Scientific Management as a Philosophy and Technique of Progressive Industrial Stabilization." Presented at the Congress of Social Economic Planning under the auspices of the International Industrial Relations Association, Amsterdam, Holland, August 24, 1931.
[6] Sanford E. Thompson, "Smoothing the Wrinkles out of Management," *Bulletin of the Taylor Society*, Vol. XIII, No. 2, April, 1928.
[7] Nahum I. Stone, "Productivity of Labor in the Cotton-Garment Industry." Bulletin No. 662, U. S. Department of Labor, Bureau of Labor Statistics.
[8] Nunn-Bush Labor. *Fortune* Magazine, November, 1938.
[9] Sanford E. Thompson, "The Sales Basis of Today's Industrial Management," in *For Top-Executives Only* (New York: The Business Bourse, 1936).

Chapter 12

[1] Industrial Accidents. Bulletin No. 78, U. S. Bureau of Labor Statistics, 1909, pp. 5, 6.
[2] *Waste in Industry*, Committee on the Elimination of Waste in Industry of the Federated American Engineering Societies (New York: McGraw-Hill Book Company, 1921), p. 331.
[3] Carroll M. Daugherty, *Labor Problems in American Industry* (Revised Edition, Houghton Mifflin, 1938), p. 101.
[4] *Ibid.*
[5] W. H. W. Heinrich, "Cost of Industrial Accidents to the State, the Employer and the Man," *Monthly Labor Review*, Nov., 1930, p. 1118.

NOTES AND REFERENCES

[6] "Coverage Limitations of Workmen's Compensation Laws," *Monthly Labor Review*, June, 1939, p. 1267 ff.
[7] Boris Stern, "Safeguarding Workers Against Occupational Diseases," *Labor Information Bulletin*, June, 1939.

Chapter 14

[1] "Science at the Cross Roads." Papers presented to the International Congress of the History of Science and Technology, London, 1931. Published by Kniga Ltd.
[2] *Ibid.*
[3] Fred Henderson, *The Economic Consequences of Power Production* (New York: John Day, 1933).
[4] *Ibid.*
[5] Walter N. Polakov, *The Power Age; Its Quest and Challenge* (New York: Covici Friede, 1933).
[6] *Yale Review*, Vol. XVII (1908), pp. 156-184.

Chapter 15

[1] Clinton S. Golden, "Making the Collective Agreement Work." Address at the Ninth Annual Conference on Industrial Relations at University of Michigan, April 12-15, 1939. Also, "Getting on Together," before Industrial Relations Assn., Phila., Nov. 21, 1939. Harold T. Ruttenberg, "The Strategy of Industrial Peace." *Harvard Business Review*, Winter 1939. Robert B. Wolf, "The Conservation of Industrial Capitalism: A Challenge to our Collective Intelligence." A paper before Bureau of Personnel Administration, Feb. 9, 1939.

Chapter 16

[1] J. B. S. Hardman *et alii*, *American Labor Dynamics* (Harcourt, Brace, 1928).
[2] American Steel Foundries, 257 U. S. 184.
[3] Release of the National Labor Relations Board, May 30, 1939.
[4] Jones and Laughlin Corporation, 301 U. S. 1.
Associated Press, 301 U. S. 103.
Friedman-Harry Marks, 301 U. S. 58.
Santa Cruz Fruit Packing, 303 U. S. 261.
Mackay Radio, 304 U. S. 333.
Fansteel Metallurgical, 59 S. C. 490.
Consolidated Edison, 305 U. S. 197.

Chapter 17

[1] One of the authors has expressed some of the same views to be found in this chapter and, in part, in the same words, in an article, "Preparedness Plus—Democracy Knocks at Industry's Door," by Morris L. Cooke. *American Federationist*, February, 1939. The reader's attention is directed to the other points raised in that article.
[2] "Hands Entrance" is a sign still found at the entrance gates of factories.
[3] Z. Clark Dickinson, "Suggestion from Workers—Schemes and Problems," *Quarterly Journal of Economics*, August, 1932.

Paul L. Stanchfield and Z. C. Dickinson, "Suggestion System in 1932 and 1933," The *Personnel Journal*, December, 1934.

[4] Wallace Clark, *Biography of Experience* (Privately published in Paris in 1939), p. 51.

[5] "Union-Management Cooperation: a Selected Bibliography," *Monthly Labor Review*, October, 1927.

[6] See *Production Problems: a handbook for committeemen*, issued by the Steel Workers Organizing Committee, Pittsburgh.
Also: "Working Together on the Railroad" in The Kiwanis Magazine, September, 1939.

Chapter 18

[1] *General Report of the Regents' Inquiry into the Character and Cost of Public Education in the State of New York: Education for American Life* (New York: McGraw-Hill Book Company, 1938).

[2] Gunnar Myrdal, "The Defenses of Democracy," *Survey Graphic*, June, 1939.

[3] R. F. Seybolt, "The Evening School in Colonial America," Bulletin No. 24, Bureau of Educational Research, College of Education, University of Illinois, 1925.

[4] *Adult Education*, American Association for Adult Education, 1936.

[5] Newbold Morris: Address before the Committee of Seventy, Philadelphia, February 17, 1939.

Dialogue between the Authors

[7] See also *Scientific Management in American Industry* by the Taylor Society, H. S. Person, Editor; Harper & Bros., New York, 1929, pp. xix, 479.

INDEX

Abundance, economy of, 17
Affiliated School for Workers, Association of Bryn Mawr; Berkeley, California; Madison, Wisconsin; Asheville, North Carolina; Chicago, Illinois, 226
Amalgamated Association of Iron, Steel, and Tin Workers of North America, 40
Amalgamated Clothing Workers, 112, 153, 264
market research by, 169
American Association for Labor Legislation, 147
American Doctor's Odyssey, An (Heiser, Dr. Victor G.), 153
American Engineering Council, Committee on Safety and Production of the, 146
American Federation of Hosiery Workers, attitude toward technology, 169
share costs as well as benefits of new technology by, 169-170
American Federation of Labor, 40, 41
cases handled by NLRA, 203
complaints of, 209
workers' education, 226
American Management Association, 167
American Steel Foundries, 199
American Telephone and Telegraph Company, 253-255
Appalachian Agreement, 169
Arkwright, 26-27
Associated Brotherhood of Iron and Steel Heaters, Rollers, and Roughers of the United States, 40
Associated Press case, effect of NLRA on, 206
Authority, functional, 88
Authority to hire and fire, 103, 104

Berle and Means, 34
Brotherhood of Teamsters, 208
Business, attitude toward labor, 18, 31
laying out details of, 73-74
organization of responsibilities in, 75
Byrnes Anti-Strikebreaking Act, 66

California State Medical Association, 127
Capital, 12-14
earned income, extracted from consumer, 18
Carnegie Nutrition Laboratory in Cambridge, Massachusetts, 219
Cartwright, 26, 27
Central Trades and Labor Council of New York City, 153
Chamberlain, John, 4
Chamberlain, Prime Minister, 86
Chase, Stuart, 24
on strike of 1877, 197
Check-off, 48
Civil Liberties report on employer associations, Senate Subcommittee on, 257-258
Civil rights, 188, 189
Clark, Wallace, 218
Clarke, Hon. John H., 251
Closed shop contract, 48
Collective action, necessity of, 39
Collective bargaining, 4, 44, 61, 89
as aid to shorter hours, 131
as check on strikes, 54
conditions of, explanation of, union as bargaining representative, 185-186
grievances, 193
plan for development in, 192
union need for expert assistance in negotiation of, 257
value of, practicability of, 264-265
Colorado Museum of Natural History in Denver, 219

INDEX

Congress of Industrial Organizations, 40, 41, 43
   cases handled by NLRA, 203
   complaints against NLRA, 209
   contract between RCA Communications, Inc., and, 168-169
   San Francisco Convention, 61
   workers' education, 227
Consolidated Edison case, effect of NLRA on, 207
Conveyor systems and assembly line, 100
Co-operative Medicine, Bureau of, 152
Coronado Coal case, 64
Corporations, control of business by, 14
   dependence of small business on, 16
   development of, 17
   growing power of, 34
   impersonal spirit of, 18
   increase in size of, 134
   as obstacle to purchasing power, 18
Crompton, 26, 27

Dalton, H. G., 251
Danbury Hatters case, 64
Daugherty, Carroll M., 145
Democracy, cooperation of workers in industry, 19-20, 22
   extension of economic opportunity under, 234
   in leadership, 89
   political and free enterprise in, 245-246
   See also Industry.
"Dependents," growth of, 33
Device of the Common Rule (standard hours and rates of pay), 129-130
Dialogue between the authors, 250

Economic income, chart of, 245
Economics, complicating factors of, 16
   need for balance in, 259
   replacement of physical labor by functional in modern, 17
   two fundamental errors in, 254

Economics—(*Continued*)
   Utopian needs from government in, 247-248
Education for workers, A. F. of L. committee on, 226
   Amalgamated Clothing Workers, 227
   California State Dept. of Education course in union leadership, 230
   College of New York Board of Higher Education under La Guardia Administration, 220
   CIO unions, 227
   SWOC at McKees Rocks, 229-230
   University of Rutgers, 231
   WPA, 227, 231
   See also Affiliated School for Workers.
"Efficiency engineer," 261-262
"Efficiency system," 261
Electric eye, 177
Electricity in industry, 174
   as uniform fluid commodity, 175
Employment, economy of continuous, 98, 99
   in expanding economy, 254-255
Ezekiel, Dr. Mordecai, 238, 239

Fansteel, 59
Fansteel Metallurgical Corporation case, effect of NLRA, 207
Farm Security Administration, 219
Federal Employment Compensation, 154
F.O.B. Detroit (Wessel Smitter), 100
Follett, Mary P., 88
Friedman-Harry Marks case, effect of NLRA on, 206

"Genetic," 181
Georgia Power Company, 218
Gower, John, 31
Grapes of Wrath, The (John Steinbeck), 34
Guilds, 32

Hargreave, 26
Harvard Law Review, 60

INDEX

Heaton, Herbert, 30
Heinrich, W. H., 146
Heiser, Dr. Victor G., 153
Hobson, John A., 26
Hoffmann, Frederick L., 144
Hosiery Code under NRA, 129
Hughes, Chief Justice, 57

Industrial planning, schemes of national, 238
Industrial Research, courses organized for business executives at Massachusetts Institute of Technology, Pennsylvania State College, Princeton, and the University of Michigan, 229
Industrial Revolution, 24-35
 the challenge of America in the, 28
 effect of steam power on, 27
 expansion due to increase of cheap raw materials, 26
 growing power of corporation in, 34
 influence of colonization on, 25
 origin of, 25
 penalty of leadership in, 29
 role of invention in, 26
 technological superiority of Great Britain, 27
 working conditions in, 30
Industrial Workers of the World, 55
Industry, accident records in, 144-146, 149
 application of science to, 136
 attitude toward personnel, 215
 basic assets acquired from nature by, 13
 early American conditions in, 12
 employer practices in, 51
 high cost of accidents in, 145-146
 military traditions in, 85-86
 necessity of democracy in, 265
 position of finance in, 22
 representative democracy in, 20-21
 safety campaign in, 146-148
 two camps of American, 264
Injunctions, governmental use of, 198
 National Labor Relations Board affected by, 209
 restraint of, by Norris-La Guardia Anti-injunction Act, 66
Insurance, salvation by, 238-239

International Association of Machinists, 208
Inter-industry, problems of, 216
International Pressmen's Union, 168
Intra-industry, problems of, 216
Iron, Steel and Tin Workers of North America, The Amalgamated Association of, 40
Iron Puddlers' Union, 40
Iron and Steel Electrical Engineers, Association of, 146
Iron and Steel Roll Hands' Union, 40

Johnson, Gen. Hugh, on John L. Lewis, 258
Johnstown Citizens' Committee, 260
Jones & Laughlin Steel Corporation case, effect of NLRA on, 206
Jones and Laughlin Steel Corporation, 260

Keynes, John Maynard, 241

Labor, considered by employer as flexible economy, 171
 controversial practices and attitudes of, 51
 distrust of employers' motives by, 258
 education in, 215
 effect of new trends on, 13
 future for, 252-253
 interest in the conduct of business, 251-252
 the new technology and consideration due, 254-255
 primary importance of welfare of, 257
 safety codes for, 149
Labor Board, organization created by, 208
 techniques used for organizing amendments to, 209
Labor espionage agencies, 260
Labor legislation: Combination Act of 1800, 32
 Fair Labor Standards Act, 132
 Hosiery Code under NRA, 129
 Norris-La Guardia Anti-injunction Act, NLRA, 206
 Railway Labor Act, 57

INDEX

Labor legislation—(*Continued*)
  railway reorganization law, 169
  safety codes, 146, 149
  severance compensation, 169
  Social Security Act, 68
  Wages and Hours Act, 118
  Wisconsin Law, 154
  workmen's compensation, 146-147, 154
Labor movement in the United States, 250-251
  fallacy in loss of interest in the, 264
Labor relations, value of personal contact in, 19
La Follette Civil Liberties Committee, 105
Layoffs, as cause of decline in wages and orders and general depression in business, 16
  collective bargaining in relation to, 188
  through NLRA protection and reinstatements for, 203
Leiserson, William M., 57
Lewis, John L., 258
Lockout, 104-105
Longshoremen and Harbor Workers Compensation Acts, 154
Lubin, Isador, New York Commissioner of Labor Statistics, 164
Luddites, 32, 35, 51

Machay Radio & Telegraph Company case, effect of NLRA on, 207
Madden, J. Warren, Chairman Labor Board, 204, 208
Management, techniques in, barrier of technology, 213
  check-off system, 48
  controversial practices, 94
  conveyor system and its misuse, 100
  "efficiency system," 261
  functional, 87
  helpful practices, 90
  labor's role, 85
  leadership, 87-89
  management engineering, 261-263
  merit systems, short ballots, democracy in industry, 213

Management, techniques in—(*Cont.*)
  motion study, 116-117
  output, 63
  overtime, 120
  shop management modeled on military lines, 212
  shop politics, 94-95
  "suggestion box," 212
  time study, 96-98, 116-118
Mandeville's Fable of the Bees, 240
McKinley, President, labor commission appointed by, 198
Morris, Newbold, 233

Napoleon, 72
National Association of Manufacturers, as "voice of American industry," 257-258
National Civic Federation, 50
National Industrial Conference Board, 128
National Industrial Council, 258
National Labor Relations Act, 47, 56, 57, 59, 66
  A. F. of L. cases handled by, 203
  accomplishments of, 203
  amendments to, 209
  CIO cases handled by, 203
  criticism in 1937 of, 202
  Chairman Madden's report on, 204
  effective date of, 205
  one-sidedness, 201
  precedents made by, 206
  protection given by, 203
  as remedial law, 196, 200
  validity upheld of, 201
National Safety Council, 145, 146, 149
Naumkeag Mills, 21
New Republic, 4
New York Gazette, 223
New York State Labor Department, 154
Norris-La Guardia Anti-injunction Act, 57, 66
Notes and References, 266-269

Ogburn, Charlton, 218
Operating control, 136, 138, 139, 143

INDEX

Optimum productivity, 22
Organization, planned, 69, 70, 72
   line and staff, 75
   of labor, 20
   of responsibilities, 75
   set-up for a single plant, 78
   set-up for more than one plant, 79
Owen, Robert, 31
Ownership, responsibilities of, 80

Patten, Simon N., 181
Pennsylvania Greyhound Lines case, NLRA effect on, 206
Person, Harlow S., 138
Picketing, 55, 56
Planning, national inter-industry, 83
   subsidy of industrial and agricultural products for home consumption, 240
President's commission on industrial relations in Great Britain and Sweden, 54
Pressure groups, 172
Production, control of, 139-143
   factors of, 124
   restriction of, 83
   straight-line, 141
Prudential Life Insurance Company, 144
Public Education in New York State, Regents' Inquiry Into the Character and Cost of, 223
Public Health Service, U. S., 127
Public investments as check to depression, 243-244
Purchasing power, effect of spending on, 242
   figures for, 241
   increase for masses in, 167
   prime mover in economics, 235
   reduction during crisis, 241
   WPA as aid to, 167

Quasi-judicial, explanation of, 206
"Quickies," 55

Railroad Brotherhood and Railroad Shop Craft Unions, 169
Railroad reorganization bill, 169

Railway Labor Act, 57
"Register control," 177
Republic Steel strike, 52, 53
"Republicans and Levellers," 32
Roberts, 26
Rockefeller, Jr., John D., 251
Rorty, Malcolm, 240
Russia's Five-Year Plan, 182

Safety Codes of the American Standards Association, 149
Safety and health in industry, 144
   use of psychiatry for, 148-149
Sales, control of, 142
Santa Cruz Fruit Packing Company case, effect of NLRA on, 206
Scientific Management, 137-138, 214, 256, 261-263
   applied in relationship among businesses, 82
   cooperation of organized labor in, 216
   factors involved in, 262
   labor practices and education in, 215
   research, 217
   training of labor leaders, 225
   See also Management.
Senate Civil Liberties Committee, 152
Senate Committee on Education and Labor, 201
   statement of Chairman Madden on effects of NLRA on American life to, 204, 208
Seniority rules, application of, 65
Severance compensation, 167
Shotwell, Dr., 24
"Slow-down," 55
Social Security Act, 66
Society for the Promotion of Engineering Education, 228
"Soldiering," 111
Soviet Union, industrialization of, 30
Span of attention, 72
Spending as a solution to depression, 240-243
Standards, group, 116
   living, 83, 258-259
   methods of determining performance, 116

INDEX

Steel Workers Organizing Committee, grievance adjustment machinery of, health and safety committee of, 44
history of, 43
as incentive to civic pride, 44
monthly educational experiment at McKees Rocks, near Pittsburgh, 229
pamphlets on labor methods, 21, 52
and on production problems, 84, 169, 260
relief committee of, 45
Steel Labor, organ of, 44
Straw boss, 44
Stretch-out, 101, 102
Strikebreaking, 55
Strikes, anthracite coal, 1902, 54
bituminous coal, 1897, 54, 198
Colorado coal report of 1912, 198
conduct in, 215
high cost of, 57
management practices in, 53
railway shopmen's strike of 1922, 198
Republic Steel, 52
rights to, 56
show of force by employer in, 105
sit-down, 58, 60
spontaneous (stoppage), 54
steel, 1919, 54
strike of 1877, 197
sympathetic and general, 61-62
union preparation for, 52
working days wasted in 1937 due to, 202
Supreme Court of U. S., decision on, *System Federation No. 40 v. Virginian Railway Co.*, 57
in Fansteel sit-down strike, 59
NLRA upheld, 205
Texas and New Orleans case, 57
Survey of all national operations, need for continuous, 246

Taft, Chief Justice, decision in American Steel Foundries case[2], 199
Taylor, Frederick W., 119, 137
Taylor Society, Bulletin of, 263
Taylor System, 138

Techniques in Industry, 181-182
changing labor techniques, 517
necessity of form for worker, 81
restrictions in trade and worksharing programs, 189
Technocrats, economic plans of, 237-238
Technology, 159
effects of progress in, 164
high prices as a result of, 170-171
mechanical and non-mechanical steps in advancement of, 160-161
regulation of introduction of new, 256
unemployment due to improvements in, 161
"Teleological," 181
"directive" approach also called, 182
Temporary National Economic Committee, 164
Textile Workers' Organizing Committee, 168
Trade-unions, evolution of, 31
free public education result of, 222
growth of industrial unions from, 40
obsolescent skills, 168
organization of early crafts in, 39
trade councils in, 40
See also Unions.
Travelers Insurance Company, 146
Tugwell, Redford, 179

Unemployment, challenge of, 155
as chronic condition, 252
collective bargainings' effect on, 191
Commissioner Lubin's statistics on, and aid towards solution of, 164-167
dangers of, 236-237
individual problems of skilled labor in, 9
labor-serving devices and economic nature of technological, 170
military solution in Germany and Russia of, 237
nation-wide cooperation necessary for, 172

INDEX

Unemployment—(Continued)
 program for, 171
 technological cause of, 164, 253
Union Health Center, 153
Union leadership, effect of company opposition on, 260-261
Unions, combated by blacklist, 65
 company courses for leaders of, 230
 craft and industrial, 40
 criticism of accounting in, 64
 evolution of leadership in, 42
 "excesses" of, 259-260
 federations of national, 40
 incorporation of, 63-64
 jurisdictional dispute in, 61
 organizational activities of, 46
 organized workers under Labor Act in, 207
 parallel development to business, 42, 43
 percentages of those in, 207
 policy in collective bargaining of, 187
 relief committee of, 44
 as result of necessity for group action, 49
 sole bargaining agent, 47
 source of income of, 41
 as stimulators of civic pride, 44
 variety in, 41
United Auto Workers, health clinic, 154
United Mine Workers, 42
United Nailers, 40
United Sons of Vulcan, 40
United States, class consciousness in the, 33
U. S. Bureau of Labor Statistics, Chief of the Division of Accident Statistics of the, 154, 208
United States Department of Commerce, 82
United States Steel Corporation, 84
 experiment in shorter hours, 128
United Textile Workers, 42

Veblen, Thorstein, 29
Virginian, The (Owen Wister), 105

Wage systems, 17, 109
 annual, 121-122
 base wage, 111
 bonus plan, 114
 factual basis for, 110
 gain-sharing or premium plan, 114
 incentive plan, 111-113, 115
 piece work, 113, 114
 point systems, 114
 salary plans, time payment plan, 112
Wages and Hours Act, Federal, 120, 131, 132, 134
Wages and Hours Administration, 133
Wagner Act, 56
 as new opportunity for labor, 252
 Section 2 (3), 60-196, 211
War Labor Board, 197
Waste, Committee on the Elimination of, 95, 98
Watt, James, 24, 26, 27
Way, Judge, 57
Webb, Beatrice and Sidney, 129, 130
Wharton School, 181
Whitney, 26
Wickenden Report, 228
Wood, General Robert E., 88
Workers, conditions in early industry for, 30
 responsibilities of modern, 80
Working hours, 123
 effect of shorter, 124-131
 regulation of maximum, 131-132
Workman's Protective Association, American, 258
World War, effect of, on labor, 50
Wyatt, 26

Youngstown Sheet and Tube Company, 251

American Labor: From Conspiracy to Collective Bargaining

AN ARNO PRESS/NEW YORK TIMES COLLECTION

SERIES I

Abbott, Edith.
Women in Industry. 1913.

Aveling, Edward B. and Eleanor M. Aveling.
Working Class Movement in America. 1891.

Beard, Mary.
The American Labor Movement. 1939.

Blankenhorn, Heber.
The Strike for Union. 1924.

Blum, Solomon.
Labor Economics. 1925.

Brandeis, Louis D. and Josephine Goldmark.
Women in Industry. 1907. New introduction by Leon Stein and Philip Taft.

Brooks, John Graham.
American Syndicalism. 1913.

Butler, Elizabeth Beardsley.
Women and the Trades. 1909.

Byington, Margaret Frances.
Homestead: The Household of A Mill Town. 1910.

Carroll, Mollie Ray.
Labor and Politics. 1923.

Coleman, McAlister.
Men and Coal. 1943.

Coleman, J. Walter.
The Molly Maguire Riots: Industrial Conflict in the Pennsylvania Coal Region. 1936.

Commons, John R.
Industrial Goodwill. 1919.

Commons, John R.
Industrial Government. 1921.

Dacus, Joseph A.
Annals of the Great Strikes. 1877.

Dealtry, William.
The Laborer: A Remedy for his Wrongs. 1869.

Douglas, Paul H., Curtis N. Hitchcock and Willard E. Atkins, editors.
The Worker in Modern Economic Society. 1923.

Eastman, Crystal.
Work Accidents and the Law. 1910.

Ely, Richard T.
The Labor Movement in America. 1890. New Introduction by Leon Stein and Philip Taft.

Feldman, Herman.
Problems in Labor Relations. 1937.

Fitch, John Andrew.
The Steel Worker. 1910.

Furniss, Edgar S. and Laurence Guild.
Labor Problems. 1925.

Gladden, Washington.
Working People and Their Employers. 1885.

Gompers, Samuel.
Labor and the Common Welfare. 1919.

Hardman, J. B. S., editor.
American Labor Dynamics. 1928.

Higgins, George G.
Voluntarism in Organized Labor, 1930-40. 1944.

Hiller, Ernest T.
The Strike. 1928.

Hollander, Jacob S. and George E. Barnett.
Studies in American Trade Unionism. 1906. New Introduction by Leon Stein and Philip Taft.

Jelley, Symmes M.
The Voice of Labor. 1888.

Jones, Mary.
Autobiography of Mother Jones. 1925.

Kelley, Florence.
Some Ethical Gains Through Legislation. 1905.

LaFollette, Robert M., editor.
The Making of America: Labor. 1906.

Lane, Winthrop D.
Civil War in West Virginia. 1921.

Lauck, W. Jett and Edgar Sydenstricker.
Conditions of Labor in American Industries. 1917.

Leiserson, William M.
Adjusting Immigrant and Industry. 1924.

Lescohier, Don D.
Knights of St. Crispin. 1910.

Levinson, Edward.
I Break Strikes. The Technique of Pearl L. Bergoff. 1935.

Lloyd, Henry Demarest.
Men, The Workers. Compiled by Anne Whithington and Caroline Stallbohen. 1909. New Introduction by Leon Stein and Philip Taft.

Lorwin, Louis (Louis Levine).
The Women's Garment Workers. 1924.

Markham, Edwin, Ben B. Lindsay and George Creel.
Children in Bondage. 1914.

Marot, Helen.
American Labor Unions. 1914.

Mason, Alpheus T.
Organized Labor and the Law. 1925.

Newcomb, Simon.
A Plain Man's Talk on the Labor Question. 1886. New Introduction by Leon Stein and Philip Taft.

Price, George Moses.
The Modern Factory: Safety, Sanitation and Welfare. 1914.

Randall, John Herman Jr.
Problem of Group Responsibility to Society. 1922.

Rubinow, I. M.
Social Insurance. 1913.

Saposs, David, editor.
Readings in Trade Unionism. 1926.

Slichter, Sumner H.
Union Policies and Industrial Management. 1941.

Socialist Publishing Society.
The Accused and the Accusers. 1887.

Stein, Leon and Philip Taft, editors.
The Pullman Strike. 1894-1913. New Introduction by the editors.

Stein, Leon and Philip Taft, editors.
Religion, Reform, and Revolution: Labor Panaceas in the Nineteenth Century. 1969. New Introduction by the editors.

Stein, Leon and Philip Taft, editors.
Wages, Hours, and Strikes: Labor Panaceas in the Twentieth Century. 1969. New introduction by the editors.

Swinton, John.
A Momentous Question: The Respective Attitudes of Labor and Capital. 1895. New Introduction by Leon Stein and Philip Taft.

Tannenbaum, Frank.
The Labor Movement. 1921.

Tead, Ordway.
Instincts in Industry. 1918.

Vorse, Mary Heaton.
Labor's New Millions. 1938.

Witte, Edwin Emil.
The Government in Labor Disputes. 1932.

Wright, Carroll D.
The Working Girls of Boston. 1889.

Wyckoff, Veitrees J.
Wage Policies of Labor Organizations in a Period of Industrial Depression. 1926.

Yellen, Samuel.
American Labor Struggles. 1936.

SERIES II

Allen, Henry J.
The Party of the Third Part: The Story of the Kansas Industrial Relations Court. 1921. *Including* The Kansas Court of Industrial Relations Law (1920) by Samuel Gompers.

Baker, Ray Stannard.
The New Industrial Unrest. 1920.

Barnett, George E. & David A. McCabe.
Mediation, Investigation and Arbitration in Industrial Disputes. 1916.

Barns, William E., editor.
The Labor Problem. 1886.

Bing, Alexander M.
War-Time Strikes and Their Adjustment. 1921.

Brooks, Robert R. R.
When Labor Organizes. 1937.

Calkins, Clinch.
Spy Overhead: The Story of Industrial Espionage. 1937.

Cooke, Morris Llewellyn & Philip Murray.
Organized Labor and Production. 1940.

Creamer, Daniel & Charles W. Coulter.
Labor and the Shut-Down of the Amoskeag Textile Mills. 1939.

Glocker, Theodore W.
The Government of American Trade Unions. 1913.

Gompers, Samuel.
Labor and the Employer. 1920.

Grant, Luke.
The National Erectors' Association and the International Association of Bridge and Structural Ironworkers. 1915.

Haber, William.
Industrial Relations in the Building Industry. 1930.

Henry, Alice.
Women and the Labor Movement. 1923.

Herbst, Alma.
The Negro in the Slaughtering and Meat-Packing Industry in Chicago. 1932.

[Hicks, Obediah.]
Life of Richard F. Trevellick. 1896.

Hillquit, Morris, Samuel Gompers & Max J. Hayes.
The Double Edge of Labor's Sword: Discussion and Testimony on Socialism and Trade-Unionism Before the Commission on Industrial Relations. 1914. New Introduction by Leon Stein and Philip Taft.

Jensen, Vernon H.
Lumber and Labor. 1945.

Kampelman, Max M.
The Communist Party vs. the C.I.O. 1957.

Kingsbury, Susan M., editor.
Labor Laws and Their Enforcement. By Charles E. Persons, Mabel Parton, Mabelle Moses & Three "Fellows." 1911.

McCabe, David A.
The Standard Rate in American Trade Unions. 1912.

Mangold, George Benjamin.
Labor Argument in the American Protective Tariff Discussion. 1908.

Millis, Harry A., editor.
How Collective Bargaining Works. 1942.

Montgomery, Royal E.
Industrial Relations in the Chicago Building Trades. 1927.

Oneal, James.
The Workers in American History. 3rd edition, 1912.

Palmer, Gladys L.
Union Tactics and Economic Change: A Case Study of Three Philadelphia Textile Unions. 1932.

Penny, Virginia.
How Women Can Make Money: Married or Single, In all Branches of the Arts and Sciences, Professions, Trades, Agricultural and Mechanical Pursuits. 1870. New Introduction by Leon Stein and Philip Taft.

Penny, Virginia.
Think and Act: A Series of Articles Pertaining to Men and Women, Work and Wages. 1869.

Pickering, John.
The Working Man's Political Economy. 1847.

Ryan, John A.
A Living Wage. 1906.

Savage, Marion Dutton.
Industrial Unionism in America. 1922.

Simkhovitch, Mary Kingsbury.
The City Worker's World in America. 1917.

Spero, Sterling Denhard.
The Labor Movement in a Government Industry: A Study of Employee Organization in the Postal Service. 1927.

Stein, Leon and Philip Taft, editors.
Labor Politics: Collected Pamphlets. 2 vols. 1836-1932. New Introduction by the editors.

Stein, Leon and Philip Taft, editors.
The Management of Workers: Selected Arguments. 1917-1956. New Introduction by the editors.

Stein, Leon and Philip Taft, editors.
Massacre at Ludlow: Four Reports. 1914-1915. New Introduction by the editors.

Stein, Leon and Philip Taft, editors.
Workers Speak: Self-Portraits. 1902-1906. New Introduction by the editors.

Stolberg, Benjamin.
The Story of the CIO. 1938.

Taylor, Paul S.
The Sailors' Union of the Pacific. 1923.

U.S. Commission on Industrial Relations.
Efficiency Systems and Labor. 1916. New Introduction by Leon Stein and Philip Taft.

Walker, Charles Rumford.
American City: A Rank-and-File History. 1937.

Walling, William English.
American Labor and American Democracy. 1926.

Williams, Whiting.
What's on the Worker's Mind: By One Who Put on Overalls to Find Out. 1920.

Wolman, Leo.
The Boycott in American Trade Unions. 1916.

Ziskind, David.
One Thousand Strikes of Government Employees. 1940.